Alexander the Great in the Early Christian Tradition

Bloomsbury Studies in Classical Reception

Bloomsbury Studies in Classical Reception presents scholarly monographs offering new and innovative research and debate to students and scholars in the reception of Classical Studies. Each volume will explore the appropriation, reconceptualization and recontextualization of various aspects of the Graeco-Roman world and its culture, looking at the impact of the ancient world on modernity. Research will also cover reception within antiquity, the theory and practice of translation, and reception theory.

Also available in the Series:

Ancient Magic and the Supernatural in the Modern Visual and Performing Arts, edited by Filippo Carlà and Irene Berti
Ancient Greek Myth in World Fiction since 1989, edited by Justine McConnell and Edith Hall
Antipodean Antiquities, edited by Marguerite Johnson
Classics in Extremis, edited by Edmund Richardson
Frankenstein and its Classics, edited by Jesse Weiner, Benjamin Eldon Stevens and Brett M. Rogers
Greek and Roman Classics in the British Struggle for Social Reform, edited by Henry Stead and Edith Hall
Homer's Iliad and the Trojan War: Dialogues on Tradition, Jan Haywood and Naoíse Mac Sweeney
Imagining Xerxes, Emma Bridges
Julius Caesar's Self-Created Image and Its Dramatic Afterlife, Miryana Dimitrova
Once and Future Antiquities in Science Fiction and Fantasy, edited by Brett M. Rogers and Benjamin Eldon Stevens
Ovid's Myth of Pygmalion on Screen, Paula James
Reading Poetry, Writing Genre, edited by Silvio Bär and Emily Hauser
Sex, Symbolists and the Greek Body, Richard Warren
The Codex Fori Mussolini, Han Lamers and Bettina Reitz-Joosse
The Classics in Modernist Translation, edited by Miranda Hickman and Lynn Kozak
The Gentle, Jealous God, Simon Perris
Translations of Greek Tragedy in the Work of Ezra Pound, Peter Liebregts
Victorian Classical Burlesques, Laura Monrós-Gaspar
Victorian Epic Burlesques, Rachel Bryant Davies

Alexander the Great in the Early Christian Tradition

Classical Reception and Patristic Literature

Christian Thrue Djurslev

BLOOMSBURY ACADEMIC
LONDON • NEW YORK • OXFORD • NEW DELHI • SYDNEY

BLOOMSBURY ACADEMIC
Bloomsbury Publishing Plc
50 Bedford Square, London, WC1B 3DP, UK
1385 Broadway, New York, NY 10018, USA
29 Earlsfort Terrace, Dublin 2, Ireland

BLOOMSBURY, BLOOMSBURY ACADEMIC and the Diana logo
are trademarks of Bloomsbury Publishing Plc

First published in Great Britain 2020
Paperback edition first published 2021

Copyright © Christian Thrue Djurslev, 2020

Christian Thrue Djurslev has asserted his right under the Copyright,
Designs and Patents Act, 1988, to be identified as Author of this work.

For legal purposes the Acknowledgements on p. vi constitute
an extension of this copyright page.

Cover image © Alexander the Great's Entry into Babylon, 1822. Begun by Pietro Galli in
1822, executed in reduced size and with alterations of Inv.no. A503 (The Alexander Frieze).
Courtesy Thorvaldsens Museum, Copenhagen

All rights reserved. No part of this publication may be reproduced or
transmitted in any form or by any means, electronic or mechanical,
including photocopying, recording, or any information storage or retrieval
system, without prior permission in writing from the publishers.

Bloomsbury Publishing Plc does not have any control over, or responsibility for,
any third-party websites referred to or in this book. All internet addresses given
in this book were correct at the time of going to press. The author and publisher
regret any inconvenience caused if addresses have changed or sites have
ceased to exist, but can accept no responsibility for any such changes.

A catalogue record for this book is available from the British Library.

Library of Congress Control Number: 2019949565

ISBN: HB: 978-1-7883-1164-9
PB: 978-1-3501-9446-5
ePDF: 978-1-3501-2039-6
eBook: 978-1-3501-2040-2

Series: Bloomsbury Studies in Classical Reception

Typeset by RefineCatch Limited, Bungay, Suffolk

To find out more about our authors and books visit
www.bloomsbury.com and sign up for our newsletters.

Contents

Acknowledgments		vi
Conventions and Abbreviations		ix
	Introduction	1
1	Apologists and Co.	21
2	Classical Themes and Christian Tradition	35
3	Tales from Judea and the Diaspora	83
4	History and Rhetoric	145
	Conclusion	191
	Epilogue: Writing Alexander, Writing Constantine	199
References		203
Index Locorum		215
General Index		227

Acknowledgments

This book is a substantial revision of parts of my dissertation, *The Christian Alexander: The Use of Alexander the Great in Early Christian Literature*. I wrote the original version under the supervision of Professors Daniel Ogden and Richard Flower in the Department of Classics and Ancient History at the University of Exeter between 2012 and 2015. The purpose of this rewrite is to offer an accessible account of my research into some relatively obscure material. After two years of teaching at the University of Edinburgh, I worked intensively on the manuscript in serene surroundings of Aarhus University, Denmark. This writing was made possible by a grant from the Carlsberg Foundation. I also want to acknowledge the support of the Foundation of Peter Mariager and Wife in producing the final text. I finalized the manuscript in December 2018 and have not included scholarship published since then, however excellent.

The tidy narrative above precludes productive research sessions elsewhere. Two trips to the Fondation Hardt in Geneva offered an inspiring social setting for scholarship. I am grateful for generous bursaries from the Classical Association, UK, and the Fondation Hardt visiting fellowship scheme to make my visits possible. I visited the Danish Institute at Athens at various stages of the research. I want to thank the staff at the Institute, the Nordic Library, and the British School, for their assistance. Professor Josef Wiesehöfer kindly invited me to Kiel for a prolific research period in 2016, and I am thankful for the invitation. Conference circuits also gave me the opportunity to test ideas in Exeter, Wroclaw (twice), Kassel, Aarhus, Copenhagen, Edinburgh, Boston, and Edmonton. I want to extend my thanks to all the audiences for helpful suggestions and to the respective conference/seminar organizers for their hospitality.

I feel privileged to have grown up in a country where education is celebrated and students are financially supported. This kind of support allowed me to concentrate on my studies at the University of Copenhagen and, later, at the University of Exeter. I am fortunate that my doctorate, also at the University of Exeter, was funded by the A. G. Leventis Foundation. For this, I am indebted not only to the Department of Classics and Ancient History for selecting me, but also to the trustees of the Leventis Foundation. Their promotion of a long line of doctoral Exonians before and after my tenure reflects but a small part of their philanthropic endeavors in this world.

Having duly acknowledged the book's ventures and patrons, I come to the people who have helped to shape the work. Daniel Ogden comes first. He took on the role of my academic mentor, my anchor, the moment I timidly stepped into his office on a September afternoon in 2011. He has since become a collaborator and a friend. He guided and encouraged me from essays to thesis and, eventually, this monograph. In a sense, he is the grandfather of this book, and I hope that the result will not disappoint.

Other key contributors to the creation of this book: two Richards galvanized me into studying Alexander and early Christianity. Richard Stoneman preached the gospel of the *Alexander Romance* when I studied at Exeter and in our conversations since then. His 2008-book had brought me to England in the first place. Richard Flower taught me the importance of late antique scribes and scholars, as well as a thing or two about Christian rhetoric. I thank them both for sparring intellectually with me. I am also grateful to the examiners of my doctoral thesis, Robin Lane Fox and Lynette Mitchell, for challenging and clarifying my thinking. I took this book in one of the directions they suggested. Debts to other scholars will be evident from the bibliography. This space is also the place to record my thanks to the staff at Bloomsbury Press, first and foremost to Classics editor Alice Wright, for seeing the project through its final stage and onward to publication. Benjamin Garstad, reader for the press, commented on the whole manuscript, which greatly improved the text. I thank Gary Vos for thorough editing at an advanced stage of the writing process.

In alphabetical order I would like to express my indebtedness to: Jacqueline Arthur-Montaigne, Sulochana Asirvatham, Elizabeth Baynham, Kim Czajkowski, Benedikt Eckhardt, Andrew Erskine, Benjamin Garstad, Gavin Kelly, Haila Manteghi, Ignacio Molina Marin, Sabine Müller, Aaron Pelttari, Chr. Gorm Tortzen, and Yvona Trnka-Amrhein, as well as former colleagues at Exeter and Edinburgh, and current ones at Aarhus.

Peter Bruun Hansen, Paschalis Gkortsilas, Anders Grunnet, Sam Hayes, and Patrick Ussher provided much-needed moral support in various countries and at various stages of writing. I offer this book as a small token of the heartfelt thanks I feel towards my close family, who endured my absence. *Forældre og brormand, af hjertet tak. I er de bedste!* Now I welcome a new member to the family, my wife Taylor Grace FitzGerald, not only a princess among proofreaders, but also a former Leventis PhD fellow herself. With love, thank you.

I wish to dedicate the book to someone, whom I wish would have been able to read the book. I dedicated my thesis to the memory of Mary Redmond Ussher (1951–2015), and this book is dedicated to the memory of Kirsten Skovholm Tortzen (1951–2018).

CTD
Aarhus, December 2018

Conventions and Abbreviations

Any book-length study will have its own conventions and idiosyncrasies. Here follows a formal outline of those found in the present work. This study straddles multiple academic fields from Ancient History to Theology. Since expert or lay readers will have different frames of reference, I have made an extra effort to make the content accessible to readers of all backgrounds.

Transliteration of personal names and toponyms follows the practice in the *Oxford Classical Dictionary* (*OCD*), which is now available in print and on-line form. For accessibility, I have chosen the *OCD* for abbreviations of ancient authors and modern scholarship. The online edition is particularly sympathetic to Christian authors, even at the expense of some crucial classical authors, such as the Augustan geographer Strabo of Amesia. For the Christian authors not covered by the *OCD*, I have consulted the abbreviations in the handbook of style for the Society of Biblical Literature.

The combination of academic fields also causes some complications with names: "Alexander" can denote King Alexander III of Macedon or Alexander, the fourth-century bishop of Alexandria (who was also "Great," according to the fifth-century bishop Theodoret of Cyrrhus). Again, an unqualified "Justin" may evoke either Justin Martyr or Justin, epitomizer of Pompeius Trogus' *Philippic History*. I have tried to contextualize names as much as possible for the sake of clarity, especially the more obscure Christians (for further reference, see Quasten 1950–1986; Di Berardino et al. 2014). Moreover, some Christian sources exist only in one or more of a range of non-classical languages, such as Syriac, Coptic, and Armenian. Fortunately, most are translated into at least one modern language. Where possible, I have adapted translations or translated texts from the original.

For the sake of consistency, all references to the Old Testament (OT) and the New Testament (NT) are to the New Revised Standard Version (NRSV) in the fourth edition of the New Oxford Annotated Bible (NOAB, 2010). All references to the Greek *Alexander Romance* (*AR*) and its subsequent versions follow the conventions in Ogden (2017: xii).

ACCS	*Ancient Christian Commentary on Scripture.* Downers Grove, IL.
BEEC	*Brill Encyclopedia of Early Christianity Online.* Leiden.
CHAP	*Clavis Historicorum Antiquitatis Posterioris*, L. Van Hoof and P. Van Nuffelen, eds. Online database.
CPG	Clavis Patrum Graecorum, Maurice Geerard, 1974—2003. Turnhout.
CPL	Clavis Patrum Latinorum, E. Dekkers, 1995. Turnhout.
FRH	*The Fragments of the Roman Historians*, ed. T. Cornell et al., 2013.
GCS NF	*Die griechischen christlichen Schriftsteller der ersten Jahrhunderte. Neue folge.* Berlin.

Introduction

In 1986, Iron Maiden released the music album, *Somewhere in Time*, featuring an eight-minute track called "Alexander the Great." Steve Harris' epic song parades the king's life and military exploits. In verse five, towards the end, front man Bruce Dickinson sings that Alexander spread Hellenism far and wide, the Macedonian learned mind, and that Macedonian culture was a western way of life. Alexander "paved the way for Christianity."

Iron Maiden's anthem to one of ancient history's most famous persons makes a relatively modern claim. Few before the Enlightenment believed that King Alexander III of Macedon (356–323 BC) had paved the way for a small religious sect (Bichler 2018: 640). Not even the earliest adherents of that faith credited Alexander with such a feat.

Ancient Christians took an acute interest in other aspects of the historical character. For example, they discussed Alexander's personal life or select events of his grand conquest of Achaemenid Persia (*c.* 335–323 BC), stretching from Asia Minor to the Indus Valley. They were not alone. Such topics were on the standard curricula in the schools of the Roman Empire. But Christians were also engaging with much material from Hellenistic Judaism that they had to combine with the classical accounts. For all, Alexander played a prominent role and so made a strong imprint on the formation of the Christian outlook, even if he never heard the Gospel message.

The present book tells the story of what the first Christians said about Alexander and why. It may already appear too controversial in some parts of the world. What has heavy metal music to do with Christianity? Did Iron Maiden suggest that Hellenism was Macedonian and not Greek? How dare I insinuate that Alexander was not an orthodox Christian in the view of the early church? As will be self-evident, he truly was not. From the outset, we need to bear in mind that ancient conditions, priorities, and views of the church differ from those of Christian denominations today. We cannot assume that Christians then imbued Alexander with the same meanings as we might do now. This study serves as a reminder of the great gap between past and present.

To many modern readers, the subject matter may still seem a strange combination. Some might even ask how much longer we can care about going on military campaigns with warlords like Alexander (Bichler 2010). Others may not find the religious dimension agreeable. Classicists, historians, and theologians tend to have their separate spheres of interest and frames of reference. But impatient readers may be relieved to learn that Alexander and religious studies is a match made in heaven.

We know more of Alexander's religious activities, personal and public, than about those of any other individual of the ancient world. Almost a century ago, scholarship could trace religious change from Alexander to St Augustine (Nock 1933) and, in today's world, the first life of the king with a religious focus is hot off the press (Naiden 2019) with more to follow. Alexander, who was himself worshiped in cults all over the Mediterranean world, entered the cultural orbit of multiple ancient religions on three continents. He later entered the scriptural texts of Judaism, Christianity, and Islam (Doukifar-Aerts 2010). While we possess excellent studies of Alexander in the Arabic and Jewish traditions (Amitay 2010; Klęczar 2018), no monograph covers early Christian receptions specifically. And that is despite the fact that the church controlled much of the memory of Alexander until the European Enlightenment (Briant 2017).

In the present study, I have endeavored to address that imbalance. I have not written another biography of Alexander. Such books are in no short supply, and many histories have withstood the test of time (e.g., Lane Fox 1973; Green 2013; Bosworth 1988: preface). Introducing an immense discourse about a celebrity presents a different sort of challenge, and a host of difficulties will present themselves shortly. The rest of the introduction outlines how such issues will be addressed. We begin with the parameters of the book before our protagonist is introduced.

How early?

Chronology is the first point on the agenda. We do not know of any Christian references to Alexander before the mid-second century AD. Hence this book is not concerned with the Christians of the New Testament or their immediate successors, the so-called "Apostolic Age." For present purposes, "early" refers roughly to the period between the reigns of the Roman emperor Marcus Aurelius (r. 161–180) and Constantine I (r. 306–337). Scholars now question Constantine's "revolution" as a watershed moment (e.g., Van Dam 2007), though we cannot ignore the emperor's tolerance and support of Christian institutions. This timeframe roughly corresponds to the ante-Nicene period of writers (*c.* 100–325), that is, Christianity before the Nicene Creed, which originated in the first ecumenical council of Nicaea in Asia Minor (modern Iznik, Turkey). The chosen period thus constitutes a neat political and religious frame.

Given the topic of Alexander, however, the parameters of the study may seem arbitrary to some readers. For example, changes in everyday experience under various emperors had little bearing upon how much Christians wrote about Alexander, just as developments in church doctrine did not affect Alexander's legacy. Moreover, Alexander's afterlife in the Christian tradition did not end with the age of Constantine—quite the contrary. Nevertheless, I argue that these three centuries marked the formative stage. The period constitutes a self-contained unit, as most of the Christian ideas about Alexander were generated at that time. Once we reach the last days of the Constantinian Christians, Lactantius (*c.* 260–325/6) and Eusebius of Caesarea (*c.* 265–339), we discover the end of an old era and the start of a new. We are thus concerned with an important chapter in the intellectual history of Christianity.

There are at least two immediate benefits to be gained from this chronological purview. First, the chronological scope permits us to make observations on the change and continuities from the second to the fourth century. From a classicist's perspective, the third century is a dark void, at least with regards to primary texts in Greek and Latin, but Christian texts illuminate the period. Second, the massive geographical area in which Christianity took hold allows us to detect empire-wide and local nodes of Alexander-related lore. This geographical focus over time also enables us to discover that much literary activity took place beyond the city of Rome. The gradual decentralization of education seems to have affected areas locally, but it will emerge that there were still some solid literary patterns on a greater scale. We need to examine the extent to which Christian writing in Greek and Latin took an interest in the same topics and treated them in similar ways in both languages. The emerging unity in topics and treatments suggests not so much a direct line of communication, but rather that certain topics were already embedded within the literature of both languages.

Which Christians?

In this period of Christianity's history, the foremost group of Christian thinkers were the so-called "apologists" (Edwards et al. 1999; Young et al. 2004; Engberg et al. 2014). Clergy members, such as Justin Martyr (*d.* before 167) and Tertullian of Carthage (*fl. c.* 200–220s), rose to the challenge of defending their faith in a hostile world. Joining the illegal Christian sect had major consequences for one's social status. It was risky to expose your Christian identity in public, an identity of choice, not birth (Tert. *Apol.* 18.4). The religion made demands of strict loyalty over earthly commitments. This self-proclaimed "third race," which was just visiting the world before taking up residence in heaven, stood outside imperial society (*Diogn.* 5).

At least that is the old story told in early Christian texts. The clergy invested heavily in generating this image of a separate Christian identity, and many texts focus on imperial persecution as a way of giving Christians a certain cultural coherence in the face of suffering. However, modern studies have demonstrated that the clergy's claims did not match the reality (Rebillard 2012: 35–42). The dangers of the religion were not as bad as advertised. Persecution was not a permanent threat, nor did it take place empire-wide, but was usually conducted sporadically by local governors. Christianity did not pose a threat to empire *per se*, for the movement was too small. So Christian communities enjoyed long periods of peace. With the rise of Christian institutions, it became desirable and even rewarding to become a member of the Christian laity in the late second century (Eshleman 2012: 65). "Christianness," understood as a unit within a wide set of identity memberships, was rarely activated in everyday life, except in special religious circumstances, such as at the Eucharist. Some members of the clergy called for the laity to put their "Christianness" first at all times but, fairly often, other identity memberships took precedence in civic social settings (Rebillard 2012: 79).

Realistically speaking, early Christianity defies communal definition for Christians told many stories about themselves and their communities (Brown 2013). From the New Testament, especially the Acts of the Apostles, we get the impression of a Messianic movement with roots in Palestinian Judaism, which was a lawful religion even in the eyes of the Romans. The members appear to be from a lower social register than the rest of society, but they claim to have taken the higher ground in terms of morality. They vehemently promote their way of life. Early texts center their missionary activity around the Mediterranean basin, away from Jewish critics, such as Rabbi Tarfon (*fl.* 100), who proposed to burn the Gospels. Other missionaries took the religion further east. Like Alexander, Christianity penetrated into Mesopotamia and India (*Acts of Thomas the Apostle*, with Andrade 2018).

On the way to India, Christianity made a considerable impact. An extraordinary, if unlikely, tale has the great kingdom of Osroëne convert through an epistolary correspondence between Abgar V, ruler of Edessa, and none other than Christianity's founding father, Jesus Christ. Jesus allegedly made a written reply to Abgar's request, saying that he would send one of his twelve to heal the terminally ill ruler. A certain Thaddaeus went in Thomas' stead. His journey beyond the Roman frontier yielded miraculous results, as Abgar and the entirety of Edessa converted to Christianity (Euseb. *Hist. eccl.* 1.13). In other legends, kingdoms outside the empire first converted later, close to the reign of Constantine I: Armenia (*c*. 301), Aksum in Ethiopia (*c*. 325), and the region of Caucasian Albania (under the Arsacid King Urnayr in *c*. 314). Such stories asserted that there was a universal Christian community, however flexibly defined.

For Eusebius of Caesarea, the self-declared "first historian of the church" and our earliest source for the Edessan story, the account meant much more. Including the conversion story at a prominent juncture, the very end of the first book of his *Church History*, he frames it as taking place at the end of Jesus' life. This epistolary exchange thus replaces the Passion narrative that readers would have anticipated. The new epistolary "Passion-narrative" becomes something else entirely, according to one recent study (Corke-Webster 2017a). First, the story presented the Jews as responsible for Jesus' death, and Eusebius makes that explicit by putting a speech to that effect into the mouth of Thaddeus, which the messenger delivered to King Abgar. It follows that the Romans were blameless, and Eusebius makes no further remarks on the crucifixion. Second, the story transformed a simple religion into an imperial power: Christianity was not a small and insignificant religion on the borders of Rome, but was even known far beyond the boundaries of Palestine. It promoted philosophical teachings with a wide appeal that had cultivated "barbarian" nations in the same civilizing way as Rome did. Its principal figure was much more than a simple carpenter; he was a lettered leader, who could decline the requests of kings and send his own emissaries to heal and bring peace. Jesus' followers were no longer exhorted to suffering and martyrdom, but could worship by laborious writing and reading of the written word—no doubt a reassuring point for Eusebius' literate Christian readership. The story posits that the church had always been such a cultivated institution throughout Christian history. In other words, Eusebius used Jesus' Abgar correspondence to present a relatable version of the humble origins of the Christians acceptable to his fourth-century audience of Christian elites.

We need to recognize Eusebius' literary project because of the importance of the *Church History*. It remains one of the only narrative accounts we possess of the earliest Christian communities. We rely on his account for much information, but his imperial context colored the representation of this knowledge. Writing ten books on the church from Christ to Constantine, Eusebius told a story that directed the world empire toward the universal peace vouchsafed by Christianity. Constantine's ascendancy heralded the end of three hundred years of adversity, which Eusebius linked to Roman appreciation of the Christian faith. For instance, Jesus had been born in the peaceful reign of Augustus (r. 27 BC–AD 14), a peace that only lasted through Jesus' lifetime. The so-called "little peace of the Church" (c. 259–303) came about because of imperial toleration of the Christians until the time of the Diocletianic and Tetrarchic persecutions (c. 303–313, sporadic and confined to the eastern parts of the empire). As Constantine's rule marked a return to the blessed Augustan age, so did the peace of the Lord reappear. Empire and Christianity were better together and had been so since the foundation of the faith and state. Indeed, the Sees of Jerusalem, Rome, and Alexandria that Eusebius often mentions in the same breath united imperial centers under one Lord and God. While readers of Eusebius, ancient and modern, may not fully endorse his glossy vision of Constantine's universal regime and Christian origin history, they need to be aware of how his construction of Christian community went much further than the New Testament and the apologists, whose heir he was.

The increasing amount of archaeological evidence complements some of the claims from the textual record. For example, coexistence seems the norm from early on (Borg 2013: 89–91). The evidence from material culture comes primarily from funerary contexts, such as sarcophagi, tomb inscriptions, and paintings in catacombs. Apparently, Christians shared burial sites with non-Christians without issue. Promising archaeological excavations from Rome have located the foundations of church structures and burial monuments that inhabit the same space as non-Christian structures. Modern scholarship suggests that Christian art and architecture appropriated the best features of Greco-Roman design to the extent that it is challenging for the modern eye to see the difference. Porphyry of Tyre (c. 233–305), a Neoplatonist philosopher and Christianity's greatest critic, complained that Christians imitated temple building for their places of prayer when they should rather worship at home (Porph. *Christ.* F82; cf. Euseb. *Hist. eccl.* 8.1–2). Houses did find use as churches, and excavations at Dura Europos in Syria unearthed the earliest preserved house church (c. 200) with an ornate baptistery. What the evidence, primarily from Rome, has in common is that, for the first few centuries of Christianity, the Christian remains are much less expensive and extravagant than those of the non-Christian

Romans from the higher classes. This picture suggests that the Christians generally came from a lower social status, thus supporting the image of the textual sources. It is difficult to imagine a Christian like Eusebius, with patrons in the upper echelons of society, thriving in this early period, even if we do know of a few Christians with contacts in the top stratum of society.

Literary sources vastly outnumber artwork and other artifacts. Accordingly, our main concern will be with Christianity as a literary movement. Again, Eusebius' *Church History* is a prime example of Christian canon formation. On almost every page of his work, we encounter some important Christian writer, who helped shape the new literature in some way. This grouping of writers naturally foregrounds Eusebius' selectivity. In the style of Irenaeus of Lyons (*c.* 130/40–200), Eusebius constantly dealt with questions of the inclusion and exclusion of self-proclaimed "Christians." He branded some heretics, such as the Egyptian Valentinus in Rome (*c.* 140–200), Marcion of Sinope (*d. c.* 160), and the Edessan Bardesanes (154–222), whom Eusebius chastised for thinking that he had come back to orthodoxy when he was still covered in "the filth of heresy" (4.30.3). This tactical dismissal of "heretical" writers defined what was orthodox and the "proper" literature for Christian readers.

The authors praised by Eusebius for their faith are legion. In Book 6, we find the most elaborate encomium of a scholarly character, namely Origen of Alexandria (*c.* 185–254). Eusebius had inherited Origen's grand library in Palestinian Caesarea, so his approval and detailed knowledge of his predecessor will surprise no one. Eusebius' representation of the man reads as paradigmatic as his own version of Jesus, however. With his father martyred at an early age, Origen was himself bent on martyrdom in youth, but abandoned that plan for the study of scripture as he matured (6.1.3). He visited the grand centers of learning, such as Rome (6.15.10) and Athens (6.32.2), while communicating via letters with the imperial court (6.36.3–4) in the same way as Jesus corresponded with King Abgar. At the end of Origen's life, he dealt with foreign heresies in Arabia (6.37) and Syria (6.38), as Jesus had dealt with foreign requests. Just as Eusebius omits the Passion narrative, he does not narrate Origen's death, directing readers to information about it elsewhere (6.39.5). Origen's life story without end thus supports the program of the whole *Church History*: past Christians were not suicidal simpletons but cosmopolitan authorities. Their work was pivotal for the piety and maintenance of the Roman Empire, just as that of Christianity's founding figure had been.

What is most telling about this image is the framing of the moment in Origen's youth in which he realized that he did not need to be a martyr like his father.

Eusebius carefully zooms in on this event to legitimize Christians turning away from martyrdom to authorship. Ultimately, his inclusion of Origen and so many other writers is no doubt because Christianity had attracted and cultivated many by his day, but it is also a claim that writing was what a follower of the lettered Jesus did. The rose-tinted image of Origen, Eusebius' illustrious predecessor at the Caesarean library, neatly reinforces the credibility of that claim.

The present focus on literature and canon formation calls for comparisons with the non-Christians in the later Roman Empire. We know well how non-Christians also canonized their own literature. The most frequently noted contemporary non-Christian movement is the so-called "Second Sophistic," although this term divides modern scholars of imperial culture (Borg 2004; Richter and Johnson 2017, with the overview of rhetoricians in Janiszewski et al. 2015). Coined by the Greek intellectual Philostratus in the third century AD (*VS* 481, 507), the phrase referred to a self-proclaimed "new phase" of Greek learning after the Greats of classical Athens (Anderson 1993; Whitmarsh 2001, 2005). It defined a special group of performing orators, some of whom held chairs of rhetoric in the urban schools of the Roman Empire from Nero to Alexander Severus, *c.* 60–230. Philostratus' efforts to imbue the movement with a certain historically significant character had been very successful, although it is not at all clear how different the activity was from previous Greek and Latin literature or imperial culture in general. For example, his *Lives of the Sophists* by no means included all the people we might consider part of the same movement, such as the satirist Lucian (*c.* 120–180?). It also includes people who did not want to be labeled "sophists," such as Aelius Aristides. As Eshleman has demonstrated (Eshleman 2012: 125–148), Philostratus organizes the top orators loosely but closely around the circle of Herodes Atticus, the greatest patron of the arts in second-century Athens, thereby promoting their rhetorical competences at the expense of all other contemporary intellectuals. Philostratus claims to have been taught by three of Herodes' students—more than anyone else in the *Lives*—and so represents himself as possessing the ultimate authority on the sophistic canon.

Canons can be misleading, and usually intentionally so. Eunapius of Sardis, who studied rhetoric in mid-fourth century AD Athens, made an updated if different selection from that of Philostratus. What is excluded from that compilation is as important as what is included. For example, such literary connoisseurs found no room for an ordinary rhetorician like the Greek-speaking non-Christian Maximus of Tyre (*fl.* 180–190s), whose lectures delivered in Commodus' Rome still survive. These lectures on quasi-philosophical matters have much classical content in common with the Christian writings of Clement of Alexandria (c. 150–215), who Eusebius posits had a special Alexandrian school that Origen himself inherited (6.6; 6.13). Highly educated Christians and non-Christians were thus preoccupied with identity formation through the inclusion and exclusion of intellectual peers.

We also notice this tendency to self-define a social group in the Christian exclusion of non-Christians and vice versa. For example, in terms of sheer rhetorical panache, Clement outclasses Maximus by far (Trapp 1997: 1). He would definitely deserve a place in non-Christian literary canons, had he not been a Christian or covered Christian topics. His stylistic superiority may seem surprising at first glance but Christians received the same education as non-Christians and could compete on terms of equality. We know from school exercises on papyri from Egypt that Christians attended the same schools and taught in the same schools as non-Christians (Kaster 1988; Cribiore 2017). To take another instance, Eusebius notes that Ammonius Saccas taught Origen in Greek philosophy at Alexandria (6.19.10). He knew that there were issues with this arrangement between non-Christian teacher and Christian student, so he insisted that Ammonius had remained a Christian throughout his lifetime and rejected Porphyry's claim to the contrary, that Ammonius had had Christian parents, but converted during his studies to Neoplatonism, a branch of Greek philosophy. Porphyry's own teacher, Plotinus of Lycopolis in Egypt (c. 203–270), also studied with Ammonius (Porph. *Plot.* § 3), so that this classroom had held the two best philosophical minds of the age, at least in their respective biographers' views. Confusingly, Porphyry also talks about an "Origen," and Eusebius even says that the Christian Origen went to study with someone else called "Ammonius." While Christians and non-Christians readily locked horns in intellectual battles, they went to great lengths to avoid acknowledging that the training they had was the same. The main difference was the priority of texts, i.e., what constituted their treasured canon, and the interpretation of those select texts (Watts 2006: 155–67).

As an irony of history, Clement appears in Eusebius' text, and both Plotinus and Porphyry appear in Eunapius' *Lives of Philosophers and Sophists*, but even so, not all of their many works are extant. All of Maximus' forty-one or so lectures survive to this day through the transmission of manuscripts. Somewhere in time copyists have had other standards and made other choices than the first who sought to define the literary canons. In a similar way, I have adopted an open-minded and inclusive approach in terms of collating the evidence. I do not wish to speculate on what there was once, when we have yet to cover what is left. There is a great deal. I have made no greater distinctions in the material on a greater scale. For example, even if Eusebius stigmatizes Tatian of Assyria (*c.* mid-second century) as a heretic (4.29.1–4), I still include his works under the Christian rubric (4.29.6–7) and consider them part of the Christian voice of that particular time, even though at least one later Christian rejected them. I have generally taken this approach in order to ensure the greatest range of comparative material across early Christianity, for otherwise we will not detect greater literary patterns or phases of thought. The assumption must be that heretics used Alexander in their writings too, for the "Orthodox" writers certainly used the king to dismiss their opponents in turn.

I do not deny that the Christian intellectuals discussed so far and their non-Christian peers represent a narrow "expert" layer of imperial society, not the great majority. This group consists almost exclusively of males with a high level of education in a world in which less than twenty percent were literate (Marrou 1982). Some readers may consider this a "top-down" approach, especially when the theme is a monarch. Nevertheless, as we shall see, Alexander was so popular at every level of society that virtually any person with basic training in rhetoric would have encountered a certain set of ideas revolving around him, which papyri from Egypt make clear (Denuzzo 2003; Prandi 2010). I also trust the above focus on Eusebius' literary project has shown (cf. Corke-Webster 2019) that there is much new to be said on the well-established authors from whom we must normally deduce the conditions of other layers of society. Indeed, much scholarly energy has gone into fundamentally changing our views of Eusebius over the past decade (Johnson 2014). This book presents a similar endeavor to understand the literary projects of other Christian authors surveyed in Chapter 1 and the collective discourse to which they were contributing.

Innovating tradition

"Tradition" is a useful, if vague, term. The label neatly encapsulates a range of primary source material from the era under scrutiny and suggests that the key ideas within this material cohere. It does not imply that material was handed down tralatitiously from Christian to Christian, but rather that there was a familiar frame of reference among Christians. "Early Christian tradition" primarily comprises evidence in the form of literary texts produced within three centuries critical for the formation of Christian thought. Tradition then means the discourse on Alexander within this text-world.

There are naturally immediate issues with this assumed tradition. The common curse of antiquity haunts the Christians too: our source material is not what it once was. Many texts are lost, others survive in a fragmentary state, and some are marred by mistakes, etc. Although it is hard to imagine that new evidence discovered in manuscripts, inscriptions, or papyri would seriously alter the picture offered here, it remains impossible to reconstruct such a comprehensive synthesis of Alexander's reception in the same way that recent series have managed for the Middle Ages (Harf-Lancner 1999; Zuwiyya 2011; Gaullier-Bougassas 2011, 2014) and later periods with their abundant wealth of material (Briant 2017; Moore 2018). And yet, I have adopted a quantitative approach because collocation of evidence is "scholarship's first and highest goal" (Ogden 2013: 2 n. 2). A systematic treatment of what survives does tell us more about the general points of interest for the Christians; which stories only they covered; and their own ways of making Alexander relevant to other Christians.

With regret, I will only touch briefly upon material culture in this book. I was disappointed but not surprised to find that, compared to written evidence from the second to fourth centuries, Christian art has little to no bearing upon the reception of Alexander in the same span (Stewart 1993). There are, of course, notable exceptions. From just outside our period, a most stunning image of Alexander is visible on a mosaic in the 1984 UNESCO site of Heliopolis in Lebanon (Baalbek). Located in the colossal structure presumed to be an Odeon, this later fourth-century "Alexander mosaic" displays scenes from the Greek *Alexander Romance*, an ever-expanding biography that Byzantine Christians came to love. The gorgeous mosaic includes a scene that is not documented in our written versions, namely a nymph bathing an infant Alexander in what appears to be a fount. Not only is it astonishing to have an image of Alexander's youth, because accounts of his pre-campaign life are so scarce, but the iconography also reminds one immediately of baptism. Scenes of John's baptism of Jesus begin to appear in Christian art from the third century onward, and they also represent Jesus as an infant. This prototype image stands in stark contrast to the Gospel narrative in which Jesus is an adult at the time of baptism (Mark 1; Matthew 3; Luke 3). For the Christian onlooker, the childlike Jesus instead symbolizes the sinless innocence that viewers themselves would return to upon baptism. Without a firm point of reference, it is much harder to interpret the image of the childlike Alexander. But the iconography shows that, if the artists were Christian, they also thought from Jesus to Alexander, not just the other way around. By contrast, we will also encounter writers who criticized non-Christian art of Alexander that they encountered in the ancient cities.

Approaching Alexander

Of the feats of the monarch styled "the Great," taking longer to record than to achieve, I shall not speak.

Manilius, On Astronomy, 3.22–23 (trans. LCL)

As ever, paralipsis exaggerates. It did not take long to list the achievements of Alexander from a Roman perspective. From a third-century AD compilation of memorable material, we hear what the ordinary student needed to know:

> Alexander, son of Philip and Olympias, from the city of Pella in Macedon crossed into Asia with 40,000 soldiers and defeated Darius, the Persian King, first at the Granicus River; then at Issus in Cilicia; and a third time at Arbela. In the three battles he conquered 300,000 enemy troops, a legion of cavalry, and 2,000 scythe-bearing chariots. Next he forced the kings of India and all of Asia's nations under his rule and seized the most notable cities of Asia: Sardis, Bactria, Susa, and Babylon in which he also died—whether by intoxication or poison is unknown—but not before he had traveled all the way to Zeus Ammon and been the first of all to navigate the Ocean.

Lucius Ampelius, Liber Memoralis, 16.2

This short review of Alexander's actions reads as a highlight reel of military exploits. The record of the battles against the Persians is largely correct, at least that they number three; the other numbers are anyone's guess. The proportion of importance between the conquest of Persia and India is correct, although Bactria was not a city, but a region in Central Asia. Only towards the end do we hear of cultural achievements, and those of a rather Roman sort. From Seneca's declamations or set speeches, we learn that it was commonplace to discuss whether Alexander would have sailed the Ocean (Sen. *Suas.* 1.pr.1). Lucius Ampelius granted Alexander that honor. He did not grant him other achievements, however. In line with other Roman historians, such as the Augustan writer Livy (*Per.* 45.9), Lucius Ampelius did not record the foundation of Alexandria, the city that became Alexander's primary long-lasting achievement.

Rome indeed lurks behind the representation of the line of Macedonian kings in which Alexander features. Lucius Ampelius rightly arranged Alexander's reign after that of Philip II, Alexander's father, but after Alexander, he turns immediately to Philip V (238–179 BC) and his son Perseus (212–166). Both lost Macedon to Rome in crucial battles. For Lucius Ampelius then, Alexander's reign was like a brilliant flash of lightning that reflected his personal greatness but short life span

(App. *B Civ.* Prooemium.38.1, προσέοικεν ἀστραπῇ λαμπρᾷ). His legacy was a wasteland of war, and Rome eventually surpassed his military might.

Rome spear-headed the formation of Alexander's ancient reception. The distortion of his image had already begun in the king's lifetime. We know of more than twenty contemporaries presenting his life story from different points of view. Fewer wrote of the Peloponnesian War (431–404 BC), which was such a crucial war for the classical Greek world. The writers range from Macedonian members of the inner circle and others, such as the Greek historian Callisthenes of Olynthus, who fell out of favor in 328 BC, to technical staff and the odd courtesan (Pédech 1984). Such contemporary sources were constantly reworked in the emerging Hellenistic kingdoms, whose rulers looked to Alexander and Argead Macedon for legitimacy. One successful rewriter was Clitarchus of Alexandria, whose dating is currently contested. Citations of his now-lost history attest that he was widely read in imperial Rome.

The Romans took full control of Alexander's image three hundred years after the king's death. They made revisions so successfully that the first-generation witnesses ceased to be used and, therefore, to exist. Modern studies routinely refer to these towering, if secondary, authorities: Diodorus Siculus (*fl.* first cent. BC), Pompeius Trogus (*fl.* under Augustus), Quintus Curtius Rufus (*fl.* under Vespasian?), Plutarch (*c.* 45–120?), and Arrian of Nicodemia (*c.* 86–after 146?). Of these five writers, who were spread across the geographical expanse of the Roman world, only Plutarch wrote a biography. This work provides a full account of Alexander's youth. The other four were narrative historians who, unlike Lucius Ampelius, began their work with the king's succession to the throne in 336/5 BC. Like Ampelius, they fastened their seatbelts and hastened after Alexander as he overran Asia. When he stopped dead at Babylon on a summer day in 323 BC, they continued his story with a new cast of characters, who were fighting one of the fiercest succession wars in world history.

Writing a serious account of the whole campaign was no small task. On it, Plutarch (Hamilton 1969) and Diodorus (Prandi 2013) each offer one substantial book, Trogus two in Justin's abridgment (Yardley and Heckel 1997), Arrian seven (Bosworth 1980–), and Curtius ten (Atkinson 1980, 1994, 2009). Plutarch may also have written another two show-orations on Alexander, and Arrian wrote *Events after Alexander*, a ten-book sequel to his popular *History of Alexander*. There is no correspondence between quantity and quality, however. In earlier scholarship, Arrian reigned supreme above the four remaining authors, the so-called "Vulgate." He was considered a more serious historian and had used ostensibly better primary authorities, Aristobulus and Ptolemy. In past assessments, Arrian came closer to what was perceived to be the historical truth. Scholarship has offered some subtle nuances to this assessment since the Enlightenment (Badian 2012), but it was not until relatively recently that we have begun to question this prioritizing. Arrian has much in common with his Roman contemporaries, and Aristobulus and Ptolemy were not infallible. New discoveries of sources from Egypt and Persia offer other perspectives, and scholarship makes major advances in unearthing what is "Achaemenid" (Briant 2010), "Macedonian" (Carney 2015), or "Roman" (Spencer 2002; Welch and Mitchell 2013) in and beyond the five historians. Much energy still needs to be directed into these areas, as we re-evaluate what we think we know about the continuous literary narratives of Alexander history.

But the "great five" are but a dune in a desert of story. One need only consult the standard sourcebook to find an astonishing number of imperial writers referring to Alexander in passing, such as the Tiberian Valerius Maximus and Athenaeus of Naucratis (Yardley and Heckel 2004). Outside the major accounts, the imperial geographer Strabo may well be the best witness to the first-hand sources, because he preserves much cited material from Callisthenes to Clitarchus. In terms of quantity of explicit first-hand references, Strabo may even be a better witness than some of the five historians we normally mine for information. A case has also been made for re-examining the second-century BC Greek historian, Polybius, as a source on Alexander history (Billows 2000).

In imperial literature, there existed also other full-scale narratives, such as the Greek *Alexander Romance* (Ausfeld 1907; Stoneman 2007–; Nawotka 2017). In three books, the anonymous author tells the life story of the king from cradle to grave, like Plutarch or one of the Evangelists. There are indeed many notable parallels with the New Testament. Alexander is the result of divine seed from Ammon's chosen astrologer Nectanebus, the last Pharaoh in exile at Philip's court; Alexander is the constant source of prophecy; he performs miraculous deeds; he institutes a cult for himself in his own city; his will is written to ensure that people follow his precepts after his death, and so on. Even the textual structure is similar. Just like the New Testament, which is overwhelmingly composed of Apostolic letters, large swathes of the *Alexander Romance* consist of letters, purportedly sent to or from Alexander. In many ways, the letters imbue the narrative, however unbelievable, with the ultimate authority of the monarch whose word was law (why would a king tell a lie?). Like the Gospel, the *Alexander Romance* was hugely influential and used much more widely than the "great five," at least until the Enlightenment (Sainte-Croix 1775, with exposition in Briant 2017: 33–36).

The *Alexander Romance* is a curious text. I briefly compared the *Alexander Romance* to the Gospels—I am not the first to do so (Pfister 1989: 87)—but others may argue that Plutarch takes up many of the same themes. For example, he frequently refers to Alexander's letter collection as serious documentation, whereas the letters in the *Alexander Romance* are typically entertaining or rhetorical by nature. Plutarch also discusses Alexander's upbringing, religious devotion, great deeds, and influence (Asirvatham 2018). He is assumed to be reworking stories from his sources, though it is difficult to say what they were, unless he expressly says so. Similarly, the letters of the *Alexander Romance* have roots in a much earlier historical time. For example, one letter between Darius and Alexander is cited separately on papyrus (*P. Hamb.* 129) and on the *Tabula Iliaca* (SEG 33.802, I, ll. 1–4), a stone miniature in the J. Paul Getty Museum in Malibu, California. Other portions of the text contain earlier and separate items, such as Alexander's Will (3.34 of early Hellenistic date) and the Egyptianizing narratives surrounding Nectanebus, Ammon, Serapis, and Alexandria (1.31–34). These previous texts woven into the *Alexander Romance* have attracted some scholarly attention (Merkelbach 1977; Jouanno 2002), but not as much as the burst of studies on the text's transmission and reception in later periods. Having saved the ancient *Alexander Romance* from ignominy, we still need to place it in the company of the other accounts and the surrounding literary landscapes.

In fact, even the established sources still need to be contextualized within Greco-Roman culture as a whole. They have not yet found their place within that rhetoric-driven culture, because we have only recently moved beyond expert studies of source issues, such as the assumed "duality" or "binary relationship" between the Vulgate and Arrian (Hammond 1983, 1993). We have been reluctant to escape Alexander and study the contemporary context of our sources on him, with its overwhelming amount of material. We rarely occupy ourselves with the daunting task of examining the entirety of the discourse on Alexander, or "der ganze Alexander" (Demandt 2009: xii). In 2016, Pierre Briant drew attention to this situation. In his book on commonplaces of Alexander, he demonstrated the remarkable continuity in how writers, ancient and modern, covered the same problems or material over and over to the point of creating "overflow and emptiness," a phrase from his paper read by Jacqueline Arthur-Montaigne at the 2018 Annual Meeting of the Society for Classical Studies in Boston.

But exploring commonplaces may also be a productive endeavor in a new direction. It can tell us more about how Alexander was filtered through discourse. We can study clusters of references that constitute commonplaces. For example, in the *Alexander Romance*, we recognize many of the stories as inversions of school exercises that schoolmasters taught, such as the sack of Thebes (*AR* 1.46). A popular setting in Greek tragedy, Thebes was the ultimate episode to employ for crafting Alexander's tragic character, and the anonymous author completely rewrites the story to create a new character arc for the king. The author engages with the topic of Thebes without seeming to draw upon any kind of clear source, save for his imagination. In the same way as school exercises, a catalog of stories was memorized and altered, as appropriate, for a given work or situation. A *topos* (plural: *topoi*; Latin: *locus/loci*) can thus be altered as prompted by rhetorical context regardless of genre. Rhetorical handbooks, from the pseudo-Ciceronian *Rhetoric to Herennius* (4.31) to Menander Rhetor of Laodicea in the late third-century AD, give us an idea of what these general topics were and how to use them. Their ubiquity in the literature means that we are perhaps in the wrong to focus solely on sources rather than on a wider curriculum of topics. Ancient intellectuals knew such topics by heart and so could deploy material from the inculcated material without exertion or reference to a particular work. This kind of "Alexandrology" or "Alexandrography" must be much more widespread and influential than hitherto recognized.

We witness the same tendency to systematize episodic scenes in our treasured historians (Bridges 2018: 32–57). In the opening of Books 16 and 17 of the *Library of History*, Diodorus states that he is organizing the histories of Philip (16) and Alexander (17) around the topical headings of their actions. The pair is so illustrious that they each fill a complete book on their own. From reading the tables of contents, we may deduce that many of the stories recounted were commonplaces in Alexandrology. Diodorus at least provides us with a long list of potential themes. Other sources confirm that many of the stories display moral character, and each unit is normally known as an *exemplum* (plural: *exempla*; Greek: *paradeigma/paradeigmata*). Despite its length, the list is not as complete as the modern mind may like it to be. For example, Diodorus' catalog does not include Alexander's most famous acts, such as the cutting of the Gordian Knot. The list is nevertheless useful for displaying how important discourse on morality was for the historian (Hau 2016). For Diodorus, recounting the actions of historical characters is the most efficient method of narrating history. Ironically, however, these two books are the first and final time that the subject matter is so focused on a single person that Diodorus can use his preferred method in his forty-volume work.

Only through systematic study of this "*exemplum* literature" can we identify the building blocks for the discourse on Alexander in antiquity and see how they fitted together. The best proponent of this method remains Gerhard Wirth's study of the fate of the ancient knowledge on the historical Alexander. Wirth argued that Alexander's death caused an instantaneous pitfall in the knowledge of the king that would only decline throughout antiquity on "the road to oblivion," the words of his main title. I disagree with his hypothesis of "decline"—for it assumes erroneously that (1) all living witnesses to the historical Alexander recorded the truth impartially, which they did not (Mederer 1936); and that (2) later writers distorted knowledge because of ignorance rather than because they had an agenda in writing an Alexander appropriate for their own cultural needs (Koulakiotis 2006). But I find Wirth's way of seeing the discourse through *topoi* worth testing. This approach presents itself as a possibility, precisely because there is so much data on the king still available in and beyond the standard histories (Djurslev 2018c: 560). Some studies have gone some way in collating the evidence (Hoffman 1907; Weber 1909; Eicke 1909; Stoneman 2011; Pernot 2013), but the corpus remains incomplete. By focusing on the early Christian evidence, we access an extraordinary source of ancient discourse, and new patterns will be revealed. Furthermore, by approaching Alexander's ancient reception from this direction, I challenge some of the traditional methods and means that primarily focus on Roman politics (Croisille 1990; Carlsen 1993). Previous studies take the form of diachronic (Frugoni 1978; Pfrommer 2001) or synchronic surveys of the highlights in certain periods (Gagé 1975; Zecchini 1984; Döpp 1999; Angliviel 2003). Others have traced the transition of individual stories from classical to Christian literature (Cracco-Ruggini 1963). I advocate a more holistic approach. It may be in the minority at present, but I hope that this book will make a new case for understanding the ancient discourse on Alexander. Taking a more sympathetic view of the later material may also give us a new appreciation of what went before.

I pose some of the typical reception-related questions one may ask of an uneven corpus of written work on such grand historical characters:

1. In what ways do Christians accommodate Alexander in a new cultural context?
    a. Which *topoi* proliferate and which ones disappear?
    b. Do new *topoi* come into being?
    c. Do education and language play a part in the selection process?
2. What methods do Christians use to embellish the representation?
    a. Do representations depend on genre?
    b. Which literary devices are more popular?

3. How does Alexander's Christian tradition match up with the contemporary non-Christian use?
    a. Do Christians emphasize the same points of reception as non-Christians?
    b. Is positivity or negativity about Alexander significant or irrelevant?
4. What, if anything, is uniquely "Christian" about Alexander's literary tradition in early Christianity?
    a. Do Christians attribute specifically Christian purpose to Alexander?
    b. Do Christians represent him with Christian features—i.e., do they make him a "proto-Christian"?

Plan of attack

I develop the overarching argument in four chapters, a conclusion, and an epilogue. Chapter 1 briefly introduces the main sources and *dramatis personae* of the study. It surveys Christian writers that mention Alexander from Tatian of Assyria to Jerome of Stridon. We notice that the learning range of authors matches that of those learned Christians introduced on previous pages; these figures came from a high social standing that could compete with that of educated non-Christians. We will see which ones used classicizing material, Jewish texts, or a combination. This chapter should be taken as a point of reference for the remaining chapters.

Chapter 2 explores three major themes Christians developed from their "pagan" peers: Alexander's education; his letters; and his wish for deification. Material pertaining to these topics was only lightly altered, if at all, and Christians were at least as good as pagans to use it, if not better in some instances. The first theme of education was generally used to dismiss pagan philosophy through the example of Alexander and Aristotle. The second theme concerns a letter that Christians seized upon, whereas pagans did not. The letter proved useful in Christian arguments against paganism. The third theme of deification was not as popular as the former two; I argue that the Christians rarely discussed deification through Alexander, which pagans did. Instead Christians preferred other mythological characters to denigrate.

Chapter 3 investigates what the Christians appropriated from Hellenistic Judaism. Christians took Jewish literature seriously in that they appropriated stories about Alexander from Hellenistic Jewish writers to the same degree as they used the pagan textual tradition. Three principal themes emerge: stories about

Jews in Alexandria, the books of the Old and New Testaments, and Josephus' story about Alexander in Jerusalem. Christians generally omitted stories that gave special privileges to the Jews, such as citizenship in Alexandria, but emphasized stories that revealed the lesser power of Alexander in relation to God. The Christian reading of the Old Testament gave Alexander history an important place in Christian thought, as a way of reorienting world history. I argue that this is the place in which the most profound changes to Alexander's prior legacy occur, for it is here that the king becomes directly relevant to the Christian world.

Chapter 4 elaborates on the last point by analyzing how the Christians fitted together material from both Jewish and pagan founts in their historiography and rhetoric. These genres are important because they allowed Christians to experiment within a well-established tradition, and Christians innovated by making new synchronisms and juxtapositions between Alexander and others. While some material remained the same as before, especially in miscellaneous texts, we find that the framework of Christian history outlined in the previous chapter makes demands on the historiographer, with ramifications for Alexander and his successors' history. Finally, we shall investigate some Christian comparisons of Alexander and key Christian figures, such as the Apostle Paul and Constantine.

The Conclusion summarizes the contents of the chapters and stresses some central points pertaining to Alexander across the Christian corpus until Constantine. The Epilogue compares Eusebius' *Life of Constantine* to the Alexander tradition, as a point of departure for studying later Christian receptions.

1

Apologists and Co.

Introduction

Not many early Christians have achieved the status of household names. The casual reader cannot be expected to be familiar with these esoteric figures, so I offer a short survey of the key Christian authors that mention Alexander. I include brief introductions and textual references with summaries, which will be discussed throughout this book. I lay out the evidence chronologically within entries, insofar as this is possible. The structure does not mean that I believe that the discourse developed linearly from author A to B, etc., although sometimes a source relationship can be detected. I intend the present chapter for quick consultation, not necessarily for continuous reading.

Tatian of Assyria

A pupil of the apologist Justin Martyr, Tatian flourished in the mid- to late second century. Born a non-Christian in the east, it is possible that he converted at Rome before residing at an unknown location in the eastern empire, perhaps Antioch-on-the-Orontes in Syria. Other Christians branded him the founder of a heretical sect, known as the "Abstinents" or *Encratites*, whose extreme beliefs included claiming matrimony was adultery, abstaining from eating meat and drinking wine, and drinking water at the Eucharist, for which they were also labeled *Aquarii*. We know these details from the Heresiologists, i.e., catalogers of heresies, and from Tatian's own works. In his day, his most famous work was the *Diatessaron* ("through four versions"; full reference in Clavis Patrum Graecorum, CPG, no. 1106). This work was a harmony of the four Gospels used locally in the churches of Syria. The text has not reached us in its early form, which was perhaps Syriac, but it is partially preserved in the Syrian Ephrem's (*c*. 306–373) commentary on it, as well as in Arabic and Latin adaptations from the Middle Ages.

While Tatian is described as an ascetic and apologist, his *Oration to the Greeks* (*Oratio ad Graecos* or *Pros Hellenas*; CPG 1104) is a vituperative outburst against everything Greek, especially the tenets of philosophy (§§ 1–3, 25–28). He attacks every aspect of Greek philosophy and morality, arguing that the only good things in the Greek world were taken from the "barbarians," such as the wisdom of the Hebrews or Indians. "Alien" wisdom was a latent theme in the imperial period. Despite his lambasting of the Greeks, Tatian's own Greek education shines through the text. But the content is distinctively in the vein of other apologetic writing of the period, especially arguments about demonology (§§ 8–20) and the priority of the Christian religion (§§ 31, 36–41).

It is in the context of this criticism that Alexander appears. First at § 2.1–2 in a few contemptuous remarks on Aristotle and, second, at § 36.1–2, a passage on the Babylonian writer Berossus, who lived in the times of Alexander. The former will be discussed in Chapter 2; the latter in Chapter 4.

Athenagoras of Athens

If Tatian launches an offensive on behalf of Christianity, Athenagoras takes a defensive stance. From his principal work, *Supplication for the Christians* (the Greek *presbeia* also suggests "address" or "embassy"; CPG 1070), we learn some ostensible details of his life. The title page suggests that he is an Athenian philosopher, although other notes from the biographical tradition call him a teacher at a school in Alexandria. The elegant style of his Greek suggests rhetorical training, and scholars routinely praise him for his Atticizing eloquence. Unlike Tatian, he was not afraid to cite sources directly from prose or poetry, supporting the doctrine that the writers were divinely inspired. His addressees are none other than the highest authorities, the emperors Marcus Aurelius and Commodus, whose co-rule lasted from 176/7 to the former's death in c. 180. Whether he delivered the oration before them or not, it is telling that he directed it to them instead of the local governors, who were normally in charge of regional persecutions. The speech seeks to repudiate three major accusations against the Christians. They are as follows. The first is that the Christians were atheists (not believing in the Roman gods); the second is that they were cannibals (in the Eucharist); and the third is that they were incestuous (all of them being brothers and sisters).

In the *Supplication*, Athenagoras argues vehemently for monotheism, not only through divine revelation, but also through dismissal of other religions. In

§§ 26–30, he takes issue with how demons tempt humans with idol and ancestor worship. His "evidence" is taken from Herodotus, Hermes Trismegistus, and Alexander's *Letter to his Mother* (§ 28). The pseudo-letter was very popular with Christians and non-Christians, as we shall see in Chapter 2.

Clement of Alexandria

Titus Flavius Clemens was one of the most brilliant apologists of the late second century. He tells us himself that his thirst for knowledge led him from Greece (Athens?) to Sicily and Syria before he found his way to a compelling teacher in Alexandria, namely Pantaenus (Euseb. *Hist. eccl.* 5.10–11). Tradition has it that Clement left Egypt during the alleged persecutions of emperor Septimus Severus (r. 193–211) and died somewhere in Cappadocia. At Alexandria, Clement received a comprehensive education, but his abilities went much beyond the common curriculum. His extraordinary skills emerge in his impressive range of knowledge and rhetorical flair in three extant works: *Exhortation to the Greeks* (*Protreptikos*, like Aristotle's work of the same name; CPG 1375); *Pedagogue* (*Paidagogos*; CPG 1376); and a miscellany, known as the *Stromata* ("Carpets" or "Tapestries"; CPG 1377). These immensely learned works are famous for bridging Hellenistic Judaism, Greek philosophy, and Christianity in the most profound way. Long conceived of as a tripartite initiation to the Christian mysteries, the books contain no real serial unity. As they represent only some of his surviving works, we can hardly consider it a specific educational program. These three give the impression that he is targeting the wealthy and already well-educated stratum of society, supported by the fragmentary text, *What Rich Man is Saved* (CPG 1379). This personal appeal to the well-to-do hardly fits well with his role of teaching ordinary Christian catechumens, but the wider interests evident in his writing suggest that he was immersed in all aspects of the church, not just raising the religion to a higher social register. For example, Eusebius speaks of Origen's attendance of Clement's classes and, at 6.13–14.9, he records the works of Clement, primarily at 6.13.3. Finally, Christian tradition is also persistent in associating Clement with the successors of Apostolic teaching through his assumption of headship over Pantaenus' school. This is done in order to maintain that Christian teaching proceeded unchanged and uncontaminated from the days of Jesus.

Alexander appears in all of Clement's surviving works, though not with the same frequency: *Exhortation* three times, *Pedagogue* once, and *Miscellany* six times. Clement sometimes extracts the passages by quoting other texts with full reference to the author, but he contextualized the citations with his own agendas. We will encounter him in Chapters 2 and 4.

Hippolytus "of Rome"

Few figures from the early third century have caused the same amount of controversy as Hippolytus "of Rome." Scholarly interpretations of the rich textual and iconographical evidence have split him into two different persons, one from the East and the other from Rome. Other scholars have confused him with a third martyr of the same name because the author also suffered martyrdom in the mines of Sardinia, "the island of death." Hippolytus' legend is tied to his resistance to Calixtus' election for the bishopric of Rome, which led some to brand him the first "Antipope." Later writers on his identity must be excused for the confusion because the uncertainty arose already in antiquity. Eusebius records a fraction of the writings attributed to him (*Hist. Eccl.* 6.22.1–2) and other details of his authorship abound. A late story tells us that Origen heard Hippolytus preaching the lost homily *On the Praise of the Lord our Saviour* when he visited Rome (6.15.10; Eusebius' silence on this meeting is telling). One key feature of the meeting is that it links the two intellectuals with the highest literary output of third-century Greek Christianity, although the comparison may not have been meant to be flattering during the heated time of the so-called "Origenist controversy" (AD 380–410s). Ignoring the debatable historicity of this meeting, the shadowy Hippolytus (c. 170–235) was, as far as we can tell, an older contemporary of Origen.

For the purpose of this study, I have chosen to present Hippolytus as the author of a single corpus, which is also done in the CPG nos. 1870–1925. Many of his texts survive intact in Oriental and Caucasian languages, as well as in more fragmentary Greek remains. Our main concern is with the following four works: *Refutation of all Heresies* (after 222, books 1, 4–10 extant; CPG 1899); *On the Christ and the Antichrist* (c. 200, fully preserved in Greek; CPG 1872); *Commentary on Daniel* (c. 204, Greek in fragments; CPG 1873), and the *Collection of Chronologies* (c. 234, later Latin adaptations; CPG 1896). Hippolytus wrote a great deal on Alexander from various perspectives. For example, he is the first to use both Jewish and classical material in tandem. Most of his sixteen references occur in the *Commentary on Daniel*. We shall regularly encounter Hippolytus in the following chapters.

Julius Africanus

The next author seems an anomaly in the third-century church. Even his name is contested: the praenomen Sextus is poorly attested, and "Africanus" is a misnomer for someone presumably born in Aelia Capitolina (the Roman refoundation of Jerusalem) in c. 170. Unlike some of his Christian contemporaries, Julius Africanus rose through the ranks and became a high-profile citizen in the empire. Reconstructing his life through his fragmentary works unveils a story fit for the big screen: early on, he served in the imperial army of Septimus Severus, which brought him as far as Edessa and its ostensible Christian ruler, perhaps in 195. He admired Abgar VIII and taught his son. He conversed with the "regretful heretic" Bardesanes, whom Eusebius later despised. Still in Edessa, Julius Africanus may have seen the famed tent of Jacob, whose cycle of exile and restoration is described in Genesis 28–33. His haphazard travels took him back to the Mediterranean. He had intriguing encounters in Alexandria (with the future bishop Heraclas and perhaps Origen), work at Rome (establishing the library of the Pantheon for Alexander Severus), and duties in Palestinian Nicopolis (the town Emmaus of Luke 24:13–35), which he seems to have restored through his imperial influence. A polyglot (Greek, Latin, Hebrew, and perhaps Syriac) and polymath, late in life he entered into a correspondence with none other than Origen. His letter concerned the authenticity of Susanna's story in the Book of Daniel. The letter is dated to 240 after which his story ends. In short, Julius Africanus was every bit as cosmopolitan and erudite as Eusebius wanted his Christians to be in the *Church History*. Eusebius even recognized Africanus' authority in several places (*Hist. Eccl.* 1.6.2, 1.7, 6.31).

Africanus' two principal works are the *Chronographies* (*Chronographiae*; CPG 1690) and the *Miscellany* (*Kestoi*, "stiches" or "embroideries"; CPG 1691). Both works are lost in their complete form and exist only as excerpts in later writers. The fragments are now available in accessible editions that have properly contextualized Africanus in the Severan period (*Chronographs* in GCS NF 15; *Miscellany* in GCS NF 18). The extensive mining of information from Africanus is the reason why his works are lost: if the original is reworked often enough, it ceases to exist in its original form. New copies may alter content or later writers may use a text's authority to write an updated version. Africanus' *Chronographies* was the first Christian history, a five-book synchronism of world histories from Creation to c. 221, whereas the *Miscellany* was a compilation of scattered encyclopedic information with little to no Christian content in nine (according to George Syncellus), fourteen (Photius), or twenty-four (*Suda*) books. Though miscellanies were common, Julius Africanus' version presents a rarity for its variety and its dedication to the emperor Alexander Severus (r. c. 222–235).

Alexander appears briefly in both works in the context of warfare and Macedonian kingship. He features several times and for different purposes. Since both topics have historiographical implications, we will consider them in Chapter 4.

Tertullian of Carthage

Quintus Septimius Florens Tertullianus, better known as Tertullian, rose to fame in the Severan period. He was the first Christian to write primarily in the Latin language, although he is also known to have composed Greek works (full reference in Clavis Patrum Latinorum nos. 1–31). The only uncontested detail of his life is that he spent it in Roman Carthage. Scholars have rejected the identification with the Roman lawyer mentioned in a later Roman digest, but maintain the idea that he was a presbyter in a local branch of the church organization. This role makes sense, as his extensive literary output primarily addresses pastoral and behavioral matters (sixteen out of thirty-one extant works). He was by no means a meek preacher as some of the other apologists might seem. He preached fire and brimstone, as Tatian had done. Described as a "rottweiler" (Corke-Webster 2017b: 250), Tertullian's many snarly sermons consisted of doctrine, polemics, and apologetic arguments, forcing his audience to put their "Christianness" first. He also sneered at non-Christians (four texts), but he was much more aggressive towards heretics (six) and their ideas (five). This distribution discloses who, in his view, presented the greatest danger to his Carthaginian congregation.

Given his large textual output, it is no surprise that Tertullian offers the most wide-ranging catalog of references to Alexander before Jerome of Stridon (d. 420). Tertullian's ten references occur in various contexts from fashion to heresy, and he does not shy away from praising or rebuking the Macedonian king. We will encounter Tertullian's writings in Chapter 2 above all, because he focuses on Alexander's education and deification.

Minucius Felix

A most elegant writer, Minucius Felix flourished in Severan Rome. He was the only Latin apologist based in the capital and may have worked there as a lawyer,

unlike Tertullian. Scholars normally pair the two because Minucius Felix seems to have used Tertullian's *Apology* in his *Octavius* (or less likely, vice versa). His unique location indicates that the center of Latin Christian activity lay elsewhere in the empire, primarily North Africa, and Minucius Felix himself demonstrates an awareness of African matters. We know little else of him. The Christian biographical tradition provides no information beyond his literary pursuits. His singular masterpiece, the dialog *Octavius* (CPL 37), is uniquely preserved in a ninth-century manuscript, which is appended to the work of another apologist, Arnobius of Sicca (see below). The earliest date for the composition is AD 197, whereas the upper limit is 248 (Schubert 2014). Despite the chance survival of this text, it offers a rather remarkable narrative. Taking place in Ostia, the narrative unfolds as a conversation between the Christian Octavius of Cirta and the pagan Caecilius of Rome, with Marcus Minucius Felix as arbiter. The outcome is inevitable, as Caecilius is convinced of Christianity's viability, but only through a mosaic of arguments marshaled from what on the surface seems to be Stoic philosophy and quotations of classical writers, such as Cicero and Virgil. The author makes not a single reference to Christian dogma or Jesus. He couches the religion in traditional language and thought. Indeed, the dialog format is also part of the persuasive strategy to advance the position that Christianity was culturally compatible with Roman values. Athenagoras had adopted a similar strategy of presenting quotations in the *Supplication*, emulating Plato's courtroom *Apology* for Socrates, whereas Minucius Felix attempts to outdo Cicero's philosophical dialogs.

At *Octavius* § 21 Kytzler, Minucius Felix provides further details of Alexander's *Letter to His Mother*. Athenagoras had conferred authority upon the letter as if it were a source as authoritative as Herodotus himself, whereas Minucius Felix juxtaposes it with arguments from Greek philosophers on the doctrine of human deification. The letter is studied in detail in Chapter 2.

Origen of Alexandria/Caesarea

We briefly met Origen in the Introduction. His importance is evident from the attention he received. Eusebius and Jerome devote the long sections to Origen's life and thought, and we still have access to many of his works, despite the Origenist controversy. As the master of Alexandrian allegory, his contentious readings of Scripture made him friends and enemies. His patron in Alexandria was the wealthy Ambrose, who encouraged Origen to take up writing at the age of thirty. Origen's success at home and abroad caused him to clash with the local bishop Demetrius, whose authority was undermined in several instances by bishops in Jerusalem and Palestinian Caesarea. Bishops in these cities granted Origen the right to proceed to the priesthood. Origen eventually lost the battle in Alexandria and was exiled to Palestinian Caesarea around *c.* 232 (Euseb. *Hist. eccl.* 6.26). Alexandria's loss was Caesarea's gain, as his work there made him the most prolific writer of his day (Jer. *Ep.* 33). Always on the move, he was involved in the main Christian debates, and became known to the imperial authorities. For example, Jerome adds to Origen's extensive travel catalog that he visited Antioch by imperial invitation and communicated with Philip the Arab, whom Jerome says was the first Christian emperor (Jer. *De vir. ill.* § 54). Neither Eusebius nor Jerome want to speak of Origen's death under Decius, perhaps because Origen outlived the emperor's persecution by a few months, dying in Tyre at the age of sixty-nine (*c.* 254).

Alexander appears in three works: Origen's fragmentary *Commentary on Genesis* (CPG 1410); *On the Psalms* (CPG 1429); and his famous apologetic work *Against Celsus* (CPG 1476). In the first instance, Origen makes use of the prophecies of Daniel to discuss content in the first Mosaic book of the Old Testament. Alexander was important for the author of Daniel, and Origen uses prophecies concerning Alexander to verify information in that book. We will consider the Biblical material in Chapter 3. Origen's second reference to Alexander occurs in the context of a comparison between the king and the Apostle Paul (Chapter 4). The third and fourth references concern separate material: the former refers to Homer, Alexander, and Jesus on the Cross (Chapter 2), whereas the latter tells the story of Alexander's visit to Jerusalem (Chapter 2).

Methodius of Olympus

From Origen we proceed to his opponent, whom Eusebius, Origen's heir, omitted from the *Church History*. Details of Methodius' life are scarce: scholarly tradition associates him with bishoprics in Philippi in Macedon, Tyre in Phoenicia, and the small town of Olympus in Anatolian Lycia. Dates are uncertain too, but he is believed to have suffered martyrdom in the city of Chalcis on Euboia, presumably in the persecutions of 311. He may have studied at Origen's school at Caesarea, but he did not agree with the master's interpretation of scripture. He wrote critically of Origen in several works, though few survive intact or at all. One of his lost writings is a dismissal of Porphyry's *Against the Christians* (c. 270; CPG 1818), the first of many Christian responses, and this defense shows that Methodius was well-equipped to take on the philosophical debates of his day. His most famous work remains the *Symposium* or *On Virginity* (*peri hagneias*; CPG 1810) in which ten virgins come together to praise the Christian way of life, ending with Thecla's song about God, the bridegroom (Christ), and the bride (the Church).

Methodius makes a brief mention of Alexander in the *On the Resurrection* (§ 28; CPG 1812). Notice of Alexander's reign helps Methodius to prove that Jerusalem was sacked six times. I will delve further into historiographical context in Chapter 4.

Arnobius of Sicca

From Roman Sicca Veneria (El Kef in modern Tunisia) came a Numidian teacher of rhetoric, Arnobius Afer. His only surviving work, *Against the Nations* (single ms. = BnF Par.lat. 1661) or *Contra Gentiles* (CPL 93), marks him as a recent convert during the Diocletianic persecution, perhaps the early stage of 302–305, if we ignore the fact that Jerome placed him in 326–327. Jerome further claims that Arnobius was led to his conversion by divine dreams, but not accepted by the local bishop at first, for he had formerly been a critic of Christianity. He may have written *Against the Nations* to revoke his former views, so that the bishop was persuaded that Arnobius was sincere in his new faith. But writing was not enough. He also needed to pledge loyalty to be admitted into the church, which he finally was. We know little else beyond Jerome's brief biographical outline and what emerges from Arnobius' sole work (Simmons 1995).

The seven books of *Against the Nations* follow the philosophy that the best defense is a strong offense. Books 3–7 read as an all-out assault on traditional Greco-Roman cult and myths. In many ways, this part of the text is reminiscent of philosophical attacks on Christianity by Porphyry and others, a format that Arnobius must have been used to as a former critic. He deploys classical myths from authoritative sources, such as Plato and Virgil, in line with how philosophers had employed incredible scriptural stories to discredit Christians. Arnobius does also draw upon arguments from previous Christian authors—without naming them. The first two books are more apologetic in nature, as they respond to the following charge: Christians were the cause of recent evils for imperial Rome. In addition to this accusation the Christians were ridiculed because they had deified a man who died by crucifixion, and were praising the name of Christ, which pagans hated. The allegation is closely associated with the main concern behind the Diocletianic persecution, namely that Christians refused to worship the pantheon of polytheistic Rome. In doing so, they were believed to cause calamities in the Roman world. Arnobius' violent counter-argument is that evil has always existed; the present hardship is not greater than those afflictions in the past. Alexander was apparently such an evil, for which Christians could not be held responsible (1.5). We will consider such an argument in Chapter 4, with a comparison of the Christian historian Orosius (CPL 571).

Lactantius

Although a famous African teacher, Arnobius was eclipsed by his student Lucius Cae(ce)lius Firmianus Lactantius (*c.* 260–325/6?). For his life we rely again on Jerome's account, this time his compilation of illustrious authors (Lactantius at § 80). After his education, Lactantius left Africa for Bithynian Nicomedia (Izmit, Turkey), a new imperial center during the first rule of four co-emperors, or the "Tetrarchy" (293–305). In this city, he taught rhetoric until his resignation during the Diocletianic persecutions. Jerome supposed that Lactantius' teaching in Latin saw limited success with students in a Greek city, and so he posited that Lactantius spent the time there writing a great many works. Modern research suggests, however, that all his works were published *after* the Diocletianic persecutions. Late in life, perhaps around 315 or earlier, he was summoned to the imperial court once again, now to teach Crispus, Constantine's son, in the new seat of power in Gaul. At Augusta Treverorum (now Trier, Germany), he may also have stayed close to Constantine himself, with whom he perhaps became acquainted years before, when the future emperor resided at Nicomedia. But such speculation about a ruler and his teacher of choice can keep historians fruitlessly preoccupied, as the example of Alexander and Aristotle reminds us. In Lactantius' case, we know of the invitation to Constantine's court at Trier and, in 325, he dedicated the epitome of his *Divine Institutes* (written in 324) to the emperor.

Lactantius' story must detain us for a moment. First, because his movements display the continued high mobility of sought-after scholars in the later Roman Empire. Second, because they indicate a divide between the imperial languages, but this division may be truer for Jerome's time than Lactantius'. Third, because his long life suggests a personal ability to adapt to the course of events, avoiding martyrdom while in the imperial center during the ostensible "worst of all" persecutions. This last point, together with the Diocletianic inception of his oeuvre, hints at why he may have been prompted to undertake his literary pursuits in support of the church. Instead of dying, he took up the pen to become what Eusebius would actively promote in the *Church History*: a writer for the faith. Lactantius' five extant works—*On the Work of God* (*De Opificio Dei*; CPL 87); *Divine Institutes against the Pagans* (*Divinae Institutiones*; CPL 85); *The Deaths of the Persecutors* (*De Mortibus Persecutorum*; CPL 91); *The Wrath of God* (*De Ira Dei*; CPL 88); and the *Epitome* (CPL 86)—reflect a radical shift in the literary production among Christians. This shift also manifests itself independently in the works of Lactantius' contemporary, Eusebius of Caesarea (next entry).

Given Lactantius' importance and output, it is disappointing that Alexander features only twice in his corpus, both times in the *Divine Institutes* (1.6.8, 2.7.19). Like Arnobius' *Against the Nations*, this work was also written in seven books and shows some similarity in terms of method. For example, many of the supporting quotations are collected from classical sources and interspersed with arguments of earlier apologists, although remarkably not Arnobius. The *Divine Institutes* breaks with tradition in many ways by being the first attempt at a *summa theologiae* rather than a simple broadside against the "pagans."

Eusebius of Caesarea

Like Lactantius, Eusebius had a complex relationship with the court of Constantine, which too seems to have provided him with the impetus for literary pursuits. Before Constantine's ascendancy, he worked in Origen's school under Pamphilius, whose name he took when Pamphilius suffered martyrdom in the Diocletianic persecution after two years of imprisonment (from November 307 to February 310, Euseb. *Hist. eccl.* 8.13.6-7; *Mart. Pal.* 7.4-7). From birth until Pamphilius' death, Eusebius had himself enjoyed "the little peace of the church," but the last persecution forced him to flee Greek-speaking Caesarea through Tyre and the Egyptian Thebaid to no avail. He too was imprisoned but released when the Emperor Galerius' edict of tolerance came into effect in 311. Ordained Bishop of Caesarea in 313, he played a key role in the long Arian controversy over the nature of Christ. Of his contact with the imperial court, Jerome says that Eusebius flourished under Constantine and Constantius, presumably Constantius II ($r.$ 337-361), though he only outlived Constantine by a few years ($d.c.$ 339). He delivered two official addresses to Constantine in 325 and 335, and famously composed his biography, the *Life of Constantine* (CPG 3496), unfinished at

Eusebius' death. Jerome does not include this biography in his brief entry on Eusebius' corpus (§ 81). Independently of Lactantius, Eusebius embarked on a similar literary project to modernize Christian literature in Greek.

Eusebius' mission required an extensive reworking of history. Accordingly, he is most famous for his historiographical works. In the Introduction, we focused on his *Church History* (CPG 3495), because it is available in full, whereas fragments remain of other Christian attempts at history writing, such as Hegesippus (c. 110–c. 180), Hippolytus, and Julius Africanus. The *Church History* does not discuss Alexander at all. Eusebius' first historiographical work was the *Chronicle* (CPG 3494), which was concerned with Christian prehistory from the Old Testament Patriarch Abraham onward. The two-book text was extensively recopied, revised, and supplemented, and so does not survive in Greek, but exists in Latin adaptation and continuation by Jerome and in an Armenian translation. Its synoptic account of Alexander history is analyzed in Chapter 4. The *Life of Constantine* also features a powerful digression on Alexander, discussed in Chapter 4 and the Epilogue.

Eusebius also produced apologetic works. The *Preparation for the Gospel* (CPG 3486) and *Demonstration of the Gospel* (CPG 3487) present readers with mosaics of quotations from previous authors, organized artfully in order to provide what is to be taken as evidence in support of the author's case for Christianity. Just like Arnobius and Lactantius, Eusebius used information from Christian and non-Christian sources, and the works contain much material not found elsewhere. Alexander was especially important in the *Preparation* (eight references) and less so in the *Demonstration* (two). We will revisit these works where appropriate, as they contain various pieces of information, some of which are rather vestigial.

Eusebius' Biblical exegesis also features Alexander in two instances: the *Commentary on Isaiah* (CPG 3468) and the *Commentary on Psalm 50* (CPG 3467). These mentions follow Hippolytus and Origen in using Alexander for other parts of the Old Testament than the book of Daniel. We will discuss these remarks in Chapter 3.

Jerome of Stridon

Although Jerome (c. 350–419/20) of Stridon (a fortification in the Roman province of Dalmatia) lived and worked outside the chronological parameters of this study, his significance earns him a place in this catalog. Perhaps most famous for his revisions to the Latin Bible, which became the *versio vulgata* and formed the basis of Scripture in the medieval western church, he was also a well-connected and formidable player in the Christian communities in which he was involved. Many influential contemporaries, including Pope Damasius I (366–384), and other wealthy patrons saw his intellectual promise. These sponsorships gave him the time and leisure for study. They also provided him with access to a wealth of material, such as the Caesarean library of Origen and Eusebius, which he utilized with his impressive knowledge of languages. Adaptation and appropriation through critical reading is perhaps a fitting description of his literary pursuits, for he did not save all his bitterness and polemics for his opponents. His venomous pen made him a controversial figure, more so than Tatian and Tertullian. He made powerful enemies, but that is probably also evidence of his prominence. He ends his own catalog of great Christian writers with himself (Jer. *Vir. Ill.* § 135; CPL 616). For various reasons, Jerome spent much of his life traveling from city to city, sometimes with his benefactors, in all the corners of the empire. Bethlehem brought him the peace necessary to compose his exegetical project and, in old age, he died where his Savior had been born.

As previously mentioned, Jerome's works are full of references to Alexander. One might attribute this to his ardent fascination with the Classics, but the impression from the preceding pages indicates that he was not the only Christian to be interested in Alexander. We might also say that Jerome was well-traveled in the East, and so was more inclined toward a positive view of Greek history, but his fellow Latin-writing Christians made the same kinds of references to Alexander, based on the Latin writers. In fact, he makes the vast majority of his references in exegetical contexts, just as Hippolytus and Origen had done. Jerome makes more than forty references to Alexander, with most of them appearing in his *Commentary on Daniel* (15/42; CPL 588). Many references to the king depend on Old Testament readings, especially the prophets, rather than classical sources. Like Eusebius, he also preserves material that other Christians and non-Christians used. For instance, Jerome is one of our principal witnesses to Origen's *On the Psalms* (CPL 592). We depend on him for fragments of their work. In many ways, Jerome looks back on his predecessors and neatly ties all the threads together on his own terms. In this sense, we may see him as a Janus, looking backwards and forwards at the same time—although he would no doubt have failed to appreciate the image.

Observations

From this sporadic survey, we may glean some general tendencies that we will continue to witness:

1. Christians operate in various parts of the empire, not only in the principal cities, but also—perhaps especially—on the periphery. Cultural productivity thus depends on both local and empire-wide associations between Christians from the outset.
2. Advanced education is the principal currency of cultural exchange. Most Christian texts do not necessarily activate a sense of Christianness in readers. Some genres make specifically Christian arguments, but many writers simply accept and re-purpose knowledge widely available.
3. Wealthy patrons supported Christians from at least the Severan period onward, which meant that Christians could pursue various avenues of knowledge in scholastic communities, just as their pagan counterparts did.
4. Christians do not seem to achieve imperial patronage until Julius Africanus and Origen, who received support on account of their learning, not their Christianity.
5. From the late second century, Christians consistently make reference to matters pertaining to Alexander, and the material depends on previous or contemporary historiographical data, i.e., Christians do not overtly invent stories without some basis in what has gone before. They are aware of the same matters as the non-Christians.
6. The distribution of references to Alexander is random. Comparatively, there is no higher frequency of references in Greek authors; of course, there are more Greek-writing Christians in the period, for Christianity came from the Greek East.

2

Classical Themes and Christian Tradition

Introduction

Plato might not be the first philosopher one would associate with Alexander. Aristotle, who taught the young king at the Macedonian village of Mieza (343–340 BC) and rose to fame in Athens while his illustrious student was away in Asia, seems a more fitting choice. Nevertheless, Sextus Empiricus, a skeptic philosopher who flourished in the late second century AD, combined Plato and Alexander (Sext. Emp. *Math.* 5.89). The passage in question concerns Babylonian horoscopes with which Sextus took issue. He argued against the idea that people born in the same month had similar destinies as Chaldean astrology proclaimed, insisting that newborns of the same month would not necessarily grow up under the same conditions. Some would be kings, others poor. As evidence, he said that no one born in the days of Alexander matched the king, nor was anyone Plato's equal. Given the fame of the pair, his juxtaposition makes a persuasive case.

In fact, Sextus' argument worked so well that Hippolytus of Rome recycled it (Hippol. *Haer.* 4.5.5 Marcovitch). The Christian writer did not even alter the statement, nor did he change the roles of Plato and Alexander, who were perceived as contemporaries (cf. Ps.-Justin *Or.* § 12; Euseb. *Praep. evang.* 10.14.17). The pair were exceptional individuals of the same century: the Athenian philosopher died (347 BC) while Alexander (*b.* 356) was just a boy. In Hippolytus' view, the Babylonian seers also inspired heretical ideas about the universe, and so their horoscopes needed a proper dismissal. Sextus had done the job well enough.

Hippolytus' appropriation is not an isolated instance. The opening paragraphs of the fourth book borrow most of Sextus' critique of the Chaldeans verbatim but without acknowledgment, which was no problem in a time with a very liberal concept of plagiarism. Publishing an idea confers authority upon it and so has a higher chance of convincing readers. Hippolytus found Sextus' ideas worthy of his composition, even if they were set in circulation by a contemporary Greek philosopher.

We detect the same takeover of non-Christian learning throughout the second, third, and fourth centuries. One of many examples occurs in the second book of Lactantius' *Divine Institutes*. Here the author is discussing the origins of traditional belief in the Greco-Roman pantheon when he turns to stories of the deities' manifestations. He naturally does not believe them and argues that one should use reason instead of trusting false tales that tradition has enshrined. Among the many Roman heroes mentioned, only two foreign figures appear, Pyrrhus and Alexander, whom Lactantius affords little space. Pyrrhus died in a shipwreck outside Locri because he stole from Proserpina's temple there (2.7.18, cf. Val. Max. 1.1.ext1), whereas Alexander's men were blinded when they plundered the shrine of Ceres in Miletus (2.7.19), probably during the sack of the city in 334 BC. Lactantius reproduces the Miletus episode from Valerius Maximus' collection of memorable anecdotes (Val. Max. 1.1.ext5). It is worth noticing the agency asserted in each case, as Lactantius first targets the individual ruler, and then the army of the other king. Another noteworthy fact is his minor alteration of the story. In the Miletus story, he omits the reason why the soldiers were blinded. Valerius Maximus explains that it was the goddess' punishment for men seeing what should only be known to women, but this piece of information did not interest Lactantius.

The Christian author has carefully selected the two stories from Valerius Maximus and arranged them together. Valerius Maximus had not connected the two, but interspersed other stories. Lactantius selected the two Hellenistic ones for a reason. It displays his erudition: Pyrrhus, another great commander, was typically compared to his predecessor Alexander, and Proserpina was naturally connected to her mother Ceres. The chiasmus of goddesses and great generals is striking, and it is also Lactantius' last example of punishment for sacrilege. He saved the best for last. Although he ultimately proceeds to reject the traditional beliefs, his illustration of the argument matches that of any intellectual believing in Roman religion.

These two introductory vignettes showcase how Christians engaged with contemporary or earlier pagan authors. Some material could be accepted and passed on without comment; other material reused, even if later Christians rejected it. Hippolytus does not seek to overturn Sextus' argument, whereas Lactantius has to use something Romans would recognize to achieve his goal of undermining Roman religion. Moreover, the authors use the anecdotes to support whatever their arguments are. The cast of characters is clearly not the most important feature, but one among several pieces of information from the available channels of knowledge. For example, Alexander features because he is a familiar figure, not because the writers wish to pass judgment on him. While Hippolytus and Sextus do so inadvertently, if only making a general point that the king was famous, Valerius Maximus and Lactantius focus on the period of Alexander's campaign and the actions of the soldiers. In both cases, the primary point of reference is to Alexander's lifetime as a period of history, which is a common tool in imperial historiography (see Chapter 4).

The previous chapter exemplified how embedded Christian intellectuals were in imperial society, at least from the Severan period onward. The two stories above suggest a close link between Christian and non-Christian learning. In the rest of this chapter, we will explore three major classical themes concerning Alexander that Christians appropriated: education, epistolography, and deification. Christians developed the same *topoi* from the Classicizing pagan literature to the same level as pagan intellectuals, if not better; Christians did not stand outside imperial culture and found the same topics useful for their own purposes. The main departure from pagan models is found in what Christians chose to omit, such as stories about Alexander and Diogenes the Cynic. Key patterns emerge. For example, the references reveal a Christian unity when the intellectuals handle the same kind of material, such as catalogs of criticism and certain pagan myths. Frequency in repetition of *topoi* reinforces consistency and agreement.

Previous scholarship has argued for discrepant and negative representations of Alexander in apologetic discourse, but below we shall find coherence. If the representations of the king are predominantly negative, it is only because the three themes about him could hardly be presented in a positive fashion. For instance, no Christian could accept the pagan practice of deification, despite the fact that Christianity's founder could be seen as a man made God. I believe that scholarly confusion has arisen because we tend to examine the same set of references, which convey this hostile representation. We then err when we accept these negative references as representative of the entire discourse. There is safety in studying the same material, although the conclusions reached will not advance scholarship. In what follows, I shall reverse the operation by showing how Christians were not seeking to pass individual judgment, but generally used the stories to counter greater points made by intellectual opposition (pagans, Jews, "heretics"). In fact, the frequency of negative reference to Alexander stories was not as high as one might expect, and we should take that as a sign that Christians had very different interests in the king, as explored in Chapters 3 and 4.

Educating Alexander

Note below the extensive length of the Christian lists of mythological material. A long list confers authority upon its constituent elements and the argument they are intended to support and illustrates the authors' erudition, essential aspects of the rhetorical strategy in early Christian literature.

Do clothes make the Christian?

The association between Alexander and Greek learning went far beyond Plato and Aristotle. A number of Greek and Latin texts address the connection, beginning already in the immediate period after the king's death. One writer from the first generation of historians, Onesicritus of Astypalea, claimed that a leader of Indian philosophers had recognized the king as the only "philosopher in arms" they had seen, μόνον γὰρ ἴδοι αὐτὸν ἐν ὅπλοις φιλοσοφοῦντα (Str. 15.1.64 (715) incorporating Onesicritus *FGrH/BNJ* 134 F17a Whitby). The passage is problematic, and even the wording is contested. The Augustan geographer Strabo tells us that Onesicritus needed three interpreters to communicate with the Indians, so the conversation was muddled at best. In turn, we only possess Strabo's paraphrase of the encounter. Nevertheless, the episode indicates the philosophical mindset that ancient authors ascribed to the king, either through his own actions or through chance meetings with various philosophers—in Strabo, Alexander sends Onesicritus in his stead; elsewhere Alexander goes himself (see below). Plutarch dedicated a whole oration to the topic of Alexander in philosophical action (Plut. *De Alex. fort.* 1). Although the speech is an excellent example of Alexander's image in virtuoso rhetoric, the contents were influential (Asirvatham 2012: 311–312). In the second century AD, a Macedonian author proclaimed that Alexander had aimed to unite all of humankind in order to make everyone "Alexanders" instead of human beings (Polyaenus *Strat.* 4.3.1). While this grandiose claim found modern admirers, including W. W. Tarn (1869–1957), the philosophical Alexander was the product of theorizing on kingship in the Hellenistic and Roman worlds.

The king's recognizability, as well as his unlimited power and insatiable ambition, made him a useful "tool to think with" (Stoneman 2003: 328). In the past, scholars saw rigid borders between what philosophical schools were doing with Alexander's legacy, but thanks to the work of Stoneman, Asirvatham, and others, we now see the discourse as fluctuating across perceived boundaries. To think philosophically using the king as a pivot did not require an allegiance, and many used the same material to explore moral and philosophical notions. Sometimes the same concept meant different things even to a single writer. For instance, Seneca the Younger mentions Alexander's generosity to say, in one instance, that one should devote all one's time to philosophy (*Ep.* 53.10) and, in another, that everything should be done in moderation (*Ben.* 2.16). The contradiction is self-evident. The king embodied various virtues and vices, the same as everyone else, but his fame made him a common point of reference. His Macedonian background turned him into an external target and so a safe proxy to discuss, say, the current emperor. These features made the king useful for authors to make use of.

One instance of Alexander's philosophical symbolism occurs in Tertullian (*Pall.* 4.6 Hunink, *CCSL* 2.744). We easily detect his presence, for the author is referring to the king by his greatness, *magnum regem*, and his Macedonian ethnicity, *Macedo*, without mentioning his name or any other signifier. Tertullian argues that Alexander had exchanged the glory of his Macedonian war-gear for the ostentatious clothing of the East. Instead of metal armor, he began to wear Persian trousers and transparent silk shirts that fit with his newfound pride and passions. The king's new clothes, in other words, symbolized a negative shift in his royal behavior and demeanor. Tertullian associates Alexander's degeneracy with philosophers, who wear purple, as exemplified by the pre-Socratic philosopher Empedocles, who was clad in Tyrian purple (Diog. Laert. 8.73). Then Tertullian lashes out at the silk and sandals worn by Dionysus, then proceeds to the example of Roman matrons, who dressed as prostitutes when worshiping the Olympians. He uses these *exempla* to suggest that the Romans had themselves adopted a foreign decadence. He admonished them to take off their luxurious gowns, or togas, and put on the true garment of Christian philosophy, the cloak, to improve for the better rather than continuing down the spiral of immoral fashion.

The necessity of the argument makes for an interesting study in Christian identity. In *On the Philosopher's Mantle*, Tertullian professes to respond to the challenge that Christians have started to wear the cloak typically borne by philosophers. He maintains that the *pallium* could be a piece of Christian clothing, as it was also appropriate for other groups, including sophists, poets, and astrologers. To this end, he imbues the cloak with common philosophical meaning, but makes a new distinction that it exhibits the discipline and holiness of Christians (§ 6). When virtuous Christians donned the *pallium*, the clothing took on a better philosophy, a better way of life. Putting on the *pallium* removed previous identity associations with it, so that the wearer could feel justified in wearing the garment as a Christian.

The struggle for identity in antiquity was crucial. Personal appearance then, just as in any period of history, greatly influenced how people would identify the wearer. For instance, a cloak could cover both a poor beggar or a wise philosopher, as is the case in Herodes Atticus' encounter with a beggar feigning to be a Cynic (Gell. *NA* 9.2.1–11). The wearer would have to establish his status by action, speech, or other evidence, but the onlooker had to recognize that social identity in turn (Eshleman 2012: 14, 36). Herodes denied the beggar a higher status, but we do not know if Tertullian's Carthaginian audience denied him the new significance of the Christian attire. The cloak already held some importance in early Christianity. The Apostle Paul had requested this garment to be sent to Rome from Troas in Asia Minor (2 Tim. 4:13) and, while in Rome, Justin Martyr continued to wear his cloak after conversion (Justin *Dial*. 1.2, 9.2). Tertullian was making a case for bringing the apparel, symbolizing the religion of the east, into the world of the Latin west. The short composition thus gives us a brief glimpse into Christian identity formation in Carthage.

For his own purposes, Tertullian has appropriated a common representation of Alexander and inserted it into a contemporary context. The strategy is in itself unsurprising. After all, orators had the license to animate history to suit their needs. What we need to recognize is how crucial the context of the work is for what the author selects and how he represents "the facts." Alexander's clothing did not have an inherently philosophical dimension—the attire was a stock-in-trade *exemplum* that authors could confer meaning upon. For example, Plutarch says that Alexander combined different sets of clothing to appease the ruled. In one instance, the dress symbolizes the cultural fusion at the mass-marriages at Susa, from which Plutarch distances himself by citing the authority of Eratosthenes, a third-century BC polymath from North Africa (Plut. *De Alex. fort* 329f–330a incorporating Eratosthenes *FGrH/BNJ* 241 F30 Pownall). In the other, the mixed dress receives a strong reaction from the Macedonian soldiers, who detest the king's adoption of new customs (Plut. *Alex*. 45.2; cf. Diod. Sic. 17.77.5). For Tertullian, the frame of reference accepts the Macedonian view of Alexander as a tyrant, and he taps into a theme that is one of the most salient in Curtius Rufus' *History* (Curt. 6.6.1–10; cf. Just. *Epit*. 11.11.11–12). The literary motif of luxury is usually grouped with several features that signified the gradual decline of the king, along with alcoholism (Arr. *Anab*. 4.7.4). Moral decline works with the other items in the sequence: the king's clothes connect to Empedocles' royal purple, which brings up Dionysus' decadence that culminates in prostituted Roman matrons. Note how the first three were stock examples of falsely deified humans and thus nothing positive to a Christian audience.

Alexander is not the starting point of Tertullian's digression either. He is preceded by Heracles' cross-dressing for the Lydian queen Omphale and the decadent Assyrian Sardanapalus. The examples do not appear as isolated instances, but form part of a catalog of domestic and foreign deviants that illustrate what Tertullian was arguing.

Cataloging values through historical characters was commonplace. For instance, in the first century BC, Cicero classified famous rulers. One passage places together Themistocles, Pericles, Cyrus, Agesilaus, and Alexander (Cic. *Off.* 2.16); another associates Themistocles, Aristides, Agesilaus, Epaminondas, Philip, and Alexander (Cic. *De or.* 2.341). Such lists may illustrate various points, and the force of argument lies in the list's paratactic structure. When arranged together in a list, the items are equally weighted and illustrative. One thinks of Athenians versus Spartans and Persians versus Macedonians as opposites in many ways, but the list format organizes them as a unified whole to reinforce whatever Cicero, or any other writer, was arguing. To take another instance featuring Alexander, we may turn to Tertullian's masterpiece, the *Apology* (c. 197). One of many passages satirizing human deification makes the point that non-Christians had chosen morally bankrupt characters like the Olympians for gods, while they let the more virtuous characters rot in hell (Tert. *Apol.* § 11.15, *CCSL* 1.109). Tertullian pairs Greeks with Romans: Socrates, Cato (wisdom); Aristides, Scipio (Justice) Alexander, Pompey (sublimity/magnanimity); Polycrates, Sulla (good fortune); Croesus, Crassus (wealth); and Demosthenes, Cicero (eloquence). Themistocles (generalship) stands alone among the Greeks. While not quite a full Plutarchan pairing, the list evidences the classification tendency, and we shall see the method used time and time again in what follows.

Leonidas of Epirus: The failed tutor

Aristotle was not the sole teacher of Alexander. The Greek *Alexander Romance* (1.13.4; cf. *A R* Arm. § 29) lists six other teachers, but none of them is corroborated by external evidence (Heckel *Who's Who* 347). "Leuconides" may, as Heckel notes elsewhere, be an error for the tutor Leonidas of Epirus, the kinsman of Olympias. From the scattered references to this figure, we learn that he was the stern instructor of the king's youth (Plut. *Alex.* 22.9–10). Plutarch records the famous anecdote according to which Leonidas found fault with Alexander's excessive offering of incense and severely punished the boy; many years later, Alexander supposedly sent Leonidas a hundred talents worth of frankincense, so that the tutor would never again need to restrain himself in the worship of the gods (Plut.

Alex. 25.6–8, [*Reg. imp. apophth.*] 179e-f; cf. Plin. *HN.* 12.62). Quintilian preserves another, if unrelated, story about Leonidas on the authority of the Stoic Diogenes of Babylon (d. in Rome c. 145 BC, Quint. *Inst.* 1.1.9). For him, Leonidas' tutoring may have been excellent for military training, but it was poor morally and so created faults in the king that grew as he matured. The two stories reflect how intellectuals used Alexander as a tool to think with: in the former, the king developed in virtue to eclipse his tutor; in the latter, Alexander's decline was the direct result of Leonidas' poor teaching.

This second story is also preserved in Clement of Alexandria's handbook for Christian instructors (*Paed.* 1.7.55, *GCS* NF 12.122). He states that Leonidas was not able to curtail the pride, *typhos*, of the adolescent king. Clement refers to an oft-used classicizing term rather than the vague faults alluded to by Diogenes via Quintilian. The subtle change makes a strong effect, for vanity is seen as one of the key faults that led to Alexander's downfall, as we have already witnessed in Tertullian's *On the Philosopher's Mantle*. Again, Alexander and Leonidas are not singled out, but appear in Clement's list of "failed" pagan teachers and their students. Clement mentions Phoenix as a teacher for Achilles, Adrastus for Croesus' children, Nausithous for Philip, Zopyrus for Alcibiades, Sicinnus for Themistocles' children, and the various tutors of Persian kings. Clement finds faults with all of these teachers, and these faults supposedly explain the careers of their students. The Christians are, by contrast, taught by Christ and so their ethical education ranked higher than any earthly education. The argument for Christian superiority is made with quotations from the Old Testament and the New Testament, clearly separated from the paraphrases Clement makes of classicizing lore. The passages give a binary impression of Christian learning as opposed to the pagan, but Clement's creative deployment of the classical material betrays any pretense to simplicity.

Heckel notes that Jerome makes use of the story (Heckel *Who's Who* 147), which presumably Jerome extracted from Quintilian rather than from the other versions (Jerome *Ep.* 107.4, *CCSL* 55.295). The linguistic parallels between the two are close and unmistakable. Nevertheless, Jerome specifies that the faults of Alexander were the king's clever tricks and the way he moved when he walked. Quintilian's version does not define the king's faults. Jerome's version is important because it formed the basis of the many medieval versions (Cary 1956: 127 n. 29), such as that found in the Venerable Bede's *Commentary on Proverbs* (2.22). The English monk quotes Jerome, but adds that Alexander was the greatest king in the whole world. While the remark may seem flattering, the amplification stresses the faults of Leonidas even more. In my view, however, none of the above versions comes close to Clement's innovative repacking of the anecdote.

Aristotle's finest killed Clitus and Callisthenes

Leonidas' example presents us with a harsh case of a teacher being judged by his students' performance. We may now ask how successful Aristotle was, and what he taught Alexander. The question has generated curious responses over the years. Plutarch refers to an education in philosophy, politics, literature, and medicine, for the king had the hands of a healer (Plut. *Alex.* 8.1). Alexander is fully capable of disagreeing with Aristotle (7.6–7), which he often does. For example, Alexander chooses to treat the Greeks and his Asian subjects with more dignity than the philosopher proposed (Plut. *De Alex. fort.* 329b–c). Aristotle told Alexander to rule the barbarians as beasts. The 1956 Hollywood motion picture, *Alexander the Great*, captures Aristotle's politically incorrect statements when the preceptor (British actor Barry Jones) sends off a scantily clad king (Richard Burton, age 29) from the palaestra. Aristotle says that "the Greeks were the chosen, the elect, and had the best culture, the best civilization." Since Alexander does not make his rebuttal in the film, Aristotle's words suggest that Alexander's mission is to civilize the uneducated East. Rossen's script for the big screen overturned Plutarch's *Life* by omitting the rest of the anecdote, just as Plutarch seems to have retouched his own sources. We may compare his testimony with that of Strabo. Citing a third-century BC source, Strabo attributes the binary opposition between Greeks and "Barbarians" to no one in particular among Alexander's advisors, though the king still disagrees. He wants to treat people in accordance with their virtue rather than their origin (Str. 1.4.9 (66–67)). Going back to Plutarch, we notice that he offers a heavily edited version of this hostile view, carefully put into the mouth of Aristotle for Alexander to reject. We may want to dismiss many other parts of Plutarch's representations of Aristotle and Alexander, including the princeling's bookishness (Brunell 2017), but we should at least recognize what the authors are trying to say through their representation of royal education and why (Molina Marin 2018: 78–80).

Writing half a decade or so after Plutarch, Tatian, a Syriac ascetic and Christian apologist, provides readers with a rather different version of Aristotle's relationship with his illustrious student (Tat. *Ad. Gr.* § 2.1–2 Trelenberg pp. 88–89). He inserts the pair into a catalog of ostensibly flawed philosophers and their students: Diogenes the Cynic died of gluttony; Aristippus, student of Socrates, strutted about in royal purple; and Plato was sold into slavery by Dionysius, the tyrant of Syracuse. Tatian reserves the lengthiest (and harshest) criticism for Aristotle, who absurdly set a limit to providential power and defined true happiness as the things that satisfy, τὴν εὐδαιμονίαν ἐν οἷς ἠρέσκετο περιγράψας. Tatian claims that the preceptor flattered the young, hot-headed Alexander in a most uneducated manner, λίαν ἀπαιδεύτως. Alexander acted in the most Aristotelian fashion, Ἀριστοτελικῶς, when he bound someone in chains, like bears or leopards, because he refused to worship him. He feasted to the point of excess and butchered his friend at a symposium. After the killing he feigned remorse lest those around him should resent him. After this description of Alexander's actions, Tatian turns to contemporary Aristotelians, who, he posits, do not believe that Providence governs the earth, and so humanity has to look after the world themselves. In that system, only the beautiful, wealthy, strong and nobly born could achieve happiness. Tatian sarcastically asks in the imperative for people of this kind to teach philosophy, οἱ τοιοῦτοι φιλοσοφείτωσαν, probably referring to the whole catalog rather than singling out Aristotle.

Though Tatian despises Greek knowledge, the passage betrays his literary sophistication. Besides the allusions to the lives of individual philosophers and their teaching, he replays some major themes from the histories of Alexander. The story reminds us of Leonidas of Epirus in that the tutor could not set Alexander right, but Tatian adds much more detail to the portrayal of Alexander. As others have pointed out (Wirth 1993: 60; Peltonen 2018: 480–483), Tatian combines the fate of Callisthenes (*FGrH/BNJ* 124 T18a Rzepka) and the murder of Clitus the Black without mentioning them by name. These same scholars assert that the Latin texts make the most of the criticisms of these episodes, preferring to see the sentiments of Cicero and Seneca behind Tatian's selection. While I do not agree with them on this matter, *exemplum* literature in Greek and Latin certainly contains many references to the two episodes. We will examine the killings of Callisthenes and Clitus in turn. For now, note that Tatian reverses the chronological order: Clitus died in 328 BC, Callisthenes in 327 BC. Most other sources, however, also make the link between these two men's deaths, ignoring any content in between, so we should not necessarily consider Tatian's juxtaposition too confused. After all, cataloging Alexander's killings for rhetorical effect was commonplace (Val. Max. 9.3.1; Sen. *De Ira* 3.17; Plut. *Mor.* 65d, 96c, 458b), including in the major accounts of Alexander (Diod. Sic. 17.preface; Just. 11.6–7; Curt. 8.8.22–23; Plut. *Alex.* 48–55). Arrian goes so far as to pretend that he has invented the association between the deaths of Clitus and Callisthenes (Arr. *Anab.* 4.14.4), though the arrangement "was not unique, and the basic idea may be quite old" (Bosworth, *HCA* II: 46).

According to the younger Seneca, Alexander's most heinous misdeed was the killing of Callisthenes, who was once thought to be related to Aristotle, but those familial ties are no longer certain (Sen. *QNat.* 6.23.2–3; cf. Curt. 8.8.20–24). No apology, Seneca insisted, could make amends for the king's crime. Anyone acquainted with philosophy ought to be endowed with the freedom to speak freely (and therefore frankly) before the ruler, the *topos* of *parrhesia*. Despite Seneca's representation of Callisthenes of Olynthus—a city Philip II had destroyed—the Greek intellectual was at best a controversial figure of the campaign (Koulakiotis 2006: 84–86). Until his death in 327 BC, he seems to have held some office associated with writing about the campaign and teaching students. The Macedonians framed him for playing a part in the so-called "Pages Conspiracy" against Alexander, because he tutored the royal pages. Callisthenes also refused to worship Alexander in the *proskynesis* affair, which took place slightly before the conspiracy. He is said to have met his end because he could not restrain his words in the presence of the king who, "held the power of life and death at the tip of his tongue" (Diog. Laert. 5.5; Amm. Marc. 18.3.7).

We cannot say for sure how he died, because the literary sources obscure the circumstances of his death (collection at Heckel *Who's Who* s.v. Callisthenes [1]). Even the first generation of historians withheld information on the circumstances of his death, for which Arrian chastised them severely (Arr. *Anab*. 4.14.3). Arrian makes an awkward pause in the narrative to offer his critique, noting only the testimonies of Aristobulus, who said that Callisthenes was put in chains and paraded before the army (Aristobulus *FGrH/BNJ* 139 F33 Pownall), and Ptolemy, who said that the Macedonians crucified him (Ptolemy *FGrH/BNJ* 138 F17 Howe). In sowing doubt about the primary accounts, Arrian misdirects his reader to consider matters of historiography instead of considering the reasons for the death itself. We stop wondering about Alexander's questionable motives for arresting Callisthenes. Arrian's strategy is thus overtly apologetic on behalf of the king, and we may make a mental note of how Arrian excuses the king's behavior. Tatian, on the other hand, amplifies the horrible circumstances of the death by adding the animal cage and directing his readers to believe that Callisthenes died because of refusing Alexander divine honors at the *proskynesis* affair. Tatian says nothing of the Pages Conspiracy. Tapping into the discourse of Alexander's decline into barbarity, he turns history into *exemplum*.

Scholarship has recently called into question whether Tatian is making reference to Callisthenes or Lysimachus, one of Alexander's companions and later Successor (Peltonen 2018: 481 n. 15). Allegedly, Alexander threw Lysimachus to the lions, which incident Latin writers used to convey the king's cruelty. In the early Hellenistic versions, the story seems rather to have had a positive meaning, for Lysimachus defeated the lion and regained Alexander's respect. I am not, however, persuaded by the argument that Tatian was thinking of Lysimachus' lion encounter. The reference to the refusal of worship, διὰ τὸ μὴ βούλεσθαι προσκυνεῖν, proves that Tatian meant Callisthenes (the infinite form of προσκυνέω). Callisthenes was implicated in the *proskynesis* affair, and we know of no such story about Lysimachus. It is, however, easy to excuse the erroneous interpretation, because the conflation between the stories of caging Lysimachus and Callisthenes arose already in antiquity. For example, Justin says that, when Callisthenes was mutilated for his actions against Alexander and was displayed in a cage with a dog, Lysimachus felt pity and gave Callisthenes poison; Alexander then threw Lysimachus to the fiercest lion, *ferocissimo leoni* (Just. 15.3.3–7 incorporating Callisthenes *FGrH/BNJ* 124 T18f). Many other fragments of first-generation witnesses put Callisthenes in an animal cage and then send him to the lion (see e.g., Diog. Laert. 5.5; cf. *FGrH/BNJ* 124 Testimonies 1, 6, 16a–18f), so there is no need to mistake Callisthenes for Lysimachus in Tatian's text. The scholarly misunderstanding is based on a problematic understanding of primary sources, which we will return to below.

Though Seneca claims that killing Callisthenes was Alexander's worst deed, the major accounts make the death of Clitus, whom Alexander ran through with a spear, appear much more sombre. We will need to afford some space to expose the story, as four of the five major accounts devote much attention to this dark episode (Just. 11.6; Curt. 8.1.20–2.13; Plut. *Alex.* 50–52.4; Arr. *Anab.* 4.7.4–9.8; cf. Favuzzi 2014. Unfortunately, the story has fallen out of the manuscript transmission of Diodorus). The surviving texts amplify the emotional effect of the killing in various ways. For example, Curtius reminds readers at the start of the episode that Clitus saved Alexander at the Granicus River many years before and that his sister Lanice served as the king's nurse (Curt. 8.1.20–21). Justin inserts the information at the end of the whole narrative when Alexander himself realizes the tragedy in his mourning (Just. 11.6.9–11). By all accounts, Clitus was no unknown soldier. He had risen through the ranks to command the Companion cavalry with Hephaistion, son of Amyntor, and been a lifelong friend of the king. The sources also agree that the king killed his brother-in-arms in Sogdinian Maracanda (perhaps Samarcand) in the late summer/autumn of 328 BC during a banquet (Carney 2015). How the scene played out makes for a rather onerous, if important, historiographical exercise. Either Alexander himself (Justin; Curtius Rufus) or flatterers (Plutarch; Arrian) provoked the inebriated Clitus. The equally intoxicated Alexander retaliated. We do not know how long the quarrel lasted, what the murder weapon was, and whether Clitus was killed *in situ* (Justin), after he returned to taunt Alexander (Arrian; Plutarch) or when he had left the party (Curtius Rufus). The murder caused a major commotion, and the king's guards reacted too late. They took control of the situation and escorted the king to mourn in his quarters from which he only emerged a full day or more later.

For most ancient and modern writers, the Clitus episode serves as a point of no return. Clitus' tragic fate symbolizes the midway mark of the decline of Alexander's mentality, not only because the murder occurs halfway through the campaign, but also because our literary texts insist on this turn in the king's character (e.g., for Plutarch, see Mossman 1988: 88–89; Koulakiotis 2017). Even Arrian confesses that the king transformed in contact with the furthest East, though he works harder than anyone to acquit the king (Arr. *Anab.* 4.7.4–5). It is my contention that the Clitus episode also resets an interrelated narrative sequence of death at court. The sequence had begun with the death of the Persian king Darius at the hands of his satrap Bessus and ended with the surrender and death of Bessus in the same year, 330/329 BC. In between the death of the two Persian rulers, Alexander ordered the deaths of the most significant Macedonian general Parmenio in Babylon and his son Philotas, who were dubiously implicated in another conspiracy against Alexander. With no more claimants to Persian rule, Alexander, the not-so-new lord of all, dominated central Asia. Primarily Latin texts stress Alexander's growing Persianizing from killing Clitus to marrying Roxane, a local princess, during the time from the invasion of Bactria (329) to the Cophen campaign (327). The culmination of this process seems to be when Alexander kills Callisthenes, the last voice of Greek reason at court. The merciless incursion into India completes Alexander's transformation before his life's circuit ends in Babylon, now a full-fledged Persian tyrant. Hephaistion's death foreshadowing Alexander's own demise serves as a reminder that the king cannot defeat death. He dies poetically at the peak of power, isolated and lonely. The Greek and Roman texts of course have individual nuances, but the basic story template of decline and fall works well for both ancient and modern Alexander biography. For example, German novelist Klaus Mann (1906–1949) crafted his story of Alexander as a love-triangle between Clitus, Alexander, and Hephaistion. The loss of the two men leads Alexander into ever deeper agony until he is released by an angel.

But Tatian seems to have revamped this great narrative by swapping the order of Clitus and Callisthenes. If the killing of Clitus occurs last, the narrative sequence does not reflect character development, but rather two examples of studied cruelty. Tatian ends the digression on Alexander with the king's worst crime, the well-known set-piece of Clitus' death in the other literary accounts. This representation fits perfectly with the primary object of Tatian's criticism, namely Aristotle's teaching. One piece of information reveals his erudition: Alexander's faked remorse after killing Clitus to avoid the wrath of his own kinsmen, πάλιν κλαίων καὶ ἀποκαρτερῶν προφάσει λύπης, ἵν' ὑπὸ τῶν οἰκείων μὴ μισηθῇ. The negative interpretation goes against the grain of the historiographical tradition, as the sources place great emphasis on Alexander's weeping and self-imposed starvation after the murder (Cic. *Tusc.* 4.79; Just. 12.6.7–11; Curt. 8.2.1–13; Plut. *Alex.* 52.1–2; Arr. *Anab.* 4.9.2). Plutarch even proposed that the grief Alexander felt equaled that which Plato felt at the death of Socrates (Plut. *Mor.* 449e). By interpreting Alexander's grief differently than the rest of our testimonies do, Tatian does, of course, not contribute to our knowledge of the historical Alexander. But we must still appreciate that he is creating an innovative version of the episode for his own purposes. Our appreciation of his rhetorical tactics helps us to realize that every other writer who uses the episode is also working towards their own ends.

We now return to Tatian's sources. For Clitus and Callisthenes, we have seen that he made use of generally known examples that any orator may have used. He did not need to have a specific text in front of him, but could freely draw on the rhetorical repertoire. Indeed, as one third-century author remarks, "who does not know the story about Callisthenes?" (Philostr. *VA* 7.2). As a Greek-speaking orator, Tatian did not make use of Latin texts to inform his ideas, though previous scholarship has argued that the judgment Tatian passes on Alexander can only come from the ostensibly hostile Latin writers. Scholars based this view on the assumption of a distinction between a positive reception of Alexander in the Greek texts and a negative Alexander in the Latin. The opinion is old, if not also incorrect (Niese 1897). As is already clear from preceding pages, much of the content was available in both languages of the Roman Empire. We only need to remember that we have three major accounts in Greek and two in Latin. The data extracted from these, and many other texts that we do not read as often as we should, was available for interpretation, and the individual author's coloring of the *exempla*, depended on the repurposing of material (Stoneman 2003).

Take, for instance, Lucian of Samosata (modern Adiyaman Province, Turkey). Like Tatian, Lucian was a mid-second century intellectual from the eastern Roman empire, thoroughly educated in, but critical of, the Greek heritage. Orating in flawless, if borrowed, Attic Greek—by this point an obsolete language for show and art—he too engages mercilessly with Greek philosophy, education and, in one instance, Christianity (Luc. *Peregr.* §§ 11–14). In a series of entertaining dialogs, Lucian takes issue with Alexander's legacy (Luc. *DMort.* nos. 12, 13, 25 Macleod). He sets the dialogs in the underworld and lets Alexander encounter other famous people, such as his father Philip, Diogenes the Cynic philosopher, and Hannibal, the Carthaginian general, as well as Scipio Africanus, Hannibal's Roman adversary in the Second Punic War (218–201 BC). The interlocutors discuss many of the themes that Lucian's contemporaries would occupy themselves with, although these deceased persons have novel takes on individual themes, especially the deification of mortals or lack thereof. In the encounter with Diogenes, Lucian's mouthpiece, the philosopher ridicules Alexander's wish to become divine now that he is dead, asking how the rumors of his divine birth rose in the first place (13.1); to whom he left the empire (13.2); and where his body was buried (13.3). These were not only major points of interest in other literary texts, but also wonderfully sarcastic questions to ask in light of the lifeless setting. Diogenes is particularly well-informed about events, making Alexander cry for wanting his glory back, as well as deification in Ptolemaic Egypt (13.3–4, τί δακρύεις, ὦ μάταιε;). At this juncture Lucian writes something highly relevant for our understanding of Tatian's digression. Diogenes asks the weeping Alexander why Aristotle had not taught him about fickle fortune—another major theme of Alexandrography—and Alexander replies that Aristotle was the most accursed of all flatterers, ἁπάντων κολάκων ἐπιτριπτότατος (13.5). Abusing Alexander's love of learning, μου τῇ περὶ παιδείαν φιλοτιμίᾳ, his preceptor talked, or wrote, to the king all the time, complimenting him and taking interests in his beauty (κάλλος), wealth (πλοῦτος), and noble standing (τἀγαθοῦ); in fact, Aristotle was the one to suggest that Alexander should value all the earthly things highly, and that is the reason why the former king is so bitter about being dead. Diogenes prescribes water of the River Lethe to make him forget the desires inculcated by his Aristotelian education. Unfortunately, other people in Hades had not forgotten his actions. It is no surprise who comes looking for a piece of Alexander: Clitus and Callisthenes (13.6).

The parallels with Tatian's digression on Alexander and Aristotle are unmistakable. Besides flattery, worldly power, and the two murdered men, Tatian also criticizes Aristotle's ostensible interest in beauty (κάλλος), wealth (πλοῦτος), and noble status (ῥώμη σώματος, εὐγένεια). I do not contend that one author is the source of the other. I prefer to think of the themes as stock-in-trade rhetoric, associated with dismissing Aristotelians. Both Lucian and Tatian, exact contemporaries from the eastern empire, work with common assumptions about Alexander and his Aristotelian learning to construct two highly critical pieces on the king's legacy. The non-Christian writer is rather more vicious in his satire; while Tatian uses the material to mock Greek philosophy, Lucian ridicules deification and philosophy at once. What Tatian was doing was then by no means worse than what the pagans could themselves do to their philosophical champions. The aims of Lucian's satire and Tatian's exhortation were clearly different, but Tatian's readers would immediately have recognized the standard set of criticisms by which one would dismantle Greek philosophy. They were not inherently Christian. While Tatian invoked the points to criticize previous philosophies from the point of view of his own philosophy, Christianity, it is too superficial to say that the passage promotes "anti-pagan rhetoric" (Peltonen 2018: 482). After all, his entire text is meant to target Greek philosophy, and Tatian does this principally by subverting common Greek tropes. Even if Tatian presented himself as an outsider (§ 42), he knew and participated in the same kind of high culture (§ 35). He did not need to activate his listeners' or readers' sense of "Christianness" in order for them to know what was wrong with Greek philosophy.

We find the opposite approach to activating Christianness in Tertullian's *Apology* (Tert. *Apol.* § 46.15, *CCSL* 1.162). Tertullian begins his criticism in the same way through a catalog of philosophers around Aristotle and Alexander. Incidentally, the list of examples reads almost exactly like that in Tatian, but it is rearranged as follows: Aristotle (sycophant to Alexander), Aristippus (wearer of royal purple), Plato (sold by Dionysius), and the Greek sophist, Hippias of Elis (443–399 BC), who replaces Diogenes the Cynic. In terms of the Alexander material, Tertullian presents readers with none of the sophistry offered by Tatian. Tertullian briefly scorns Aristotle for not taking every opportunity to set the king on the right path. Without the elaborations, the core of the story feels much more reminiscent of Quintilian's terse Leonidas anecdote, because Aristotle is the only one to blame for the flattery. Also, unlike Tatian, Tertullian provides readers with explicit examples of Christian counter-behavior. For example, Hippias was killed for plotting against the state, whereas Christians had never even thought of such a thing when the Roman Empire persecuted them. Every example of philosopher-versus-Christian reflects a particular Christian principle, at least from the perspective of the clergy, that is, the Christians who were in charge of running the church institution at a local level. For instance, Tertullian posits that Christian men only have sexual intercourse with women and a Christian husband only with his wife, whereas Greek philosophers hire courtesans (Phryne) and seduce adolescent males (Socrates). By vocalizing the contrasts, Tertullian activates what kind of behavior the audience should regard as Christian. As a member of the clergy, he wanted to convey an image of the ideal Christian with a strict discipline and morality. He is of course using the binary examples not only to inform Christian readers what they should aspire to, but also to present a public facade to non-Christians. Despite adorning his doctrine with purely classicizing examples, he wanted to make it seem as if there were great differences between *philosophus et christianus*, and the disciple of Greece and the one of heaven, *graeciae discipulus et caeli*.

The negative reception of Aristotle's teaching in Tatian, Lucian, and Tertullian naturally does not displace the positive receptions we know from second- and third-century imperial texts. Their divergence is the reason why these passages offer so much of interest. For example, other literary texts contain much more positive receptions, even in passing remarks. The Cynic Dio Chrysostom supplies us with a hyperbolic praise of Philip's choice of Aristotle for Alexander's teacher (Dio Chrys. *Or*. 49.4–5) and the Roman miscellanist Aulus Gellius, the light of Latin literature in the second century, gives a sample of what Philip's invitation may have looked like (Gell. *NA* 9.3.3–6). These two examples were meant to illustrate Philip's brilliance in giving the philosopher responsibility for the prince's education, but they operate with the unspoken assumption that Aristotle's teaching was excellent. Aelius Aristides plays with this common assumption when he remarks that the Greeks criticized Philip for associating with Aristotle, whereas Alexander was glorified for the same association (Aristid. *Or*. 32.29).

More ambiguous accounts also circulated. For example, Diogenes Laërtius, who provides us with a biography of Aristotle at the beginning of Book 5, conjectures that Aristotle came to Alexander when the prince was in his fifteenth year (5.10). He ascribes to the wider literature the notion that the Aristotelians received the name "Peripatetics" because of Aristotle's walks with Alexander when the king was recovering from an illness (5.2). Diogenes also makes a list of Aristotle's works, noting the existence of a one-book work with Alexander's name (5.22) and four books of letters between teacher and pupil (5.27). The relationship stays strong until the king kills Callisthenes and starts to resent Aristotle, who introduced them (5.10; cf. Plut. *Alex*. 55.8–9). In Plutarch's sophisticated Alexander-biography, the author also makes a note of the later estrangement with the preface that Alexander loved Aristotle more than his father Philip (Plut. *Alex*. 8.4). Hence Alexander's gradual decline is not only linked to giving in to his vices (methomania, arrogance, self-deification, eastern ostentation) and misdeeds (incidents involving Thebes, Persepolis, Clitus, Callisthenes, India), but also the absence of Aristotle's education. As he traveled, the king behaved badly and so fell further away from the virtuous Greek life. Plutarch thus represents the campaign away from Greece as a journey from intelligence to barbaric ignorance. There is perhaps some deeper meaning to be found in Plutarch's ending, as it confers some authority upon the poison plot, purportedly organized by Aristotle himself (Plut. *Alex.* 77.3). Moreover, I also note that Plutarch's conclusion with Philip III Arrhidaeus as Alexander's successor works well, since his fate mirrors the fall of Alexander (77.8). The king's half-brother too had been of good moral character (χάριεν ἦθος) and high birth (οὐκ ἀγεννές) until the snake-worshiping Olympias drugged him, ruining his intelligence (διαφθαρῆναι τὴν διάνοιαν).

The historicity of the relationship between the king and his tutor thus licensed elaborations, however incredible. The best example is Alexander's letter to Aristotle about India, one of the longest letters in the *Alexander Romance* (3.17 with Gunderson 1980). The student reports back to his master what flora and fauna he has discovered in that country. Aristotle also wrote back, hailing him a new Odysseus for his travels (*AR* 3.26.7). Other texts generated further fictions on the basis of what people thought Aristotle had written. In yet another Christian exhortation, this time attributed to Justin Martyr but probably from the fourth century, we hear of an Aristotelian book addressed to Alexander (§ 5, *SC* 5.28). He is identified by his ethnicity, but nothing else noteworthy, except being the addressee. There is also a book with Alexander's name on Diogenes Laërtius' list, though I hesitate to take the association further than that. After all, Pseudo-Justin Martyr speaks of Aristotelian doctrine in a much more general kind of way than actually quoting the text. He is kinder than Tatian, for he at least says that Aristotle was more correct than Plato.

Gymnosophists: Indian philosophy uncovered

En route eastwards, the Macedonian expedition would encounter numerous natural philosophies. Few were more thought-provoking than what they discovered at the perceived edge of the world. At Taxila, in the Indus valley (Punjab, modern Pakistan), they chanced upon "Gymnosophists," literally *naked sophists* or *philosophers* (Molina Marin 2018: 120–121). In the early Hellenistic texts, such as Onesicritus' account, these philosophers lived in perfect tune with nature, enjoying what the land supplied them. Onesicritus had supposedly visited them himself, as already mentioned, and other primary witnesses corroborate their existence (Str. 15.1.61 incorporating Aristobulus *FGrH/BNJ* 139 F41 Pownall; Str. 15.1.66 incorporating Nearchus *FGrH/BNJ* 133 F23 Whitby). Onesicritus may have had a chance to meet them, because the Macedonians spent much of the spring of 326 in Taxila for diplomatic reasons. We cannot confirm whether Alexander spent the time interviewing the religious leaders, as much as he did meeting embassies from the local rajahs or went sightseeing with civic leaders. The primary accounts cited above, especially Aristobulus, and stories from other regions, suggest that he did, but they tend to have a fictional tone. In any case, we must be aware of the Greek, later Roman, conception of India (Karttunen 1989; Parker 2008). The Greeks, even those who visited, were very selective in what they reported back, and the cultural expectations were exaggerated. Writers imagined India to contain the most extreme wonders of flora, fauna, and peoples, which also licensed them to intensify any action the Macedonians took whether hostile or favorable. For example, while the Indian leg of the campaign (327–325 BC) is the one most enveloped in legend, the Greco-Roman sources also represent it as the bloodiest. Amplification of everything Indian occurs across non-Christian and Christian texts. Representing the utopian life of the Gymnosophists was no exception (Stoneman 2015).

The ancient authors focus on two Brahmanic figures: their leader, Mandamis/Dandamis/Dindimus, and Caranus/Calanus/Sphines, who left India behind to follow Alexander (Plut. *Alex*. 8.5, 65). We do not know if he came along of his own free will, or as one of the many hostages the Macedonians took. According to Arrian (Arr. *Anab*. 7.3.1), it was necessary to include Calanus in any history of Alexander. Arrian speaks positively of one key episode, namely Calanus' death. The Indian philosopher had fallen ill and decided to end his life on his own terms. He chose death by self-immolation on a pyre in front of the army (Arr. *Anab*. 7.3.6 incorporating Nearchus *FGrH/BNJ* 133 F4; cf. Ath. 10.49, 437a–b, incorporating Chares of Mytilene *FGrH/BNJ* 125 F19a; Ael. *VA* 5.6). The feat showed perfect self-control, and the audience applauded him for his willpower. Although Arrian couches the instance in the language of abstinence and asceticism, it appears from context that the event marked the beginning of a funeral drinking party, and so the display stands in stark contrast to the Macedonian behavior. Indeed, other authors seem to have taken issue with Calanus' method of withdrawal from the world (e.g., Str. 15.1.68 [717], incorporating Megasthenes *FGrH/BNJ* 715 F34a), and so his ascetic death developed into an *exemplum*.

More stories of Calanus circulated in Helleno-Jewish texts appropriated by Christians. One curious detail, attributed to a student of Aristotle's peripatetic school, suggests that the Syrians, of whom the Jews constituted a part, were descendants of a philosophical group from India, the so-called Calani (Joseph. *Ap*. 1.179 = Euseb. *Praep. evang*. 9.5.5 = Clearchus of Soli F6). The tribe name implies that Calanus the Indian was the founder of this community. The information appears in a fictional dialog between Aristotle and an unnamed, but learned Jew. Aristotle makes the statement. It is difficult not to think of Calanus' name in this context, and one scholar takes Aristotle's saying to refer to Calanus specifically, even if the original text is vaguer on that point (Bar-Kochva 2010: 48). Though the Indian was burned in Susa, not Syria, he fits the bill in every other respect. The ostensibly Indian background of the partially Jewish group certainly rests upon the model of the "eastern sage." From early Hellenistic authors onward (Theophrastus, Clearchus, Megasthenes), the Jews were cataloged with other eastern cultures and thus inserted into the discourse of "barbarian wisdom." While labeling the whole people, or *genos*, as philosophers may seem strange, the reference may rather point to the fact that the Jews lived an ascetic lifestyle and worshipped a god without an image. The Greeks knew of such aniconism and ritualistic behavior from their own belief systems. Hellenistic and imperial readers would find the Syro-Jewish people, among many others, recognizable and appreciate the deliberate exoticizing of the founding figure. Founding figures from abroad were popular in ancient thought (Cadmus for Thebes, Pelops for the Peloponnese, etc.), and intellectuals occupied themselves with creating fictional genealogies and succession narratives. Calanus may be a surprising example of this widespread tendency.

Another instance of the Calanus story made an impact. At the turn of the millennium, Athenaeus the Mechanic wrote a work on siegecraft in which he quoted a saying of Calanus on how Indian philosophers differed from their Greek counterparts (*Tactica* § 5). Greeks held long speeches over insignificant deeds, whereas Indians did the opposite. Philo, an Alexandrian Jew of the same period, quotes the saying partially (Philo *Prob.* § 96). He presents the *chreia* as part of a letter that Calanus sent to Alexander. In writing, Calanus declined the invitation to come with the king to educate the West. The dismissal was brave, for the king had threatened Calanus with death if he did not agree to go. The missive turns tradition upside down: the Indian philosopher was famous for going with the Macedonians, not remaining in India. The author may have confused Calanus with Mandamis, the Gymnosophist elder, who did stay behind. For Philo, Calanus' rejection recalled the Stoic doctrine of freedom (cf. Arr. *Epict. diss.* 3.24.69), and so happened to illustrate Philo's principal argument that good people were free.

No pre-Constantinian Christian used the *chreia* or noted the existence of this letter, but the document resurfaced in the late fourth-century writings of Ambrose of Milan (*Ep.* 7.34–38, *CSEL* 82(1).60–62). He does not mention Philo, even if the Jew was one of his favorite authors (Ruina 1993: 291–311). Ambrose asserts that Calanus' letter contains mere words rather than action, and he turns to the deeds of three virgins (Thecla, Agnes, and Pelagia), who had more desire for death than Calanus. We are told that Thecla and Agnes suffered martyrdom in the arena, whereas the Antiochene Pelagia leapt off a rooftop to escape the intentions of some lustful soldiers. Ambrose caps the list with the example of St Lawrence, a third-century martyr, who, while being roasted alive, said defiantly to his guards, "turn me over and eat of me." Given our knowledge of Calanus' self-immolation, the choice of Lawrence's cooking flesh seems strange, but Ambrose's readers probably did not know that version of the story. Ambrose translated and edited only the Philonic letter, thus omitting what Calanus had been most famous for.

We need not see the two different stories about Calanus as linked or competing. The whole background story was not required. Authors did not need to mention the pyre or explain differences between Mandamis and Calanus. Of course, some writers knew the full version. In the third century, Hippolytus of Rome summarizes matter-of-factly that Alexander paid Mandamis a visit because the Indian had conquered the body and so was deified, whereas Calanus was disgraced for abandoning his philosophy when leaving India (Hippol. *Haer.* 1.24.7). This summary ends the list of Hippolytus' digression on the Brahmans, the example of Alexander conferring a sense of historicity on what he has said about them. We will witness this use of the king's testimony in the next section. Detractors may say that Hippolytus' remark does not add to our knowledge, but it confirms the pattern that we have already witnessed of Christians engaging with the same information as in the historiographical sources, and on the same terms.

The existing background knowledge may of course always be elaborated into the realms of fiction. For example, Hippolytus' rough contemporary, Philostratus, wrote much more on the Brahmans on the basis of the Alexander tradition. Philostratus taught at Athens, and his famous *Life* concerns the first-century philosopher Apollonius of Tyana (Phot. *Bibl.* 44.9b). Early on in his career, Apollonius decides to pay a visit to the philosophers (Philostr. *VA* 1.18, 3.16). Book 1 follows his odyssey to Babylon and Book 2 describes the Indian leg of the journey, which is full of locations, monuments, and artifacts from Alexander's period there, including a 350-year old elephant that had fought the Macedonians at the Hyphasis (Philostr. *VA* 2.12, 2.24).

Philostratus' thorough engagement with the Greek literary tradition makes the *Life* a fascinating read. Apollonius, without much help from his companions, outdoes Alexander's travels every step of the way. Apollonius achieves this feat by visiting, and thereby overcoming, the same geographical difficulties, such as the Dionysiac city of Nysa (Philostr. *VA* 2.9) and the Rock of Aornus (2.10). In each case, Philostratus also explains what Alexander did or did not do at a given location, and the author's comments always play on the reader's expectations. For example, Apollonius learns from the Indian king Phroates (like Alexander learns from Porus) that the Macedonian king had not visited the actual Brahmans, but the warlike Oxydracae instead, who knew little except how to fight (2.33). Nevertheless, he was impressed with their "philosophy." As an aside, I note that the *Alexander Romance* uses Oxydracae as the name of the Brahmans (3.5). Amusingly, Phroates' report on the Brahmans pokes fun at the whole tradition of Alexander's important meeting with the philosophers. Apollonius already knew of the Gymnosophists back in Greece and had traveled along Alexander's route to see them, but the king himself had not even been able to recognize the *naked* wise ones. When Apollonius finally gets to meet the "real" Brahmans (Philostr. *VA* 3.16), he has surpassed the limits of both Greece and Rome, symbolized by the altars of Alexander (2.43). He is ready for his initiation into true, cosmic philosophy, going beyond the confines of the material world. The paradigm of the "eastern sage" certainly applies to Apollonius' initiation, but it is important to note that it is only the beginning. The Indian journey occupies the first part of the eight-book work, and thus reverses the usual operation of going to India last. Apollonius quickly dispenses with the Greek philosophical heritage before he takes on the great challenge of lifting the emperors' ban of philosophy by standing trial in the empire's capital. Alien wisdom therefore conquers Greece and Rome.

Writing parodies on parts of Alexander's campaign was an intellectual pastime, and Philostratus' allusive retelling proclaims him a master of contemporary high culture. Lucian supplies us with many further examples. The best appears in *The Ship* (Luc. *Nav.* §§ 28–40) in which three sailors pretend they each had a wish; one, Samippus, wishes to be a general modeled entirely on Alexander, except with regard to hereditary rule, for he does not want to inherit the power from his father. The three revisit many situations on their imaginary march to Babylon, which they take, and then they retire to excessive luxury of the ostensible oriental court. Lucian's mouthpiece Lycinus, Samippus' elder, offers his honest opinion, pouring utter scorn on the vanity of the poor Samippus. Lycinus does not think more highly of the other two, whose wishes had much in common with the greed of Midas and the ambition of Icarus. The sentiment in both Lucian and Philostratus is interesting. While Lucian defames Alexander's military achievements, Philostratus belittles both the campaign and the philosophical results. The two texts reveal that not all imperial Greeks valued the Macedonian king as highly as one may think when reading Plutarch's biography or Arrian's history. But the Christians never went so far in their critique of the campaign. As we shall see (Chapter 4), the war on Persia, its execution and timing, was important for Christian purposes, and so criticism of the king was limited to attacks on his personality and conduct.

Besides Mandamis and Calanus, the literary tradition provides us with another encounter between Alexander and the Gymnosophists (Plut. *Alex.* 64; cf. *AR* 3.5–6). The king met not two philosophers in person, but ten, and embarked upon a game of riddles in which the ten each had to answer a question with his life on the line. This trial by riddle, the German *Halsrätzel* (*Neck riddle*) is part of a much larger phenomenon in the ancient world, pitting power against wisdom, and the wise did not always win. From the case of Callisthenes, we remember the saying that the king held the power of death at the tip of his tongue. Alexander tried to catch the Gymnosophists out in a liar's paradox, but his riddles were not very good, only rather trivial (variations collated at Szalc 2011: 9–14). Which were more numerous, the living or the dead? Which was first, night or day? How can a mortal become a god? When Alexander was not satisfied with the answers he received, one of the wise men said that the king received answers as befitted the questions he posed.

The episode presumably originates in one of the major historical accounts, but evidence suggests that the exchange developed into a school exercise early on. A Hellenistic papyrus from second-century BC Abusir near Cairo contains parts of the dialog (*P. Berol.* 13044 = Cribiore 380). It lacks the introductory capture of the wise persons. The importance of the document lies in the labor of the author and others like him. Students of Greek were required to rewrite the scene and elaborate on various aspects as directed by the grammarian. Non-Christians and Christians would have equal access to the episode in their rhetorical repertoire. After all, they had pored over the same banal questions when they had learned to write. Another papyrus from the second century AD contains a written exercise loosely based on the same exercise as the Berlin papyrus (*P. Genev.* inv. 271), so we may assume that the school practice continued. The second papyrus has a distinctive Cynic flavor, for a letter of a Cynic hero, Heraclitus, also appears on the document. The papyri are translated by R. Stoneman (2012: 77–83). References in the wider literature indicates that the Gymnosophist story was well-known (see e.g., *Metz Epit.* §§ 78–84). We do not know if the dialog came with a pre-packed meaning in its original context, but it did not seem to have an inherently "philosophical allegiance" (Bosman 2010: 192), even if later versions might. At any rate, the meaning of the *chreia* could always be modified, as we have seen.

It follows that the traditional education offered a more static template as a point of departure. At least, innovating was not always the chief aim in drawing upon prior training. Clement of Alexandria provides us with a version that scholarship has considered remarkably close to that of Plutarch (Clem. Al. *Strom.* 6.4.38). As ever, Plutarch had an editorial hand in retelling the story, but so too had Clement, for he varied the length of the answers in direct speech. Many of the questions and answers remain the same, and we find relatively few major variations across all the attestations we still possess. The *Alexander Romance* contains the most differences, which can be explained either by dating that part of the text to a period before the Berlin papyrus or by positing a much later context for it. Another explanation may be that the author attempted to make an entertaining caricature of a well-known episode that students had revised so many times. For the second and third centuries AD, the story template, evidently inculcated at school, cultivated a shared intellectual practice that we will find further expressions of on the pages that follow.

One final text on the Gymnosophists demands attention, even if it lies outside our chronological purview. *De gentibus Indiae et de moribus Bragmanorum* or *On Indian Peoples and the Customs of the Brahmans*, perhaps by Palladius of Galatia (b. 364), bishop of Helenopolis in Bithynia, represents a wonderful conglomerate of the traditions discussed above (trans. at Stoneman 2012: 34–56). Palladius, if the treatise is genuinely his, wrote to his diligent reader on the matter of the philosophers, whom he had not himself visited, though he claims to have come briefly to the Indian periphery until the summer heat made him return west (1.1). Like Philostratus, Palladius claims that Alexander had not traveled past the Ganges, one of the four rivers that purportedly flow from Paradise; the king had built a monument at his kingdom's border near China, however (1.2; cf. Philostr. *VA* 2.43). After the preface follows the first part of the work. Palladius recounts ethnographic information that he had heard from a certain Theban (Greek or Egyptian?) scholar, who had traveled as far as the borders of Taprobane (1.3–14). Unlike Apollonius, the scholar had a hard time coming into the country and was taken captive and put on trial before an Indian ruler (cf. Philostr. *VA* 2.23–41 for Apollonius' trial and visit to an Indian king). The Indians released the scholar after six years because another Indian king had learned that his enemy held a Roman citizen captive and forced him to labor as a baker (1.8–10). The Indians, who feared the military might of Rome, let him leave. The next four paragraphs detail the geographical and ethnographic details of the Gymnosophists, who lived apart from the other Indians. The lore matches the wonders we hear of from Philostratus, as well as other related *Indica*.

The second part takes the form of a discourse that, Palladius advocates, will improve your life if you read it carefully. He states that he has acquired the text from Arrian, student of the Stoic Epictetus. The name in itself sounds suspicious, for Arrian was famously from Bithynia, like Palladius. Whoever the author was—probably Palladius himself, not Arrian, whose *Indica* is extant—he professes that the story derives from the authority of Dandamis himself, and so the text plays on multiple levels of literary legitimacy. A brief summary of the narrative with a view to the above themes will bring forth the parallels. Alexander comes to India wishing to visit the Gymnosophists, whom he has learned about from Calanus, who left them (2.2). The Brahmans are dismissive of the arrogant, murderous, and passionate king (2.3-10), and scorn Calanus as well, for giving up wisdom for pleasure (4, 11). Though the Greeks revere Calanus for his knowledge, he was worthless to the Brahmans. Despite the dismissal, the Indians direct Alexander to their leader. Unfortunately, the king cannot find him in the forest, so he sends "Onesicratus" to summon Dandamis (12-13). However, the Indian philospher does not do requests, and Onesicritus is forced to return with the message that the king needs to come to the philosopher (14-19). Conquered by the naked old man (cf. the Diogenes-section below), Alexander goes to speak with him for an hour, but he spends most of the time listening. Dandamis teaches him about worldly desire and invites the king to reject the material world (21-30). The king learns that an evil demon had perverted his divine spirit toward slaughter (31), apparently the goddess "Sophia" (Athene?). Alexander does not know how to repent and apologizes to God for his allotted fate. He then gives Dandamis presents for the lesson (32-36). The Indian laughs at the gold, accepting only oil to burn on a fire while offering prayers to God (37-39). As Alexander departs, Dandamis continues the lesson, covering many topics from vegetarianism to pillaging (41-56). Dandamis gets the last word, appropriately ending with God, who extends His mercy to every human being (57), but Alexander is already gone.

Scholars have previously considered the whole text a Christian exhortation to asceticism. Stoneman has now proposed that *On the Brahmans* reads as a "stylistic update" of an originally Cynic diatribe (Stoneman 2015: 7-8; cf. Steinmann 2012), lightly edited to remove the worst impieties and changing "gods" to "God." In this section, I hope to have questioned how much we need to worry about such antecedents and philosophical categories when we think of content so mutable as that concerning Alexander. Writers were fully capable of elaborating on existing tales, and few stories were more popular than the encounter with the Brahmans. From the preface and first part of Palladius' discourse, it seems to me that the author deftly exploits our expectations as much as any previous non-Christians or Christians did. Palladius' level of learning should not surprise us since urban schools taught such content. Monastic communities appear to have taken over the educational role once we reach Palladius' period (Larsen and Rubenson 2018). I see no reason why the same author should not have composed the second part of the text as well, passing it off as a treatise by Arrian (the Stoic, not the Cynic). I prefer to think of Arrian's role as conferring authority upon the whole literary project, and Palladius has already related a great deal of information from "the Theban scholar." The combined authorities work well in Palladius' favor, now that he claims only to have visited India briefly. Moreover, Christians, such as Hippolytus and Clement of Alexandria, had no difficulty in processing the material and making it their own, and so too did later Christians (cf. e.g., Aeneas of Gaza *Theophrastus* p. 18). The primary texts, including Palladius', once again point to a common cultural coherence among Christian intellectuals and their non-Christian peers.

Diogenes the Cynic: King avoids dog

The Brahmans were not the only naked philosophers Alexander encountered. Before the launch of his campaign, Alexander purportedly visited Diogenes of Sinope in his tub, perhaps in the Craneum outside Corinth. Alexander asked what he demanded of him, and the sage answered, "stand out of my light," ἀποσκότησόν μου (Diog. Laert. 6.38). Diogenes Laërtius, the philosopher's biographer, does not record Alexander's response to Diogenes' insolence, but elsewhere he notes that Alexander would have been Diogenes, had he not been Alexander (Diog. Laert. 6.32). Plutarch makes the connection between the two sayings in many places (Plut. *Alex.* 14.5; *De exil.* 605d–e; *De Alex. fort.* 331f–332a; *Mor.* 782b–c), offering various explanations for the king's positive reaction. In the *Life*, Alexander walks away jesting with his friends that he would be Diogenes for the philosopher's grandeur in rejecting the king. But, in the orations, Plutarch develops Alexander into a philosopher-king, who ranked Cynicism second after his own civilizing mission (Plut. *De Alex. fort.* 331d–332c). In terms of narrative, the meeting becomes another version of the encounter with Dandamis, who behaves like a second Diogenes. He also refuses to meet Alexander, so the king must come to him. The Gymnosophists also receive nourishment from the sun. The major themes also match up: asceticism versus personal wealth, power versus wisdom, philosophy versus kingship, and so on. The literary association did not go unnoticed. Ever the stylist Arrian arranged that narrative of his history so that the encounter with Diogenes in Corinth was followed by that with the Gymnosophists in India (Arr. *Anab.* 7.2.1).

The meeting in Corinth went viral, and legends grew up around the episode. For example, Plutarch noted that the pair died on the same day (Plut. *Mor.* 717c). The Stoic Emperor Marcus Aurelius considered Diogenes greater than Alexander (M. Aur. *Med.* 8.3.1) and Constantine's half-nephew Julian agreed with his predecessor, who was his imperial idol (Julian *Against Heraclides* § 8, *To Uneducated Dogs* 6.20). Other Greek philosophical writings contain several variations of the encounter (Arr. *Epict. diss.* 2.13.24, 3.22.92; cf. Simp. *In Epict.* p. 53). Roman literature overflows with elaborations (e.g. Cic. 5.32.91–92; Val. Max. 4.3.ext4a; Sen. *Ben.* 5.4.4; Juv. 14.308–312). We even possess three full-scale dialogs on the subject: Dio Chrysostom *Oration* 4, Lucian *Dialogs of the Dead* 13, and the 33rd Pseudo-Diogenic Letter (Bosman 2007: 54–55). Diogenes clearly enjoyed a wide and positive reputation in the non-Christian writers, even if his life story was fused with Alexander's, whom he seemed to so despise in the retellings (Stoneman 2003: 326–328; Demandt 2009: 221; cf. Molina Marin 2018: 84).

We are in for a surprise when we turn to the Christian testimonies. There is none in the extant corpus (cf. Giannantoni 1990 ii: 240–249). In fact, we do not hear of Diogenes and Alexander until after Constantine. The earliest attestation occurs in a letter to the philosopher Maximus of Ephesus, sent by Basil of Caesarea, who was a child when Constantine died in 337. The first of the great Cappadocian Fathers and later a Doctor of the Church makes passing mention of the famous meeting, requesting that his reader does not adopt Diogenes' saying, "here is as far from you as there is from us," ἴσον ἐστὶ παρ' ὑμῶν τὸ δεῦρο καὶ πρὸς ὑμᾶς ἐνθένδε (Basil *Ep.* 9.3). The saying is not attested in the previous non-Christian literature, but one might speculate that the response was what Diogenes said when Alexander unsuccessfully summoned him. Basil represents himself as the wise older ascetic, and Maximus as the young student, though he was twenty or so years older than Basil. The Christian aristocrat uses this and other sayings to encourage Maximus to visit him in his monastic community in Annesi, near Sinope on the Black Sea, around 361. Maximus was based at Julian's court at Constantinople, so they were not far apart. Because of poor health, Basil claimed to be growing roots, like a plant, at his family estate, so Maximus had to come to him. The mobility issue was feigned: he had already visited Constantinople in 359 for a minor church council and would soon be summoned to Cappadocian Caesarea (modern Kayseri, Turkey), where he would spend time as a presbyter from 362 and bishop from 370. Despite the neat vignette, we do not know whether Maximus accepted the invitation.

At first glance, the absence of the Alexander and Diogenes anecdotes in Christian texts gives a strange impression. Given its ostensible canonical status in the non-Christian texts and the patterns we have seen so far, we would expect many Christian references to the encounter. We cannot blame Christian censure or the absence of evidence, for many second- and third-century Christians knew of Diogenes and refer to him on his own (Krueger 1996: Ch. 5; cf. Koulakiotis 2006: 114–122). We witness, however, that the same pattern of absence occurs elsewhere in non-Christian literature. For example, the encounter between Alexander and Diogenes does not seem to form part of the curriculum taught at school. Papyrological evidence suggests that Alexander-related exercises mainly concerned military history, letter writing, and the odd eastern encounters (Denuzzo 2003; Prandi 2010: 85–95). If Stoneman is right in considering the *Alexander Romance* a product of a rhetorical school (Stoneman 2009), the following fact demands attention. Diogenes does not appear in the text, but the Brahmans do. In fact, Diogenes does not appear in three of the five major historians: Diodorus, Justin, and Curtius Rufus; this may be explained by the partial survival of these sources. Diodorus wrote on Calanus, whom he oddly calls "Caranus" (Diod. Sic. 17.107)—not only the name of a mythological founder of Macedon, but also one of Alexander's half-brothers.

Whatever the reason for Diogenes' non-appearance in parts of the literature, we must observe the importance of eclecticism. Selecting what content to preserve and prioritize shaped the filter through which the stories flowed. The simplest way to detect constituents of a given canon is by the quantification of the frequency of such data, but we have to be critical, for the authors evidently engaged with tradition on their own terms. Selecting what to omit also presents a choice. In spite of its popularity, we can see that the Diogenes anecdote remains an optional unit for both Christians and non-Christians. Later fourth-century references increase the number of Christian references (e.g. Jerome *Jov.* 2.14; John Chrysostom *Oppugn. PG* 47.337), but it is not commonplace in homilies until it appears in the handbooks of preaching much later in Byzantine history (Ps.-Maximus Confessor *Loci Communes PG* 91.773–774, 833–834).

Burn after reading

Leon of Pella on Alexander's letter to his mother

Prior to the Roman destruction of Pella in 168 BC, someone by the name of Leon, perhaps connected to the circle of Persaeus the Stoic (*d*. 243 BC), chanced upon an important letter. Alexander himself had written it to his mother. Leon published the confidential letter, despite the explicit order for Alexander's reader to burn it, which Olympias had not. No one else payed heed to the letter's wish, for the document found its way to Rome for the polymath Varro (116–27 BC) to read its contents. The letter interested non-Christian and Christian readers, who put its contents to good use.

Citing the letter was popular, and so the exact text unfortunately does not survive, if it ever existed, because it was reworked or summarized by many different authors. We possess a number of passing references to it in the extant literature (Lüschen 2013: 119–120). Paul Keyser has proposed the following historical reconstruction, which I reproduce here for the sake of convenience (Leon *FGrH/BNJ* 659 Keyser): prompted by the discovery of Alexander's letter, Leon of Pella produced a work. The preface began with the discovery and then followed the contents of the letter. The missive itself opened with the king's encounter with the priests at either Heliopolis or Memphis, or most probably Ammon's oracle in the Siwah Oasis. The priests informed Alexander of the great antiquity of Egypt and Mesopotamia, disclosing the secret that the pantheon arose from ancestor worship, i.e., the first gods were humans. The priests recounted the gods' discoveries on behalf of humanity, such as grain (Demeter), herding (Ammon), and weaving (Hermes). The chief priest feared divulging the confidential knowledge to the public and so begged of Alexander that Olympias should burn the letter after reading it.

While the narrative seems straightforward, readers may find the letter strange and suspicious. Why would Alexander write to his mother about such matters? The explanation lies in the ancient imagination. Writers represented Alexander as an explorer and adventurer, as well as a conqueror. His visits to places considered exotic, such as Egypt and India, corroborated various pieces of information about the perceived periphery of the inhabited world. Alexander could report such *exotica* to his mother or Aristotle and this imbued the information with the aura of authority, for why would the king lie to family members or his teacher? The oft-cited personal letters come from the *Alexander Romance* (e.g. Aristotle 3.17; Olympias 3.27–28), and this text alone provides more than thirty fictitious letters (Montaigne 2014; Whitmarsh 2013). Fabrication of royal letters was evidently a great industry in antiquity, and Leon may have added his forgery to the growing body of literature circulating as early as the Hellenistic period. The trend did not abate in the imperial period. Indeed, the frequent use of Leon's letter points to its popularity. This pattern evinces the common ground among intellectuals of various religious backgrounds insofar they drew upon a similar body of material.

One episode seems a fitting scene for the letter. The 332/1 BC visit to the oracle of Ammon in the Libyan desert famously features priests as sources of information for Alexander's desires (see e.g., Str. 17.1.43 incorporating Callisthenes *FGrH/BNJ* 124 F14a Rzepka). The exact purpose of traveling to this destination continues to elude us, but the sojourn to the Siwah Oasis clearly held great importance for Alexander, for the journey was time-consuming and arduous. Most sources present us with the motivation of the priests for flattering the king with divine honors, whatever he had done to persuade them to do so (Just. 11.11.1–8; Curt. 4.7.25; Plut. *Alex.* 27; Arr. *Anab.* 3.3.2; *It. Alex.* §50). Leon's letter taps into this sort of story by recapitulating the notion of ancestor worship, providing the reader with precedents for deification of the sort Alexander and/or the priests may have envisioned for the king. It also taps into the less flattering train of thought that the Egyptian priesthood consisted of habitual liars, and so the letter adds to the lengthy catalog of their falsehoods by saying that they lied about the gods. The dishonest flattery took other forms as well. One section of the letter (August. *De civ. D.* 12.11 incorporating Leon *FGrH/BNJ* 659 F3) concerned the chronology of the empires (Assyria, Egypt, Persia, Macedon), and this section declared that the Macedonian power would last longer than that of Persia, a mighty imperial power in the age of Alexander at any rate. Perhaps the most incriminating detail involves the burning of the letter, supplied by one late witness (August. *De civ. D.* 8.5 incorporating Leon *FGrH/BNJ* 659 F1). The request catches the eye because it intensifies the fraud. The information must not be shared with the public. The letter's contents exposed not only the priests, but also Alexander himself, who informed his mother of the deceit. In a sense, Alexander's mother makes for an apt accomplice, for she was credited with circulating her own rumors of Alexander's divinity (Arr. *Anab.* 4.10.2 incorporating Callisthenes *FGrH/BNJ* 124 T8 Rzepka). The Siwah episode and the triangulation of informant, announcer, and recipient thus provide a fitting historical framework for Leon's forgery. Unfortunately, only two fragments speak of Libyan Ammon (Leon *FGrH/BNJ* 659 F9a+b = Hyg. *Poet. astr.* 2.20; Tert. *Pall.* § 3), and so we cannot be certain that the Siwah Oasis was the location of Alexander's interview in Leon's letter.

In other ways the letter reads rather dubiously. Different writers place different points of emphasis on the testimony of Alexander. Leon may himself be the author (Tatian T1; Arnobius T2b; Scholion F4; Clement/Eusebius F7; Tertullian F8; Hyginus F9a), or he was the priest who disclosed the hidden truth to the king (Augustine T2a; Augustine F1; Augustine F3; Minucius Felix F5; Augustine F6; cf. Ps.-Cyprian [*Idol.*] § 3, *CSEL* 3.20). The first group remains more trustworthy in its mention of Leon, as the authors represented were both Christian and non-Christian witnesses, some of which one may regard as scholars. The other group consists of openly apologetic texts, and so made different emphases for effect. For example, members of this second group stress the role of Alexander as the author and Olympias as the reader, so as to highlight the confidential nature of the correspondence. Augustine of Hippo (354–430) provides many of the details from the latter group, but we will see how he was reworking an existing body of Latin apologetics by Minucius Felix and others. In order to discern patterns of similarity and dissimilarity, the following sections investigate the strategies employed by Christians when they mention the letter.

Athenagoras

Athenagoras provides the earliest explicit reference to Alexander's letter (Athenagoras *Leg. pro Christ.* § 28.1 incorporating Leon *FGrH/BNJ* 659 F3; cf. 28.7). He identifies Alexander as the son of Philip and gives the title of the letter as *Epistle to His Mother*, ἐν τῇ Πρὸς τὴν μητέρα ἐπιστολῇ. He omits Leon, both as author or Egyptian priest, preferring to confer full authority upon the notion of Alexander as the author. Uniquely, he juxtaposes Alexander's questionable testimony with the acknowledged witness of Herodotus, who reported that he had held conversations with Egyptians at three major civic and religious sites: Heliopolis, Memphis, and Thebes (Hdt. 2.3). The juxtaposition creates a powerful effect, for it forces us to accept Alexander's documentation on a par with that of Herodotus. Athenagoras does not, however, quote anything from the letter, but extracts much of his information about Egyptian ancestor worship from Herodotus. His use of the sources implies that they are both in agreement and so adds double weight to his argument, at least by ancient standards. The paratactic organization of the evidence continues when he finishes his list of evidence from Herodotus (§ 28.7, omitted by Jacoby/Keyser). For those people who considered Herodotus a fabulist, Athenagoras argues, one could turn back to Alexander or Hermes Trismegistus, plus many others, who provided similar evidence. Again, parataxis beckons readers to accept the statement, however brief the reference to the sources. This arrangement does not indicate that Athenagoras is "carelessly summarizing" (Keyser's *FGrH/BNJ* commentary on F3), but rather a careful deployment of the key authorities, supported by more dubious texts that he chooses to obfuscate. Athenagoras may use highly regarded literature, but as an eloquent rhetorician of the church, he can also misdirect for the sake of argument.

Alexander may seem the odd author out in the company of Herodotus and Hermes Trismegistus but, as previously mentioned, he was reputed to be an altruistic explorer. Athenagoras' contemporary Maximus of Tyre claimed that the king had asked for information about the sources of the Nile from the Ammonian oracle (Max. Tyr. 41.1). The passage has a rhetorical edge, however, for Maximus is insisting that Alexander would not have achieved true happiness, *eudaimonia*, no matter what he had asked the god. The pointed remark is not only tied to the trope that Alexander was not satisfied no matter how much he achieved in life (e.g., Max. Tyr. 29.2), but also contextualized within wider Greek thought. For the source of the Nile was the single biggest Egyptian mystery from Herodotus onward (see e.g., Hdt. 2.10). In Alexander's day, his court historian Callisthenes was thought to have looked for its spring when he sailed down the Nile as far as Ethiopia (Callisthenes *FGrH/BNJ* 124 F12a–d). It seems to me that Maximus represented Alexander's interview with priests at Siwah in light of this common representation. Investigating such matters of natural history was important when visiting Egypt, and Alexander and his expedition provided a key testimony on the problem. While Athenagoras took the design in another direction than Leon and Maximus, he was working with the same assumptions and in the same literary vein. We will detect a similar pattern in the next testimony.

Minucius Felix

The date of Minucius Felix' dialog, the *Octavius*, remains a hotly debated issue, but it is undoubtedly later than Athenagoras, who seems to have published his work under Marcus Aurelius and Commodus. A Severan date (*c.* 193–235) for the dialog is not unreasonable (Schubert 2014), and there may have been an African connection. Leon's work seems to have circulated widely in North Africa, as many apologists, who mention it, have ties to that continent. For example, (Ps.-)Cyprian and Tertullian were from Carthage; Athenagoras was thought to have taught at Alexandria, and Minucius Felix's Christian mouthpiece is supposed to have traveled from Cirta in Numidian Africa to Rome to visit his host. Stylistically, the level of Latin suggests a highly competent rhetorician, suitable for the third-century church that attracted intellectuals of the highest caliber. The literary genre and presentation offer the most innovative aspects of the *Octavius*, for the author seems to have primarily reworked existing arguments for Christianity's viability.

Minucius arranges the letter paratactically with other authors (Min. Fel. *Oct.* § 21.3 Kytzler, *CSEL* 2.29), just as Athenagoras did. The document lists writers who followed the belief of Euhemerus of Messene (330–250 BC) that the gods had been mortals. The list forms a new part in which the interlocutors discuss the differences between Christianity and paganism rather than the shared features (§§ 1–20). Octavius comes across as steeped in classical literature and, in the pertinent passage, he cites Euhemerus, Prodicus of Ceos (435–395 BC), and Persaeus of Citium, the Stoic to whose circle Leon may have been attached. Alexander's letter represents the final piece of evidence, practical rather than philosophical. The king described the practices of the Egyptians because he had been there, and we must believe what he said because he said it to his mother. Minucius does much to point to the independence of the document, calling it, "a remarkable work," *insigni volumine*.

Minucius' version provides more details of the content of Leon's work than Athenagoras. Alexander is no longer referred to as the son of Philip but great (*magnus*) and of Macedon (*Macedo*). Leon is not mentioned, but an unnamed priest features. The king had forced the information from the priest through fear of his power, *metu suae potestatis*. We will return to this statement below. The key piece of new information concerns the gods, for Minucius Felix states that Hephaestus (Vulcan) was the original god and the family of Zeus (Jupiter) followed after. Paul Keyser claims that this relation is "unusual" for Hephaestus sprung from Zeus and Hera, but then, he cites Diodorus for the "indicative exception" that Hephaestus was the first king of Egypt because he discovered fire (Diod. Sic. 1.13.3; cf. Keyser's *FGrH/BNJ* commentary on F5). But this detail is actually the best evidence corroborating the Egyptian context of the letter. Since Manetho wrote on Egypt in the third century BC, it was known to the Greeks that Hephaestus was the creator Ptah of Memphis, patron god of craftsmen and lord of heaven and earth (Manetho *FGrH/BNJ* 609 F3a Lang). For example, the Egyptianizing *Alexander Romance* speaks of Hephaestus as, "the progenitor of the gods" (*AR* 1.3.4, cf. Euseb. *Praep. evang.* 3.2.6–7 incorporating Manetho *FGrH/BNJ* 609 F18). Minucius Felix's reference to the Egyptian pantheon is therefore highly suitable for the interlocutor, as is to be expected when Octavius of Cirta wants to use Alexander's letter as evidence against the Egyptian religion. In order to lampoon the opposition, his proof needed to appear genuine and annexed from knowledge widely available to friends and foes.

Pseudo-Cyprian

This author is rightly not collected in the fragments of Leon of Pella, because he makes use of Leon's work only through Minucius Felix. *That idols are not Gods*, *Quod idola dii non sint* (or *De idolorum vanitate*), contains so many linguistic parallels to Minucius Felix's *Octavius* and Tertullian's *Apology*, that the text almost reads as a compilation or marginal notes to those works. Based on such sources, the text is shaped as a powerful apologetic tract against polytheism. Jerome and Augustine attributed it to Cyprian of Carthage (martyred 258), but most scholars consider the work late and spurious, and some even believe that the text is dependent upon Lactantius' *Divine Institutes* (Gassman 2018: 9–10). We may see the Cyprianic tract as evidence for the use of the first Latin Christians in the fourth century, returning to the roots of the literary movement and preferring its wisdom to non-Christian literature. Constant reworking of the literary corpus makes for a new frame of reference, as well as creating a larger corpus of updated texts. This tendency to renew previous writings by Christians was an important activity, as texts became outdated or needed to be appropriated for new contexts.

The Pseudo-Cyprianic pamphlet adapts more than it repeats its sources, as is evinced by the passage in question (Ps.-Cyprian [*Idol.*] §3, *CSEL* 3.20). The author does not arrange Leon's letter next to that of other authors' witnesses, but lets it stand alone as an authority. This omission represents a departure from both Athenagoras and Minucius Felix. Pseudo-Cyprian uses the letter as part of an argument against the religious practices abroad as opposed to those at home in Rome. Local cults deified famous ancestors in a given region, and some worshiped individuals more than others. The divergent cult practices are presented to support the overarching argument that there was no organized religion or unified worship of the Olympian or Egyptian deities across the empire, as opposed to the universal Christian religion. The author could thus represent Christianity as unified and strong in its common worship of God, ignoring the inconvenient schisms, Gnostic sects and other challenges in the early church. The letter constitutes the climax of the argument, which ends on the mocking note that no mortals-turned-gods had been born recently, perhaps because Jupiter had become too old or Juno lost the ability to bear children.

In terms of the contents of the letter, the author makes a few minor adjustments. For example, he removes Minucius Felix's epithet *Macedo* when identifying Alexander. He recycles the curious notion only found in Minucius Felix that the priest was afraid of Alexander's power, *metu suae potestatis*. The remark may seem to have been intended to represent Alexander not as a violent despot, but a scientist, who wanted the exact information from the priest. But the literary tradition contains many examples in which the king threatened oracles with violence if they did not say what he wanted to hear. We come close in the episode of the visit to Siwah in which Alexander bribes the priests to say what he wants them to (esp. Just. 11.11.7–8), but there are more convincing examples. For instance, we see the pattern in the story of the king's consultation of Apollo's oracle at Delphi. Plutarch tells the story that the king wished to consult the oracle on an inauspicious day, and the oracle was closed (Plut. *Alex.* 14.6–7). The prophetess was, however, not able to refuse Alexander's zeal, even if she had the law on her side. Breaking the law, noted twice by Plutarch who was himself a priest at Delphi, Alexander attempted to use force to drag her to the temple, whereupon she remarked, "you are invincible, my son," and he had no further need of her prophecy (cf. Diod. Sic. 17.93.4; Just. 12.2.3). The *Alexander Romance* stages a similar episode when Alexander visits the oracular trees of the Sun and the Moon. An Indian priest tries to prevent Alexander and his soldiers from hanging garlands upon the trees, citing the law, but concedes that Alexander can do what he wishes if he uses force. For a king the law is unwritten, βασιλεῖ γὰρ νόμος ἄγραφος (*AR* 3.17.37–38; cf. Clem. Al. *Strom.* 3.4.30.2). In the remainder of the episode, Alexander has full access to the oracular trees.

Summary

The representation of the encounter in Minucius Felix and Pseudo-Cyprian differs from the version in St Augustine, who said that the priest did not fear Alexander himself, but feared going public and so wanted the letter burned (Aug. *De civ. D.* 8.5 incorporating Leon *FGrH/BNJ* 659 F1). This change may seem insignificant to the innocent reader, but it confirms the tendency we have witnessed in the three previous instances. Each writer had the license to alter not only the context and the way the letter was presented, but also the contents within the letter. Strategies depended on purpose and intent. As ever, the sources were open to interpretation, and authors could employ them as they wished, however far their purposes were removed from the context of the original letter. I note that each author, whether Christian or non-Christian, takes for granted that Leon's work existed as a reliable source of information.

Given their diverging strategies, we must note that most Christians found common ground in using the letter. They focused primarily on Alexander's report of Egyptian ancestor worship as fuel for their criticisms of human deification. Most Christians preferred Alexander to Leon in terms of authorship, and some even played the king up against the most acknowledged historiographers and philosophers. Some Christians also dismissed the contents of the letter as mythological falsehoods (Tert. *Cor.* 7.6, incorporating Leon *FGrH/BNJ* 659 F8), whereas Clement of Alexandria uses the letter's notes on myths to construct a chronology of the earliest Greeks as compared to the Hebrews of the Old Testament (Clem. Al. *Strom.* 1.21.106.3). Eusebius of Caesarea cited the latter with approval (Euseb. *Praep. evang.* 10.12.23). In general, however, the letter presented a good opportunity to overturn non-Christian religious practices from within, that is, evidence based on a credible eyewitness and a document signed by a famous person, so important for capturing the attention of readers. It is ironic that, by the time we get to Pseudo-Cyprian and Augustine in the fourth century, they seem only to be quoting from Christian authorities, even if they purport to have firsthand knowledge of the original letter.

The three testimonies studied above reflect important patterns that will recur in the present and following chapters. First, Christians utilized much knowledge from traditional literature, whether they chose to accept, appropriate, or dismiss it. Feigning antipathy toward non-Christian learning was part of the rhetorical strategy, for most Christians participated in the same intellectual culture. Second, the Christians could use this material freely, even if they often followed how other Christians had employed the same information. Nuances and variations occur, but there are common points of emphasis that connect the Christians as opposed to the non-Christians. For example, the Christian focus on idolatry, ancestor worship, and religious secrecy. The same kind of pattern applies to how non-Christians use the stories. For example, they take more interest in the actual myths in the letter than Alexander's interaction with the priest. Third, we note that the Christians did not always return to the original texts, but enjoyed reading and reusing each others' updated versions. We see this pattern from the fourth century onward, and it may have contributed to the fact that little Christian literature survives from the second and third centuries. The absence may indeed reflect the constant updating of texts. Fourth, we must abandon the idea that geographic and linguistic barriers determined what was written about Alexander. Countering that argument may seem pedestrian, for imperial culture was dictated and nourished by the sprawl of the empire across the East and West. We know of local variations, of course, but few differences in the Alexander literature may be found between Greek and Latin, East and West. The same material flowed through the literary filters in the centers of knowledge, forming a solid basis for elaborations and innovations.

Deification denied

Birth myths

Zeus/Jupiter reigns supreme in most categories among the Olympians, including the less flattering ones. One of his failings is adultery. An ancient list recounts no less than forty-one incidents and names the women involved, as well as the bastard children fathered on them. The women are mythological figures, such as Europa, Io, and Hippodamia, but one historical figure stands out: Alexander's mother, Olympias (Rufinus? Clem. *Recogn.* 10.21.5, GCS NF 51.340). Pseudo-Clement of Rome identifies her as the daughter of Neoptolemus, an Epirote ruler and self-proclaimed descendant of the Homeric hero Achilles (cf. Paus. 1.11.1; Just. *Epit.* 7.6.10). The author also identifies Alexander as the result of the union between Zeus and Olympias. In so doing, he exploits the existing mythology that surrounded the siring of Alexander, now studied at length by Daniel Ogden (2011: 7–123). We know of three principal myths, supplied by the beginning of Plutarch's *Life of Alexander* 2–3, but Zeus is the offender in all three cases. The passage thus recycles a common notion rather than a specific story to expose Zeus' infidelities and thereby substantiate his overall claim that the Olympian gods were sinners and unworthy of worship. This strategy was doubly effective, for Zeus' immoral behavior reminded the initiated at least of the first (idolatry) and seventh commandment (adultery) of the Mosaic law (Exod. 20:3–6, 15; Deut. 5:7–10, 18).

In the various texts attributed to Clement, the fourth bishop of Rome, this remarkable reference to Alexander's ancestry occurs only once, but later Christians also listed Zeus' affairs. One late antique poem contains a memorable passage in which Eros is engraving his love-inducing arrows with the gilded names of the targets that he will shoot for Zeus (Nonnus *Dion.* 7.117–28, Olympias at 128). The final target is Olympias yet again, and she will be embraced by her thrice-coiled, *trieliktos*, consort, suggesting Zeus in his serpent guise. Though the reference is clearly negative in the Pseudo-Clementine *Recognitions*, Nonnus seems more positive. His mythologized Alexander heralds the last days of Greek mythology and the beginning of history.

Clement of Alexandria made the most cutting comment on Alexander's desire to appear the son of Zeus. In a tirade against idolatry (*Protr.* 4.54.2), Clement denounced man-made images of gods, as well as individuals who sought godhood. He did not spare nations (Scythians, Greeks, Egyptians), courtesans, or kings, providing supporting material from a host of non-Christian writers. Once again, Alexander is one among many persons mentioned. His sacrilege consisted of wanting the sculptors to add horns to his human portraits, so he should appear more like the Libyan Zeus Ammon, who was famous for having curly ram's horns. This depiction might have held a particular resonance for Clement, who was himself North African. From Africa, we also possess archaeological evidence that horned Alexander busts and coins were still produced in Clement's day (Fulinska 2012: 393). The artifacts provide tangible evidence that Clement's readers could themselves witness on coin portraits or on physical sculpture in Alexandria. Alexander's error was therefore familiar and apparent to Clement's audience, whether initiated or not (Wirth 1993: 61).

While Clement's remark again reinforces what a Christian might learn from the Mosaic law, the comment matches what some near-contemporaries thought of Greek mythology. For example, Lucian's *Parliament of the Gods* (Luc. *Deor. Conc.*) offers the same sentiment on horns as Clement. Momus, satire personified and Lucian's mouthpiece, derides ugly and unnatural animal additions on multiple divinities, including Egyptian deities (cf. Juv. 15), Dionysus and Zeus Ammon (§ 10). He does not think highly of statues either, nor is he impressed with the many new gods on Olympus, divinities who were previously mortals. A key target is Dionysus (alcoholic, effeminate, mad, foreign, arrogant, etc.) who brought Pan, two women, a dog, and a party of satyrs to ruin Mount Olympus. Zeus does not permit Momus to taunt Asclepius and Heracles—incidentally, Dionysus, Heracles, and Asclepius are the same three gods that the philosopher Celsus had considered more clearly deified than Jesus, a mere phantom in his opinion (Origen *C. Cels.* 3.22.1; cf. Justin *Dial.* § 69). Momus also questions Zeus' numerous affairs with women (§ 8), though not to the same extent that the Pseudo-Clementine *Recognitions* had done. As we have seen earlier, the Christian writers were using what contemporary satirists might make of the Greek pantheon and applying their criticism more broadly to a wide range of examples.

Christian exploitation of the myths concerning Alexander's birth remains rare, however. Another instance occurs in Tertullian (*De anim.* § 46.5, *CCSL* 2.851). The passage makes but a brief mention of the dream in which Philip sees himself pressing a lion signet on Olympias' womb, and the seal represents the future birth of the lion-like Alexander. To Tertullian, the story is historical fact, which he posits with a reference to his source, the Cymaean historian Ephorus (Ephorus *FGrH/BNJ* 70 F217 Parker). The story represents one of many factoids that Tertullian is using to repudiate Epicurean and heretical doctrine of dreaming, that is, that dreams were merely fancies. To represent dreams as good evidence for the existence of the soul Tertullian accepts this particular tale, along with many other notable stories from traditional texts, such as Herodotus. Again, we notice that his concern is not with Alexander *per se*, but rather with the construction of an argument for which Alexander-related stories provided recognizable evidence. And yet, few Christians mimicked Tertullian and used this birth myth of the lion seal. Conversely, the story is enshrined in the historiographical texts (cf. Plut. *Alex.* 2.4–5; *AR* 1.8.3–6).

If Christians were only concerned with Alexander's deification, one might observe that they here missed a great opportunity to deride Greek culture (Lüschen 2013: 120–121). But it is also the pattern we find elsewhere. From non-Christian texts, we know that some capitalized on such tales, disapproving of the king's own claims to divine heritage (Ael. *VA* 12.64; Luc. *DMort.* 13.1–2). Deification is a major theme in the accounts of the imperial period, although few authors develop stories from Alexander's youth. The absence of such stories can be attributed to many factors, such as the incomplete source material, but it is nevertheless striking that so few instances appear in the surviving textual corpus. With regard to the birth myths, the Christian pattern matches what we find in the non-Christian texts.

The king is dead

> *One world is not enough for the young man from Pella. / In discontent he seethes at the narrow limits of the universe / as if confined on the rocks of Gyara or tiny Seriphus. / But once he's entered the city that's fortified by potters, / his coffin will be big enough. It's only death / that reveals the minuscule size of human bodies.*
>
> Juvenal *Satire* 10.168–173 (Trans. LCL)

The death of Alexander constitutes a powerful theme in imperial literature, though few treatments equal the outburst of Juvenal. He directs his invective against the notion that the world was not enough for Alexander, a commonplace in Roman rhetoric before the elder Seneca (Sen. *Suas.* 1.pr.1; Lucan 10.25–28; Sen. *Ep.* 119.7; cf. *Rhet. Her.* 4.31). The scathing irony of the coffin's size fitting the king's corpse is incisive and was favored by a number of authors (Stoneman 2003). The pre-Constantinian Christians, however, took less interest in the king's passing, as we shall see.

I must preface this section with the observation that pre-Constantinian Christians did not make remarks on the king's tomb or coffin, as later writers did. In the fifth century, John Chrysostom asked to be shown Alexander's tomb on the assumption that nobody knew where it was, or knew the day of the king's death (*Hom. 2 Cor.* 26.5, *PG* 61.581). Though enthusiasts of the search for Alexander's lost tomb take this passage as evidence for its disappearance (Saunders 2006), Chrysostom's passage is not unique in its purpose to stress that Jesus, Christian monuments, and feasts were visibly celebrated everywhere, but not long-dead monarchs. Another Antiochene author could make the same claim for Christian superiority, adding famous Persians and Roman emperors to the equation (Theodoret *Graecarum affectionum curatio* 8.60–61). But before Constantine, no one seems to have found it proper to compare Alexander's death with Jesus' imperishability.

Clement of Alexandria comes close, though. In another passage of the *Exhortation* (*Protr.* 10.96.4, partially incorporating *Sib. Or.* 5.6), he uses an anecdote relating to Alexander's death in order to make a case against those who had argued that Christians had abandoned the pious practices of previous generations. He addresses the claim by saying that Christian ethics offered a better path compared to earlier generations, which had themselves acted childishly in their beliefs. Children would, however, not stay children forever, but would increase in virtue with time and the proper training. Abstaining from idolatry was one way to grow up, and so Clement turns to Alexander's deification as an example of the mistakes that the ancestors had made. He argues that flatterers, who had proposed to canonize Alexander as the thirteenth god, were clearly in the wrong because "Babylon proved him a corpse," ὃν Βαβυλὼν ἤλεγξε νέκυν, a line adapted from the Sibylline Oracles. To add a further criticism, Clement praises a pointed remark by Theocritus, a fourth-century BC philosopher from Chios. Theocritus had allegedly said about Alexander's death that humans should rejoice now that mortals saw gods dying before themselves. The comment is but one of the sharp remarks on Alexander in his repertoire (cf. Ath. 12.55 [540a], incorporating Phylarchus *FGrH/BNJ* 81 F41 Landucci). Clement commends Theocritus for scoffing at his fellow citizens before powering on with further examples.

The passage must detain us a moment. It presents multiple points of interest. I start with a minor philological point. Clement uses a verse from the Sibylline Oracles, possibly quoting from memory. He has omitted the last part of the line, changing the meaning slightly from the original, which read "Babylon confounded him and gave a corpse to Philip," ὃν Βαβυλὼν ἤλεγξε, νέκυν δ' ὤρεξε Φιλίππῳ. He also omits the context of the passage, which explicitly calls for Alexander's own pretensions to be the son of Zeus-Ammon. Clement has adjusted the agency from Alexander himself to the people who deified him. He is thus choosing a different strategy than in the passage above in which he instead derided Alexander's *own* wish to appear to be the son of Ammon by adding a horn to his sculptures. The subtle difference ultimately fuels the argument in each passage. In this section, it sufficed to say that the king's death in Babylon removed any shadow of a doubt that Alexander was not a god and that was quite clear to some of his contemporaries. A corollary was that people were ridiculous for worshiping him. In the other passage, Clement needed evidence for kings' deification of themselves, and so Alexander's paternity issues fitted the bill, along with the evidence from his portraits. Combining the two passages, we notice that Clement does not just target Alexander among other kings, but more so his followers, who failed to see through the king's vanity. By ancient standards, his double reference increases the persuasiveness of his case.

The second point concerns the use of the Sibyl versus the typical "classical" sources, such as Theocritus' remarks. Clement considers the Sibyl on a par with other authoritative texts and need not justify his choice. Compared to the Theocritan invective, Clement's Sibylline quotation is more succinct, but it reinforces the point that he selected material carefully from what he regarded as a common arsenal of material. The identities of the Sibyl are notoriously problematic to determine, but Clement saw little difference between her and the "classical tradition." This sort of inclusion will concern us in the chapters that follow.

Let us turn to the notion of Alexander being the thirteenth god of the Olympian pantheon. The idea presents a heated issue in modern studies of Greek historiography, for some sources report that such honors were meant for Philip rather than Alexander (Diod. Sic. 16.92.5; Apsines *Rhet.* 1.19 incorporating Demades *FGrH/BNJ* 227 T93). Clement provides an intriguing test-case, because he opts for Alexander, but also mentions the deification of Philip elsewhere in the *Exhortation* (*Protr.* 4.54.5). In so doing, he highlights—rightly or wrongly—divine Olympian honors for Philip, a passage which scholars know and discuss (e.g., Badian 2012: 268–272). But Clement does not refer to Philip as the thirteenth god of the pantheon. He is giving that honor to Alexander in Book 10, as we have seen. Though that may be internally inconsistent in his text— Alexander would surely be the fourteenth Olympian then—we cannot use Clement to make a one-to-one comparison with the historiographical accounts, for Clement applied the *chreia* differently (Baynham 1994). This fact needs to be included in future debates on the question of divine honors for Philip.

We have repeatedly seen that we need to be more aware of the *exemplum* literature and its mutability. We can achieve this awareness by casting the net wider in our search for comparative data. Locating and identifying references in the vast corpus previously took a long time, but computerized searches make matters easier. For example, it took more than half a century to refute Hermann Usener's hypothesis that John Chrysostom was the sole witness to the curious report that the Roman senate had deified Alexander as the thirteenth god (Usener 1902 *contra* Straub 1970). Usener believed that this Alexander was the emperor Alexander Severus, whereas Straub argued that John Chrysostom meant the Macedonian Alexander. But the two were commonly confused in antiquity too, although the latter was meant by default (see e.g., Epiph. *Ancoratus* § 60.4). Johannes Straub, who had the right end of the stick, suggested that Chrysostom's version was confused with a legend surrounding Pontius Pilate. After Jesus' crucifixion, Judea's governor sent a message to Tiberius, recommending divine honors to be conferred on Jesus, but the senate refused (Tert. *Apol.* 5.1; Euseb. *Hist. eccl.* 2.2.1–2). John Chrysostom had thus erred because he had conflated what the church tradition taught about Alexander (the Great) and Jesus.

In relation to the divine honors for Alexander, Clement uses the *chreia* in the same way as Lucian (*DMort.* 13.2–3) and Aelian (*VH* 5.12 incorporating Demades *FGrH/BNJ* 227 T82). The former says that the Ptolemies deified Alexander, whereas the latter prefers the Athenians. Aelian points to Demades, a fourth-century BC orator from the city. The Athenians were the usual option (Val. Max. 7.2.ext13; cf. Aeneas of Gaza *Theophrastus* p. 34), but writers had much scope for variation. Clement does not commit to a location, and so no one is singled out. He turns the statement into a general one, so as to scold as many as possible. His main point on death also follows along the lines of Lucian. This author satirized Alexander's claim to divinity by placing him in the Underworld. Here the king meets Diogenes the Cynic, who was surprised to see Alexander there, now that people worshiped him as a god. Diogenes criticized Alexander for his insistence on his own divinity, even in death, but also blasted the flatterers who built temples to the king. In another dialog (Luc. *DMort.* 12.6), Alexander bumped into his father Philip. Unfortunately, Philip was not impressed with his son and chastised him for many things, including taking other fathers and competing with the gods. He ended on the notion that Alexander should be ashamed for still desiring godhood in death. Death renders immortality useless for him, and he should recognize that fact, not hold on to his vain wishes. Death thus proves, in both the Christian and non-Christian case, that human deification was ridiculous, unless one could conquer the grim reaper.

Note once more how easily this anecdotal material could be recontextualized. The stories could concern Alexander, or his father Philip, and writers could target several groups (Athenians, Ptolemies, Romans, "pagans," etc.). For some writers, the thrust of the argument featured death, whereas others changed the focus to consider other subjects. The malleable nature of the material is important, for it brings us to an important realization. We are at the mercy of our literary sources, who had their own agendas in using a certain story. For this reason, we must remain vigilant and aware of why the writers choose to revisit the stories. The more popular the *exemplum/paradeigma*, the more attention we must invest in it, for popularity means that the idea was commonplace or useful in debates. By approaching the tradition as a whole instead of individual, the present book differs fundamentally from modern studies interested only in historical origins or seeking to pick out what is representative; we cannot determine the historical or the outstanding without awareness of the bigger picture.

In general, early Christians tended not to capitalize on Alexander's death as evidence against his deification. Only Clement makes use of this proof. It may be that other historical examples were preferred. For example, Celsus and Origen choose to denounce Antinous, Hadrian's deified plaything, who in their view had unjustly joined the ranks of the gods because of the emperor's personal affections (Origen *C. Cels.* 3.36). Contrary to expectations from earlier scholarship (Demandt 2009: 421–422), neither Alexander's death nor his birth-by-Zeus are frequent in Christian arguments. The fact may surprise readers because these items make for thematically appropriate points of criticism and occur frequently in the writings of non-Christians. But the apologists favored other historical and mythological *exempla* in this regard, perhaps due to general education and to the relative accessibility of folklore (Morgan 2007: 233).

Compared to non-Christians, Christians rarely make references to the events surrounding Alexander's death. Tertullian refers twice to the king's ostensible assassination by poison (*De anim.* § 50.3, *CCSL* 2.856; *Adv. Valent.* §15.3, *CCSL* 2.766). In both instances he mentions only a minor factoid from the wider tradition, namely the Nonacris River in Arcadia, the so-called "waters of Styx" (Vitr. *De arch.* 8.3.16). We know this potent poison well from the historiographical accounts. They claim that the conspirators had, on the council of Aristotle, carefully brought a draught from this river to Babylon in a donkey's hoof (Diod. Sic. 17.117.5–118; Plut. *Alex.* 77.1–3; Just. 12.14). At a celebration for Dionysus, Iollas, the cupbearer and Cassander's accomplice, poured the icy liquid into Alexander's wine-cup after which the ruler died some days later (cf. *AR* 3.31–32.10; *LM* § 97). While Arrian denies the historical value of this information (Arr. *Anab.* 7.27), he too needs to mention the story for good measure. Conversely, Sextus Empiricus considered the Antipatrid plot a fact and used it in a digression on what exemplified history as truth (Sext. Emp. *Math.* 1.263). Numerous references in the literature document its widespread use (e.g., Ov. *Ib.* 297–298; Sen. *Ep.* 83.23; Plin. *HN.* 30.149; Ael. *NA* 5.29), so Tertullian had the murder story on good authority.

Tertullian's purpose was, however, not to elaborate on the plot of Antipater. He used the information to dismiss the teaching of two heretics. In *On the Soul*, he disputes the doctrine of the Samaritan Menander, who was a disciple of Simon Magus and active in the era of the emperor Claudius; in *Against the Valentinians*, he dismisses the gnostic cosmogony of the Alexandrian Valentinus (d. c. 160), who lectured in Rome. Menander was associated with water, teaching that his baptism guaranteed immortality because the recipient would become eternally young (Iren. *Haer.* 1.23.5). Valentinus had spoken of a being named Achamoth, whose tears had created the waters of the world (Iren. *Haer.* 1.4.4). In the case of Menander, Tertullian required proof from living disciples baptized by the cult founder in the first century, of which there presumably were few left in the third century, at least decidedly few youthful ones. As for Valentinus' Achamoth, Tertullian describes her in an ever-sarcastic tone and style, while associating her with banalities from Greek myth and philosophy. Nonacris appears in a list of rivers and ponds that flowed from Achamoth's eyes during her deadly mood-swings: Nonacris killed Alexander, the Lyncestis River in Macedon made people drunk, and the Salmacis spring in Carian Halicarnassus turned swimmers into hermaphrodites. It is not clear if the rivers were already mentioned in Valentinian doctrine. In my view, their reappearance in *On the Soul* suggests that Tertullian himself created the list. Incidentally, heavy drinking and effeminacy are themes closely linked to Alexander's tradition, though it is not clear if the author intended such resonances. The most important thing to note is the strong sarcasm, which I believe indicates that Tertullian's remarks on the rivers are made in the spirit of mockery; he ridiculed the heretics by associating them with non-Christian myths that made their doctrine seem even more preposterous. By organizing heretics and myth in a single stream, "Orthodox" Christians could then exclude non-Christian and heretical ideas collectively at a single stroke.

One final use concerns posthumous cults for Alexander. Cults of the conqueror were common across the Mediterranean, and Arrian remarks upon local oracles in Macedon in his day (Arr. *Anab.* 7.30.2). Again, the topic seems to present a golden opportunity for Christians to mock deification, but they did not. We know of just two such instances. In the Pseudo-Clementine literature, the author speaks of cultic honors for Alexander at Rhodes (*Homil. Clement.* 6.23.1, GCS NF 42.144; *Recog.* 10.25.2, GCS NF 51.344). Inscriptions and literature confirm the existence of such a cult on the island (Dreyer 2009: 227–228), and so we may assume that the cult was widely known. The author uses this general knowledge in a passing remark against deification. He has Clement, the protagonist, list examples of such cults after noting his disdain for past people, who worshiped Asclepius, Hercules, and Dionysus (again, note the canonical tricolon of heroes receiving godhood). The examples amount to Hector at Troy, Achilles at Leuce, the "White Island" (now Snake Island in the Black Sea), Patroclus at Pontus, and Alexander at Rhodes. Note how Alexander is once again the last on the list of mythic examples, apparently associated with the other great heroes of Greek thought. This Homeric theme runs strong in imperial literature, and so it is unproblematic, even appropriate, to see a Christian author make use of the commonplace (Heckel 2015). Though the list seems crafted for the purpose and probably was, we know well Clement's other examples. Arrian refers to Achilles' island in his work on the Black Sea, focusing on the cult site and the manifestations of the hero (Arr. *Peripl. M. Eux.* §§ 21–23; cf. Plin. *HN* 4.13.93). Using cults acknowledged by literature confers authority upon Clement's list. Of course, the Christian author informs the reader of how one should interpret that list. Despite its value, the list represents the sole instance in early Christian literature that censures Alexander's cult on Rhodes or elsewhere.

Coda: Alexander, Origen's Jew, and Jesus on the cross

The above uses of material relating to Alexander's death and deification follow the pattern we previously witnessed in the case of the birth myths. Christians were well aware of, if not inspired by, what some of the non-Christians were doing with the content and deployed the same tools to bestow authority upon individual arguments. While the repurposing of stories is important for how Christians used them, it cannot be denied that not much was changed in the Alexander story itself. We are hardly surprised that these new contextualizations are typically dismissive of him. After all, we expected as much and noticed the same pattern in the Christian dismissal of Alexander's teachers and the philosophers he encountered insofar as they exemplified Greek *paideia*. Mythology too was criticized, and Alexander stood at the end of the mythological era. Yet, none of what the Christians attempted comes across as worse than what non-Christian satirists, such as Juvenal and Lucian, said. The Christian corpus contains relatively few instances of personal attacks on Alexander; he features mostly as a tool to target others. I do not make this observation to suggest he was faultless in the eyes of the Christians, but rather to emphasize that there was much more at stake than simple representations of the king.

Perhaps the most surprising tendency relates to the frequency with which the Christians use Alexander as a rhetorical tool against deification. One might anticipate that the number of such references would be overwhelming, given the conclusions of previous studies, but the actual occurrence is low. For example, Christians alluded to Alexander's pseudo-letter much more than they utilized birth myths or stories about his death, though they did know those legends well. The fictional letter seems to have been an important document for non-Christians and Christians, although the Christians valued different points from the letter than did the non-Christians. However, the general tendency in Christian writing was not to overuse the same examples, and so we actually discover a richer variety than hitherto believed. All of the Christian stories can be found in Greek and Latin literature, whether contemporary or not. This raises the issue of Christian identity in the Roman Empire. The boundaries between Christian and non-Christian use of these stories feel blurry, and the discourse feels fluid. If a story supported an argument, the writers did not need to alter anything. The key difference between Christians and non-Christians lies in how regularly Alexander was used and the interpretation of what a given story meant.

To illustrate the fluidity of the discourse, we turn to Origen's engagement with the philosopher Celsus. Seventy or so years before Origen, Celsus had published a critique of Christian beliefs. This work is important, because it shows that some non-Christians took the Christians seriously as philosophers. Celsus was not the only one to do so, and many other pagans remarked upon the Christians (Engberg et al. 2014). Celsus' account may otherwise seem remarkable in its knowledge of Christianity's tenets, if we assume that the Romans knew little of the religion in the second century. In Book 2 of Origen's text, Celsus has invented a Jewish character to address a Christian convert and deny the Christian claim to the Jewish heritage. Our passage features Celsus' Jew, who mocked Jesus' aspirations to godhead by focusing on his blood. Greek gods had celestial fluid in their veins, the so-called "ichor," and Celsus asks pointedly if Jesus' blood was "like ichor that flows in the veins of the blessed gods?" (Origen *C. Cels.* 2.36, incorporating Hom. *Il.* 5.340). Celsus assumes that blood flowed in Jesus' veins, which was a telling proof that he was not divine. Origen preserves this remark to dismiss it and, by doing so, makes a curious chain of textual culture: a Christian cites a Jew invented by a pagan philosopher, who quoted Homer, to ridicule the ostensible divinity of Jesus. In turn, Celsus must also have known something of the Passion narrative in the New Testament to apply the saying to Jesus.

The ichor-line comes from the *Iliad*, but ancient writers normally attach this use of the verse to the Alexander tradition (Bosworth 2011: 45–47). The earliest witness attributes the saying to Dioxippus, an Olympic winner in the *pankration*, who also made a career at Alexander's court (see Ath. 6.57 [251a], incorporating Aristobulus *FGrH/BNJ* 139 F47). It is not clear if Dioxippus' saying is blatant flattery, for the line refers in the *Iliad* to Diomedes' wounding of the martially weak goddess Aphrodite. Writers rarely associated her with Alexander (though see Luc. *Herod.* §§ 4–7), so the remark may have been an insult. Plutarch puts the saying into the mouth of Alexander himself, perhaps to downplay the king's own claims to divinity (Plut. *Alex.* 28.3, *Mor.* 180e, 341b; cf. Sen. *Ep.* 59.12), whereas others attribute it to Callisthenes (Sen. *Suas.* 1.5 = Callisthenes *FGrH/BNJ* 124 T13) or Anaxarchus (Diog. Laert. 9.60). Later literature tended to conflate Callisthenes and Anaxarchus, so we need not be surprised by the error. Celsus must have had the wider tradition in mind when he applied the saying to Jesus on the Cross.

At this juncture, we should not be astonished to discover that Celsus had borrowed a well-known piece of the Alexander tradition for his own purposes. After all, we have seen this strategy on display throughout the chapter. Our examples have just been by Christian writers instead of non-Christian ones. The basic rules for the literary games were set, though the intellectuals dictated the conditions for the discourse through the priority of texts, stories, and insisting on what they meant. For instance, Origen eventually dismisses Celsus' ichor anecdote with reference to the Gospel. Origen uses two stories for authority: Jesus' wounds bleeding water and blood (John 19:34–35) and the Roman centurion recognizing him as the son of God (Matt. 27:54). The centurion saw portents, such as earthquakes, that convinced him of Jesus' divinity and, Origen argues, so other Romans should recognize Jesus' divinity too. It is obvious that Origen's argument only works if we are willing to accept the authority of the New Testament and prioritize that text over Homer and Greek beliefs about the divine, as Origen did. Celsus would certainly have contested this view of the Gospel's authority, but Origen got the last word, at least in the *Against Celsus*. By then Celsus was long dead. Had they ever met, they might not have agreed on much, but they would at least have appreciated each other's attempt to exploit the communal material pertaining to Alexander.

3

Tales from Judea and the Diaspora

Introduction

The previous chapter explored the unity and diversity of the discourse on Alexander among the pre-Constantinian Christians. One topic of interest was the extent to which Christians participated in the "classical tradition" and which themes they used. In this chapter, we further problematize the notion of a classical canon by surveying the material Christians appropriated from Hellenistic Judaism. Tales about Alexander from Judea and the Jewish diaspora, the Jews outside Judea, were readily available to Christian writers, as they were written in Greek. Alexander entered the cultural orbit of the Jews early on, playing various roles in the Jewish storytelling in Greek of the second century BC to the first century AD and the historiographical writings of Flavius Josephus. After the sack of Jerusalem in AD 70, Greek ceased to be the language of choice for the Jewish textual tradition, and Aramaic and Hebrew were less accessible to Christians. The majority of Christians regarded Hellenistic Jewish texts with respect, if not reverence, and we have already seen some signs of their integration into the Christian literary canon in the example of the Sibylline texts. We will discover more examples of Christian eclecticism below. While the Jewish contexts and agendas of the composition of these stories regularly engage scholars, Christian engagement with the same tales has attracted less interest. The surveys of this chapter thus provide an important corrective to previous studies and a data set for further exploration.

Alexander's city

Jews and Alexandria

The Egyptian city of Alexandria remains one of Alexander's most important legacies. When Diodorus writes about Alexandria's glorious foundation, he asserts that the city remained the greatest in the world (Diod. Sic. 17.52.5–6). Another historian refers to it in a review of Egyptian cities as "the crown of all cities," *vertex omnium est civitatum* (Amm. Mar. 22.16.7). Alexandria vies with Seleucus' Antioch for the third place in a fourth-century poem (Auson. *Ordo nob. urb.*). Unfortunately, the author cannot decide between the two founders. The city's fame is in all cases tied to the founder's success, and the memory of Alexander fueled Alexandria's political success under the Ptolemaic dynasty and under Rome. For example, we have already observed that the city held the tomb of the king, a cult site as well as a grand attraction for visitors. The tomb, *sema*, or "body," *soma*, marked the favorite destination for a number of noble Roman tourists, starting with Julius Caesar and, later, his adopted son Octavian. The latter supposedly broke off a piece of Alexander's nose when he came to see Alexander's tomb—the tomb of a real king, Octavian asserted, not the corpses of his Ptolemaic enemies (Suet. *Aug.* 18.1). Alexandria was the major physical manifestation of Alexander's fame, as one second-century orator remarked; the only monument worthy of his stature. Dedicating his oration to Rome, Aelius Aristides says that the king had built the city, so that it would assume the second rank after Rome (Aristid. *Or.* 26.26).

The local community made the most of interest in Alexander and spread many legends about the city's founder. The Alexandrian synagogues were not behind in this sort of activity. The best example occurs in the historical writings of a famous Jewish aristocrat. Flavius Josephus, whose writings have only reached us because Christianity appropriated them, writes that the Jews had been given special civic rights allowing them to dwell freely in Alexandria (Joseph. *AJ* 14.114 incorporating Str. *FGrH/BNJ* 91 F7 Roller). This statement needs to be read alongside Josephus' claim elsewhere that both Alexander and his successor in Alexandria, Ptolemy I, had granted citizenship to the Jews because of Jewish piety and virtue (Joseph. *BJ* 2.487–488). It follows that the Jews had been allowed to pursue their own political and religious life since the very foundation of the city. The historian articulates the notion again in the polemical *Against Apion* (Joseph. *Ap.* 2.35–44, 70–72 incorporating Hecataeus of Abdera *FGrH/BNJ* 264 F22 Landucci). Strabo's text does not support Josephus' appeal to the royal authority of Alexander, however. While Strabo says that the Jews were offered rights, including a plot of land and a local ruler, an *ethnarch*, he does not connect these concessions to Alexander or the Ptolemies, but rather to their Egyptian origins. The Macedonian connection is forged by Josephus. In the same passages, Josephus also draws attention to several additional documents to support his argument that the Roman Caesars had not done anything to diminish the existing rights of the Jews in Alexandria. The words of Alexander and Roman rulers conferred authority upon the Jewish privileges; this assertion constituted a plea that Josephus' Roman contemporaries should also respect the Alexandrian Jews. Furthermore, I wish to note here that no Christians repeated the Josephan claim in the pre-Constantinian period or after. Christians were not concerned that the Jews should enjoy a special status in a city they themselves inhabited.

Even if Josephus is named, most of the Jewish legends are anonymous. That fact makes their contexts difficult to determine. Also unclear is just how early these legends were circulated. Trajan expelled the Jews from Alexandria during the Diaspora Revolt, as is evident from the near-absence of Jewish papyri in Egypt after AD 117. But some Jews continued to live there or had since returned, because, some centuries later, Cyril, then patriarch of Alexandria, could instigate a pogrom on the city's Jews (Socrates *Hist. Eccl.* 7.13). Nothing in the legends themselves reveals when they were composed. For example, one Rabbinic text speaks of Alexander's retrieval of Solomon's throne (2 Targum Esther 1.4; cf. Stoneman 1994: 44). Alexander had taken it from Babylon and sent it back to Alexandria. The story may remind readers of Alexander's recovery of the statues of Harmodius and Aristogeiton, the Athenian tyrannicides of the fifth century BC. He returned them to Athens from Babylon (Arr. *Anab.* 3.16.7–8 with Finn 2014). Although there may be a Near Eastern origin to the literary motif, it unfortunately does not tell us much about the dating for the story of Solomon's throne. A variant found in a much later Syriac text relates that Alexander brought a silver throne to Jerusalem from Alexandria, which was built for the Messiah, so that Jesus could reign in Alexander's stead. At the Advent of the Messiah, Jesus would also receive Alexander's crown and the subsequent crowns of all the Alexandrian kings from Alexander to Messiah (Budge 1889: 146–147). The throne legend establishes the importance of Alexandria in the Jewish consciousness. Writing about Alexander thus provided the Jewish community with its own social identity in Alexandria.

Another possibly Jewish tale of Alexandrian origin survives in later Christian versions, from perhaps as early as the fifth century. In one passage of John Moschus' *Spiritual Meadow* (§ 77), John suggests to Sophronius, the future patriarch of Jerusalem (*d.* 638), that the two of them should visit the Tetrapylum of Alexandria, where Alexander had buried the bones of Jeremiah, one of the major Old Testament prophets. They find three Christian hermits at the site, and they engage in a discourse on asceticism, which is only proper for Byzantine monks, who had spent time at the monastery of Theodosius the Cenobiarch near Bethlehem (east of the modern village of al-Ubeidiya). The background story of

Jeremiah's burial runs as follows: Jeremiah had been stoned to death by the locals of Daphnae (Tell Defenneh) in Egypt and buried in the region of the Pharaoh's palace. In death, the remains of the prophet repelled the asps and crocodiles from the land, which he had also done with prayers in life. The author then mentions, a unique first-person statement, that he had heard from some old men, descended from the Successors Antigonus and Ptolemy, that Alexander had visited the tomb of Jeremiah and learned of the mysteries relating to him. The king had then brought the bones to Alexandria and respectfully arranged them in a circle that warded off reptiles from the city. He then filled the circle with good serpents that would continue the purge (source texts collated at Barbantani 2014: 228–232).

Bringing venerated objects back to Alexandria evidently suggested the sanctity of the city and the importance of its Jewish community. The throne of Solomon, or the Messiah, makes a typological connection to Alexander's rule, but it is currently less clear how the Old Testament prophet fits in. Presumably, the choice fell on Jeremiah because he, like Alexander, had ties to Egypt since both were buried there. I have argued elsewhere that Jeremiah is a later addition to an existing story about the revered house snakes of the Alexandrians, *agathoi daimones*, and the author, whether a Jew or Christian, has used the prophet to provide a respectable etiology for the otherwise heathen phenomenon (Ogden and Djurslev 2018).

The Jeremiah story reminds us of another legend of the city's foundation. The circuit of apotropaic bones echoes the foundation myth of barley being used to mark the boundaries of the city (Curt. 4.8.6; Plut. *Alex.* 26.8–10; Arr. *Anab.* 3.2.1–2; *It. Alex.* § 20). Flocks of birds descended upon the edible outline and ate every grain. The king's soothsayers heralded this as a good omen and explained that the city would supply the world with food. Many other versions of this myth exist (e.g., *AR* 1.32.4; Val. Max. 1.4.ext1; Str. 17.1.6; Vitr. *De arch.* 2.preface.4). The inconsistent narratives reflect "the multiple personalities of Alexandria itself" (Erskine 2013: 170). We may think of the Jeremiah story in the same way, as an expression of the same myth reflecting the Jewish, and later Christian, communities in Alexandria. They also had to assert their connection to the city and its original foundation. Indeed, with regard to dating, if the barley myth stemmed from early Alexandria (late fourth century BC?), then nothing prevents the Jeremiah story from having originated with the earliest Jewish diaspora settlement in the city. The Jews would have needed foundational tales to legitimize their presence as soon as they entered the city, as indeed the Greeks would have.

In the case of Alexandria, we have noted some important literary tendencies. First, Josephus' reworking of Strabo's testimony reminds us of how the Christians reworked classicizing material, whether much earlier or recent in origin. Long before Josephus and the Christians, the Hellenized Jews had fully immersed themselves in the Greek textual tradition. Jewish literature from the Hellenistic period reflects the cultural contact with the Greeks in and outside Judea, and it was available to Christian writers. They thus had to engage with a literature that had already brought together the best of both worlds. Secondly, the references to Solomon demonstrate how interested Jews were in bringing material from the Hebrew scriptures closer to the Greek world in which they lived. Scriptural references needed to be explained in a new context and, in so doing, the Jews produced powerful narratives. Given the centuries of cohabitation in Alexandria and elsewhere, it is difficult to set a hard boundary for the crossing over of motifs and extricate what comes from where. The Jews did not necessarily compose such tales to speak to others; rather they needed them to help shape and express their own thought-world. Third and finally, the Christians exploited Jewish literature, especially the Tanakh, which became the Old Testament for them, with important consequences for the Christian communities. For example, the Jeremiah story survives only in certain Christian narratives, and none of them are identified with a named author, nor are they securely datable. Despite the probably quite early date of the story, no pre-Constantinian Christian had chosen to preserve the tale, as far as we know, and so we need to bear in mind that Christian selectivity applies to engagement with Helleno-Jewish literature too. As ever, Christians engaged with Hellenistic Judaism on their own terms.

Jewish precedent inspired the Christians, who had to stake a claim to an early presence in the city. According to church tradition (Euseb. *Hist. eccl.* 2.15–16, 2.24.1; Jer. *De vir ill.* 8), Mark the Evangelist had first preached his Gospel in Alexandria. Jerome said that Philo, a local Jewish philosopher, had composed a work on the first Christian community (Jer. *De vir ill.* 11.3), but Christian ascetics were easily confused with certain Jewish communities. Christians considered Mark the first bishop of the city, and Eusebius emphasized the close ties between the bishoprics of Rome and Alexandria throughout his history of the church. Moreover, the city was also home to an influential school of Platonism from the first century BC to the second century AD. The writings of the Alexandrians seem particularly attuned to this philosophical direction. We possess multiple pseudonymous texts from the Apostolic period, such as the *Epistle of Barnabas* and *Epistle of Diognetus*, that are believed to hail from Alexandria based on the teachings they inculcate. The evidence for a specifically Alexandrian school of

Christian doctrine is scant and hardly secure. For example, Athenagoras of Athens may have instructed a Christian community in the city. Clement of Alexandria found his intellectual home under Pantaenus' tutelage, perhaps succeeding him if there was a school in *c.* 200. Clement did not stay long, however, as he fled the Severan persecutions at Alexandria to Cappadocia in 202 and arrived in Jerusalem in 205. Some sort of community must have remained in the city, for Ammonius could teach the future Origen, no doubt the greatest figure of the early church. Origen's life in Alexandria lasted until *c.* 231, after which he left for Palestinian Caesarea because of a dispute with Demetrius, bishop of Alexandria.

The legend of the Septuagint translation

One of the primary Christian interests in Alexandria concerned the Septuagint translation, the earliest Greek rendition of the Hebrew scripture (Wasserstein and Wasserstein 2006). Christians relayed an elaborate legendary tradition about the text's inception, preserved in many Jewish texts, including the *Letter of Aristeas* (later second century BC). According to this legend the first Ptolemies, either Ptolemy I Soter or Ptolemy II Philadelphus, allegedly commissioned a Greek rendition of the Pentateuch, namely the five Mosaic books: Genesis, Exodus, Leviticus, Numbers, and Deuteronomy. The famous Athenian librarian, Demetrius of Phaleron, had urged his ruler—the *Letter of Aristeas* names Ptolemy II, but that ruler exiled Demetrius rather than retaining his services—to make a copy of the law. The Ptolemies set the previously captured Jews free and sent a delegation to Jerusalem, which the High Priest received favorably. He sent seventy (or seventy-two) Jewish elders from the twelve tribes to Alexandria, so that a copy of the Law could be made. Ptolemy wept when he received them, offering them hospitality and making inquiries about Jewish culture. He discoursed with the wise ones for a week—he had evidently more patience than Alexander when he asked riddles of the ten Gymnosophists of India. As if this high level of supposed royal and religious authority were not enough, the narratives imbue the legend with another layer of ostensible authority by adding divine inspiration. The Jewish translators had produced seventy (!) identical translations of the Hebrew text, although each one sat in a separate cell when he did his translation. The translation took seventy-two days to complete. The Alexandrian Jews were thrilled with the scripture in their own language, Greek rather than Hebrew, and requested further copies after which the translators returned to Jerusalem loaded with gifts from the king. The historicizing slant makes the legend compelling, even in Aristeas' letter. The historian Josephus turns to this episode right after his narrative on Alexander's campaign and the rise of the Successors (Joseph. *AJ* 12.11–118; *Ap.* 2.45–47), which suggests the legend's important connection to the new regime after Alexander.

Josephus does not, however, attach the name of Alexander to the legend of the Septuagint, although Philo does (Philo *Vit. Mos.* 2.29). The Alexandrian philosopher notes in passing that the commissioner of the translation, Ptolemy II Philadelphus, was the third in succession from Alexander since that king conquered Egypt. Ptolemy II is thus in a direct line of succession from the founder. Philo's casual remark, written almost three centuries after the death of Ptolemy II, shows how Alexandrians saw the continuity in the reign of Alexandrian kings from Alexander himself. Philo is thus a witness to the long-lived success of the early Ptolemaic language of legitimacy that appropriated Alexander as the Ptolemaic precursor. The link between Alexander and the Ptolemies appears regularly in Ptolemaic court poetry, such as Theocritus *Idyll* 17 and Posidippus' poetry. In Philo's passage, Alexander did not have anything to do with the actual Septuagint translation itself, but he was recognized as a key individual in the formation of the dynasty and a marker of the time after which the translation was carried out.

The earliest Christian reception of the Septuagint legend went in two major directions: The first major direction occurs in the Greek apologetic tradition. Some writers posited that there were several translations of the Septuagint before the one made by the Ptolemies (Clem. Al. *Strom.* 1.150.1–3; Euseb. *Praep. evang.* 13.12.1 citing Aristobulus the Jew; Ps.-Justin *Or.* § 12). They used their chronological assertion to argue that Greek philosophers, such as Pythagoras and Plato, had borrowed all their philosophical concepts from the previously translated versions of the Pentateuch. For example, Plato was thought to have spent a significant amount of time in Egypt (e.g., Amm. Mar. 22.16.22) and so could have poured over Mosaic law. A famous saying, attributed to the influential Neoplatonist Numenius of Apamea (*fl.* late second century), refers to Plato as an Atticizing Moses. The theme had a major impact on Christian literature (Euseb. *Praep. evang.* 9.6.7 citing Clem. Al. *Strom.* 1.150.1–3), and the logic showcases the ancient idea of the transmission of knowledge. If one could prove that some philosophical concept was older than another, it followed that any later insights had been borrowed from the more ancient one. Old knowledge was better than new, and all knowledge already existed in the world. Later versions were misunderstandings of what had gone before. Some of the apologetic writers had clearly recognized that the Ptolemaic dynasty was hardly old compared to the philosophies of the Greek world and so changed the date of the Septuagint. Of course, the logic behind this argument is tenuous. Just because the philosophers lived close to the time of Alexander, it certainly did not mean that they had derived their knowledge from Moses. But Christians nevertheless labored to argue the historical point. For example, in one of the most sophisticated responses to pagan criticism, Origen uses this kind of computation to dismiss Celsus' claim that the Greek philosophers had come first (Origen *C. Cels.* 4.39, 6.19).

As far as the Alexander material is concerned, the importance for this alternative Septuagint computation lay elsewhere. Clement of Alexandria and Eusebius did not attach Alexander to the Ptolemaic dynasty, which Philo had done, but instead used the event of Alexander's Persian campaign as a vague marker for the dating before which alternative Septuagint translations had been made. There had then been many translations of the Septuagint that Plato could have consulted. Alexander's campaign had obviously taken place before the Ptolemies, and so the expedition could work as a *terminus ante quem*. To take another instance, a late third-century *Exhortation to the Greeks* postulates that Socrates, Plato, and Aristotle had lived long after Moses (§ 12). The pseudonymous author makes reference to the famous *Philippic Speeches* of Demosthenes, the fourth-century Athenian statesman, in order to assert that the philosophers had lived closer to Philip and Alexander, Demosthenes' political opponents. The *Exhortation* concludes the computation with Alexander's association with Aristotle, which was known from those authors who had recorded the deeds of Alexander. All of these references support the case for Alexander's place in history, which the author then could use to say that the Septuagint had been translated before Plato, Aristotle, and Demosthenes.

Modern minds may think of such arguments what they will, but it was hard to provide serious dating for historical events with ancient calendars. Synchronisms were complicated, and thus one could allow for some creativity. We note again the misdirection of what is not said. Showing that the philosophers lived close to certain personages, regardless of the amount of evidence, does not say anything about Moses' dating or prove his influence on others. Nevertheless, the onus was then on the opponents' side to prove that Moses came after the philosophers, not before. Some non-Christians attempted this strategy. Celsus argued that Moses lived in Ptolemaic times because of the Septuagint dating that Philo and others advocated. Moses was thus a third-century Jew and no influence on Greek philosophy. Both sides evidently made use of pseudo-historical arguments. Moreover, we have previously seen that Alexander's Asian campaign distinguished time periods from each other, a topic we shall return to in Chapter 4.

The second major direction of the Christian reception of the Septuagint legend continues the Jewish story of the Ptolemaic Septuagint translation (Justin *1 Apol.* 1.32, *Dial.* § 68, § 71; Irenaeus *Haer.* 3.21.2; Tert. *Apol.* § 18). Most Christians maintained the truth of this version. The Jewish story gave some historical grounding to the legend, and the Septuagint appeared to be an ancient document from an important historical period. This dating ensured that the Christian belief was not a new faith but had been expressed in a time period prior to the advent of the Messiah. For "Orthodox" Christians, reconciling the God of Israel with Jesus, the founder of the religion, represented an important task, not only for chronological reasons. Followers of Marcion of Sinope, whom other Christians labeled a Gnostic teacher, argued that the vengeful God of the Hebrews had nothing to do with Christianity. Marcion and his followers wanted to cut the Jewish roots of the faith. Operating in Rome and elsewhere, they presented a dangerous challenge and so counterarguments had to be made. Controlling the source text of the Old Testament was one way to assert the importance of the old for understanding the new. Later Greek editions of the Septuagint, including many other books of the Old Testament beyond the Pentateuch, were composed and circulated from the second century AD onward. The names attached to these editions were Aquila of Sinope, Symmachus the Ebionite, and Theodotion of Ephesus, who sought to create their own versions of the Greek translation. Christians worked with the Greek version, as scripture in Hebrew was inaccessible to them, or else the Christians were unwilling to acquire Hebrew. There are two exceptions to this rule: (1) Origen's *Hexapla*, a rendition of Scripture in six columns (Hebrew, transliterated Hebrew in Greek letters, Aquila, Symmachus, Septuagint, and Theodotion) for comparative study, and (2) Jerome's "Vulgate" Bible begun in 382 and completed in 405. Both texts made a major impact on subsequent church tradition but, in the ancient context, they were equally important for establishing the firm connection between the two Testaments. Scriptural canon and authority are never static, not even in the present day, as we shall see.

Like Josephus, most pre-Constantinian Christians did not need to attach the name of Alexander to the Ptolemaic dynasty, though many later Christians did (Wasserstein and Wasserstein 2006: 113–131). Exceptions exist. Julius Africanus mentioned the Septuagint translation in a chronological overview of the Ptolemaic dynasty, beginning with Alexander's conquest of Egypt (and Libya). The passage confuses the enumeration of the Ptolemaic rulers, but that may be because this fragment of Africanus' historical work is found in John Malalas, an Antiochene historiographer of sixth-century Byzantium (John Malalas *Chron.*

8.6–8 incorporating Julius Africanus F86, *GCS* NF 15.254–255 Wallraff). The local context in Africanus is a list of reigning monarchs, showing who reigned at what period in the Ptolemaic regime. The addition of a significant cultural "fact," the Septuagint translation, makes sense as an insertion.

"No" Alexandria

Alexandria was not only the home of the Septuagint, but also a Biblical location in later Latin literature. The Hebrew prophet Nahum, to whom one of the minor Old Testament books is ascribed, mentioned an Egyptian city called "No-Amon" or "Thebes" (Nah. 3:8–11), and Jerome rendered the name "Alexandria" in his translation of the Biblical text. Jerome also wrote a commentary on this book and, in the pertinent passage, he again identified No-Amon as Alexandria and proceeded to offer an erudite digression on Alexandria and Alexandrian history (Jerome *Comm. Nah.* 3.8–9, *CCSL* 76a.562–563). Changing the Bible text philologically and interpretatively, he turned the once pagan foundation into a Biblical place. The evidence suggests that many other westerners followed suit—unsurprisingly, considering that Latin Christians commonly used Jerome's version. For example, Isidore of Seville records in his seventh-century encyclopedia of the world that Alexandria was built upon the Egyptian city No and established the boundary between Egypt and Asia (Isidore *Etym.* 15.1.34).

The alteration of Nahum's text is important. Mapping a space onto the contours of the Biblical landscape makes a strong claim for its inclusion in the Christian tradition. We see the tendency best expressed in a seventh-century pilgrim's guide in which Alexandria had its own entry. The guide contains lengthy descriptions of Alexandria's central sites, such as shrines of the Christian martyrs and the Church of St. Mark. Written by the Irish monk Adamnan (624–704), the ninth abbot of the Celtic monastery on the Scottish isle of Iona, the book professes to record the travels of a Gallic pilgrim and bishop, called Arculf, whom Adamnan rescued from a shipwreck. The work not only gives an account of the pilgrim's experiences in the Holy Land, but also of the Near East after the Muslim conquests. The entry on Alexandria in Egypt runs thus:

> This great city, once the capital of Egypt, was originally called No in the Hebrew tongue. This populous city, named after its famous founder Alexander, king of Macedon, by a name known in the entire world: Alexandria, because it obtained its grandeur and name from its re-foundation. [...] This Alexandria, which before it was built to a gargantuan size by Alexander the Great, was called No, as

already said, and was situated by the mouth of the Nile River at a place called Canopus and the city borders Asia, Egypt and Libya.

Adamnan De Locis Sanctis 2.30.1, 2.30.26
(cf. Jerome Comm. Os. 2.9.5–6, CCSL 76.94).

No's re-foundation and expansion evidently casts Alexander in the role of a great founder, *ktistēs* or *conditor*, as we have already seen Christians prepared to name him. Adamnan adds another dimension by insisting on the city's Biblical background and placing it on the same level as the re-foundation. The OT context gave the city a new resonance. It conferred upon the whole city the prestige of being a part of an even more ancient world, that of God's people, the world of the Biblical drama. It suggests a confluence of Hebrew, Greek, and Christian traditions. By going to Alexandria, one could visit a space that contained the best of all three worlds: a new and old Christian world.

Adamnan's seemingly factual description, based on an eye-witness account, does not diverge much from the previous works of Jerome and Isidore, however. In fact, he simply reworks what is already evident in his predecessors. Scholarship has now argued that Arculf acts as no more than a literary device for Adamnan's display of his Christian learning (O'Loughlin 2007). We noticed the same pattern in Palladius' treatise *On the Brahmans* when he brought in a well-traveled "Theban scholar" to inform readers of the Indian customs.

The later Latin identification of Alexandria depends on a common textual tradition in Jerome's Vulgate Bible. In Jerome's day, Christians contested the location of the Biblical No-Amon. Some eastern Christians believed that No should be identified with Thebes in Upper Egypt rather than Alexandria in Lower Egypt. The latter reading is maintained in modern editions of Nahum, such as the NRSV. The geographical disagreement reflects the exegetical process of identifying the sacred sites of the Christians, and it was by no means a linear procedure. For instance, the fifth-century Syrian bishops Theodore of Mopsuestia and Theodoret of Cyrrhus dismissed No-Amon's association with Alexandria. Instead they offer two different interpretations. The former noted that one Egyptian city was called Amon, but made no further identification of it (Theodore *Comm. Nah.* 3.8, PG 66.417–420). The latter made a vague case for interpreting No-Amon as what the Greeks had considered a famous Libyan oracle, noting Alexander's expedition to the Siwah Oasis (Theodoret *Comm. Nah.* 3.8, PG 81.1804). These locations do not, however, mesh well with the idea that No-Amon was a populous city or a Hebrew name. The two Antiochene theologians were reacting to the exegesis of the Alexandrian school in which some had tried to identify an obscure place (the Hebrew No) with a better known one (Alexandria). For example, Cyril of Alexandria (378–444) argues forcefully that No-Amon should be identified with Alexandria (Cyril *Comm. Nah.* 2.56–57), perhaps because he wanted to assert the Biblical origins of the city he himself presided over.

Alexander and the Bible

Why scripture matters

The case of No-Alexandria demonstrates why the interpretation of Scripture mattered. Different opinions on textual matters changed the understanding of the text that the Christians valued the highest. At first glance, it may therefore seem strange to read the following statement by the Apostle Peter in the New Testament:

> First of all, you must understand this: no prophecy of Scripture is a matter of one's own interpretation, because no prophecy ever came by human will, but men and women moved by the Holy Spirit spoke from God.
>
> 2 Pet. 1:20–21.

The Apostle insists that Biblical prophecy had a singular and unequivocal interpretation, even if we have already found divergence (*contra* Philo *Vit. Mos.* 2.191). Peter naturally has an agenda in making such a claim about prophecy's innate meaning. If Scripture had but one meaning, he could claim that only the Christians had the key to understanding Scripture correctly, namely through the teachings of Jesus. On that tenuous basis, Peter, and Christians after him, made the even more nebulous claim that they had exclusive understanding of the true meaning of prophecy and the Mosaic law. They contended that the contemporary Jews misunderstood Scripture. They made such claims to dispute the Jewish counterargument, namely that *Christians* had misunderstood the Law because the teachings of Jesus had misled *them*.

The disagreement over Scripture was no covert operation within Christianity, but one that defined religious identity. If a reader, Jew or Christian, made an exegetical explanation of a prophetic passage, he did so on the assumption that he had perceived the inherent divine meaning of the text. He had understood the message that God was revealing through his prophets. Making an interpretation on the basis of a reading of Scripture was thus regarded as more powerful than seeking the authority of any other ancient text because of Scripture's divine authority.

Understanding the meaning of Biblical prophecy proved the biggest apple of discord between Origen and Celsus' imaginary Jew (e.g., Origen *C. Cels.* 2.4, 2.8, 2.12, 2.15, 2.28–29, 2.37, 2.79, 3.17, 7.4). Celsus had created a Jewish figure to voice his criticisms of Christianity. Jews read scriptural prophecies with the expectation of a future Messiah, whereas Christians had found their Messiah in the figure of Jesus. By rejecting the interpretation that the Old Testament prophecies prefigured Jesus as the Christ, contemporary Jews could argue that Christians misunderstood or misappropriated Scripture. The Christians could respond, in turn, that Jesus was key to the fulfillment of prophecy. Appropriating the Old Testament books and their prophets as "Christian" voices was a principal task in the Christian communities because "reception and appropriation is the exegetical process whereby readers make the text their own" (Young 1997: 27).

Though Alexandria as No became a contested detail in the exegesis of a minor prophet, the identification does not seem to have concerned many before Cyril and Jerome. This is the only time that Alexandria was thought to appear in the Old Testament. Alexander appears more often than his city, and explicitly so (Torrey 1925). But pre-Constantinian Christians also read Alexander into the Old Testament. We now turn to the Biblical book in which Alexander was believed to feature the most, namely the Book of Daniel.

The Book of Daniel

The Macedonian conquest of what eventually became the Roman province of Judea was consolidated by the sacking of the cities of Tyre and Gaza (332–331 BC). After Alexander, Judea was at the mercy of the dreaded kings of the Hellenistic world. The Successor dynasty of the Seleucids had many encounters with the Jews, and the best-known example remains Antiochus IV Epiphanes' abolition of Jewish customs in the Jerusalemite community, which led to the Maccabean revolt. Between 168–165 BC (or 167–164), the persecutions raged, ending with Antiochus' death and the re-dedication of the Temple. During the reign of various Hasmonean monarchs (*c.* 140–37 BC), Palestinian Jews immersed themselves in the Hellenic textual culture, as they had not done before. Central prophetic and historical texts stem from this period of Seleucid oppression and Jewish counter-reaction to imperial repression. One key Biblical text, the Book of Daniel, was completed within this context of conflict with foreign rulers. The historical crisis demanded both an explanation and the hope for better things in the future. Daniel presents one of the strongest voices in response to a specific historical situation among the major prophets.

The Book of Daniel offers readers an absolute apocalypse, the only one of its kind in the Hebrew Bible (Collins 2016: Ch. 3). We may compare the text to Revelation in the New Testament, the final apocalypse. Long considered the canonical Jewish apocalypse, the Book of Daniel is now studied in relation to other apocalypses, such as the Enoch tradition and the Dead Sea scrolls discovered in the Qumran Caves after the Second World War. Danielic prophecy poses innumerable issues of interpretation, for the author has compiled the contents of his work from various periods of history and sources in different languages, while adding his own editorial hand to impose structure on the narrative. The historical background of the name that confers authority upon the text, Daniel, continues to elude our grasp, and so we are no closer to a firm dating for the various stories contained in his book. The two languages are Hebrew for chapters 1:1–2:4a; 8–12; and Aramaic for chapters 2:4b–7:28, and the Jewish community furnished a Greek translation in *c.* 150 BC. New additions such as the famous stories of Susanna and Bel and the Dragon, later appeared in the Book of Daniel. Furthermore, the Hebrew/Aramaic duality provides separate narrative structures. The first part tells the story of Daniel's life at the Babylonian court under Nebuchadnezzar and Belshazzar, then the Median court of Darius ("the Mede") and the Persian court of Cyrus, an unhistorical sequence of rulers to which we will return. The second part resets the chronology and speaks of Daniel's unsettling visions during the reigns of the same kings, starting with Belshazzar (chapters 7–8). The two halves of the text thus form a coherent narrative in which Daniel is first introduced as a pious seer, who could coexist with the Gentile rule, and then he was made to perceive the truth through revelations, that the earthly empires embodied by the wicked monarchs would crumble before God. In the aftermath, pious Jews like himself would enjoy an everlasting life in the starry sky with the angels—a remarkably "Greek" way to dissipate into stellar immortality.

The text adds further supernatural dimensions to the historical backdrop of the Jewish exile in Babylon. Its author suggested that the fighting took place on a cosmic level in which celestial beings fought on behalf of their subjects on earth. The Ancient of Days would judge four monstrous beasts (Dan. 7:9–12) and an angelic being covered in clouds, "one like the son of man," would receive the kingdom from the Ancient of Days (Dan. 7:13–14). In a parallel revelation, the archangel Michael would fight against the cosmic versions of the princes of Persia and Greece. The battle's outcome was already predetermined by God

(10:1–12:4). The imminent victory reassured contemporary Jewish readers that the crisis they endured would soon cease. The message to the masses promoted quiet resistance. Because the fight took place on a heavenly plane, the text does not encourage earthly violence. Instead it argues that Jewish resistance should be through justice, purification, and the belief that supernatural powers would carry the right-minded Jews through the confrontation. As such, Daniel's peaceful approach stands in stark contrast to the successful military resistance of Judas Maccabeus and his followers.

Non-Christians also read the Book of Daniel and contested Christian readings. Porphyry of Tyre, Plotinus' student, performed controversial exegesis of the historical content of Daniel in the twelfth book of his *Against the Christians*. The third-century Neo-Platonist argued that "Daniel" had predicted everything correctly up until the reign of Antiochus Epiphanes, but nothing beyond his rule, and so the prophecies applied to the Maccabean revolt of the second century BC. Conversely, Christians believed that the prophecies concerned Jesus, the Son of Man, as well as the future kingdom of God. Since they understood the prophecies to concern future events, Christians labored to interpret the prophecies in a way that supported their arguments. They rose to the challenge of proving Porphyry wrong. But much more serious was the Jewish challenge to Daniel's status as a prophet. Jewish scribes compiling the Torah and the Babylonian Talmud did not consider Daniel a prophet, but merely an example of a pious Hebrew. It is difficult to date when they discredited Daniel's prophetic power. Perhaps by *c.* 500 he had lost his mantic authority in Judaism. Claiming Daniel's history and restoring his divine inspiration became a Christian priority that distinguished them from their non-Christian peers.

The importance of the Book of Daniel comes across most clearly in the number of commentaries composed on it. Eusebius remarks that a certain Judas first composed a commentary on Danielic prophecy in the age of the Severans (Euseb. *Hist. eccl.* 6.7.1). Modern scholarship claims that much exegesis of Daniel was lost before Hippolytus wrote a commentary in *c.* 202 (Cerrato 2002: 17–22). Hippolytus' commentary survives in extensive fragments and a range of *scholia*. He also composed a treatise on Christ and the Antichrist in which he recycles much apocalyptic content from Daniel. I offer a short list of lost commentaries that we know of from Hippolytus to Jerome:

- Origen wrote a commentary before 250, completely lost save for fragments in the Catenae, that is, a chain of Biblical commentary collated by later compilers.

- Eusebius commented on Daniel in the early fourth century, but his commentary is also completely lost save for a few fragments in the catenae.
- Pseudo-Ephrem of Syria wrote a Syriac commentary on Daniel in *c.* 370 that partially survives.

Other commentaries, now completely lost, were written by:

- The Alexandrian Didymus the Blind (*c.* 319–398), a follower of Origen's exegesis.
- Titus of Bostra in Syria (*d. c.* 378).
- Apollinaris (*d.* 382), the bishop of Laodicea in Syria.

So, when Jerome published his commentary on Daniel in 407, it was the first Latin commentary on this OT book. It also remained the only one of its kind in the West. Latin-speaking Christians knew Daniel, of course, and had interpreted some material from him, but no one found a full commentary worthwhile. Their interest in the end times rested upon Revelation rather than Daniel, and this priority reveals a difference between the eastern and western Church. Revelation never achieved the same status in the Greek East. Even in the Orthodox Church of today, the text does not form part of the New Testament canon. Greek Christians preferred Daniel's apocalyptic visions, perhaps because of its contested nature and its focus upon eastern imperial power. From the foundation of Constantinople in AD 324, Daniel became a herald of Greek imperialism and a revered figure in early Byzantium (Euseb. *Hist. eccl.* 3.49 with Lane Fox 1986: 647). Jerome, who lived in the East, took pains to explain the status of Daniel to western readers. Contemporaries criticized his efforts, for he did not include every word, nor every line of the prophet, which was the normal procedure (Williams 2006: 112). His interpretations were, however, not contested. Few western Christians had sufficient knowledge to challenge Jerome and, as already said, their apocalyptic interest lay elsewhere.

In George Cary's 1956 study of Alexander in the Middle Ages, the Book of Daniel represents the single most important text for the formation of a theological conception of the king. The text is also of major importance for the early Christian reception of Alexander. Cary's study went as far back into Late Antiquity as Jerome's commentary, because Jerome "presented in his commentary an interpretation which was almost invariably upheld by later writers" (Cary 1956: 120; cf. Demandt 2009: 215). When we look at Jerome's commentary from our own vantage point, he stands at the end of a long-standing, primarily Greek, exegetical tradition. Jerome was looking back on the early Christian interpretation and often cited from previous expositions of the Book of Daniel. We now turn to how that tradition came to Jerome and how it expresses the history of Alexander in Biblical imagery. We begin with Daniel 8 in which Alexander appears most clearly and then we proceed to two less clear visions.

Daniel 8

Daniel 8 is perhaps the most well-known Biblical passage in Alexander-related scholarship. The vision features symbolic imagery in the form of an extended fight between two figurative beasts. The prophet sees a mighty ram with two horns, one greater than the other (Dan. 8:3). The unconquerable ram becomes great by extending its territory (8:4). But then a one-horned he-goat (or, possibly, a satyr) makes a flying charge from the west (8:5). As if they were jousting knights, the two animals lock horns, and the he-goat defeats the ram (8:6-7). The he-goat grows great but breaks his horn at the height of his strength. The single, huge horn breaks into four smaller ones, and they disperse into the four winds (8:8). The rest of the vision concerns the actions of another successor horn that seeks to fight heaven (8:9-15). Daniel seeks an explanation, and a voice from above commands an interpreter, apparently the archangel Gabriel, to inform Daniel of the meaning. Gabriel tells Daniel that the prophet's vision concerned the end of time (8:17). The ram symbolized the two kings of Media and Persia (two horns), and the he-goat was the king of Greece, its horn the first king (Alexander, 8:20-21). The four horns were the number of following kingdoms that would not have the same power (8:22). The little horn represents a destroyer, a prideful transgressor that would destroy the holy people (Antiochus IV, 8:22-25). The angel tells Daniel to seal the vision, and the prophet faints (8:26-27).

Since the historical setting of the text is the Babylonian exile (c. 597-539 BC), the prophecy is presented as concerning future events. Like most ancient prophecies, the Book of Daniel was written after the fact, and so the author takes into account much historical content from Hellenistic history. The task of identifying the events and agents was left to the commentator. For example, in his line-by-line analysis, Hippolytus makes the following identifications:

> For [Dan. 8:4], he says the ram is Darius, the king of the Persians, who prevailed over all nations. For he says, [Dan. 8:4]. But the male goat who comes from the west, he says is Alexander the Macedonian, king of the Greeks. And so when the male goat comes to the ram and savages him and beats him on his face and shatters and hurls him to the earth and tramples him, it signals this, which also

happened. Alexander after he had engaged with Darius in war, overpowered him and prevailed over all his army destroying and trampling the camp. Next after the male goat was exalted [Dan. 8:8]. For after Alexander ruled all the land of Persia and subjected them, later he died, dividing his kingdom to his four rulers, as is shown above, that is to Seleucus, to Demetrius, to Ptolemy, and to Philip, from whom one horn was exalted [Dan. 8:11]. It says, *and on account of him the sacrifice was disturbed* and *righteousness was hurled to the ground*. For Antiochus, who was called Epiphanes, being from the race of Alexander, became king.

> Hippolytus of Rome *Comm. Dan.* 4.26.2–7
> (*GCS* NF 7.254–256, trans. Schmidt, adapted)

Hippolytus' reference marks the first identification of Alexander and Darius with the he-goat and ram, but this identification would regularly re-appear in Christian texts. It might be thought that the frequent reference to Alexander as the he-goat indicates that the identification was well-known to Christian readers. For example, in one instance, Jerome simply refers to Alexander as "the he-goat," *hircus*, with no other signifier in his exegesis of the prophet Isaiah (Jerome *Comm. Isaiah* 5.20.1, *PL* 24.189; cf. *Vit. Hil.* Pref.). However, in many Christian homilies, the frequency of explanation make it seems more like a reminder that, "the ram is Darius, the Persian king; the he-goat is the Greek king, Alexander of Macedon" (John Chrysostom *Adv. Jud.* 5.7.1). This sort of remark seems to indicate that the identification was too obscure and so needed clarification or repetition for a preacher's audience. Often preachers needed to explain the story of Daniel as well. The preachers never knew who would be in attendance. Perhaps Jerome could expect readers to know in his work on Isaiah, published in 410, for his readership was probably the same as the one for his *Commentary on Daniel* from 407. If so, Jerome had created a frame of reference in his exegesis that only certain Christians could appreciate the full extent of.

The identification of the four Successors varied, though some names reappear frequently. Jerome refers to Ptolemy in Egypt; Philip in Macedonia; Seleucus in Babylon and Asia; and Antigonus in Asia Minor (Jerome *Comm. Dan.* 2.8.8, *CCSL* 75a.853–854). Jerome substitutes Demetrius with his father Antigonus, but otherwise gives the same names as Hippolytus. They are both consistent in the figures they mention across their corpora (Hippolytus *Antichr.* § 24, Jerome *Comm. Dan.* 7.6 [*CCSL* 75a.842–843]), so they insisted on each of their lists. We may question the historical value of such lists, for the named Successors did not all reign at one time. For example, Philip III died as king in 317 BC and Seleucus did not take Babylon until 312. None of the Successors, who had previously been Alexander's generals, proclaimed themselves king until

c. 306 BC. The naming game was commonly played by non-Christians too, even if they did not base their work on Daniel. For example, one first-century Roman biographer mentions in his work on kings that Antigonus, Demetrius, Lysimachus, Seleucus, and Ptolemy assumed the mantle of Successor after Alexander. Again, we are presented with a sequence impossible before 306 BC when the generals carved out different parts of Alexander's shattered realm for their kingdoms (Nep. *Reg.* § 3).

Hippolytus identifies the last horn as Antiochus IV with the interesting note that he was from the same race as Alexander (see below). Other Christians made the same designation, and it became the standard interpretation in early Christianity (Jerome *Comm. Dan.* 8.9a, *CCSL* 75a.855; John Chrysostom *Adv. Jud.* 5.7.4; Theodoret *Comm. Dan.* 8.8, *PG* 81.1444–1447). Hippolytus' rough contemporary, Origen of Alexandria, offers a unique interpretation:

> Another instance in the same prophet: the affairs of Darius and Alexander, of the four Successors of Alexander, the king of Macedon, and of Ptolemy, the regent of Egypt, surnamed Lagus, were foretold in this way: "Behold, the he-goat of goats (ὁ τράγος τῶν αἰγῶν) set out from the west across the surface of the entire earth. It had a horn between its eyes. It came to the two-horned ram, which I saw standing on the bank of the river Ubal, and the he-goat hurried headlong upon the might of the ram. I saw it reach the ram, rage at it, strike it down and crush its two horns. The ram had no power to stand before the he-goat; it threw the ram to the ground, trampled over it with no possibility for the ram to break free from the he-goat's grasp. The he-goat of goats grew great. While it was strong, its great horn was broken, and four smaller horns rose from it and dispersed to the four winds of the sky. From one of these, a strong and remarkably great horn went towards the south west in which the sun sets."
>
> Euseb. *Praep. evang.* 6.11.25 incorporating Origen *Comm. Gen.* 1.8 (*PG* 12.60). Cf. Basil and Gregory *Philocalia* 23.5 (p. 192 Armitage); Ps.-John Chrysostom *Homily on Luke* 2.2. (*PG* 50.234)

The principal parts of the reading are unproblematic. In fact, most of it comes directly from the Book of Daniel, and Origen has mainly added a prefatory list of names for identification. Origen interprets the animals as Darius (ram) and Alexander (he-goat, great horn) and refrains from commenting on the four Successors represented by the four horns. The strange part of the interpretation is the identification of the last horn as Ptolemy, the founder of the Alexandrian dynasty. In the Danielic prophecy the horn represents the stand-in for the Antichrist, usually identified as Antiochus, and scholarship affirms that Origen casts Ptolemy in this nefarious role (Bodenmann 1986: 283).

I contend that this scholarly interpretation of Ptolemy's role is incorrect. It seems rather unlikely that Origen, who wrote a commentary on Genesis in Alexandria in *c.* 230, would have thought or spoken so disparagingly of the first Ptolemy. In my view, we need to take a closer look at the context in which Origen quotes Daniel. Origen deploys this reference in an exposition of a passage in Genesis 1:14, "let there be lights and let them be for signs." The signs are stars, which reveal the course of a person's life. Unfortunately, this knowledge is not available to humans. Origen embarks upon the topic by talking about witnesses to the truth and accurate predictions in Scripture. The truth of the divine revelation of God foretold events through witnesses inspired by prophecy. To prove that prophecy predicted historical events, he uses numerous "fulfilled" prophecies in the Old Testament (Judas' betrayal foreseen, Zech. 11:12–13; the story of Susanna; prediction of Jesus' birth in 2 Kings; Cyrus). Then comes the pertinent passage of Daniel 8, preceded by Daniel 2 (see below). Since we have Origen's exegesis of the passage on good authority—not only is the passage extracted in full by Eusebius, but also by Basil of Caesarea and Gregory Nazianzen, who reproduce a fairly long, coherent citation in the *Philocalia*—we know that Origen did not say anything beyond the horn going southwest. Indeed, his list of evidence for prophetic truth continues with prophecies by Jesus Christ. The passage on the horn bound for the southwest thus breaks off abruptly before the next piece of evidence. By demarcating the prophecy, Origen omits Gabriel's warning to Daniel and thus the apocalyptic ending of the prophecy. The omission gives a new resonance to Daniel 8: Alexander fought Darius and won; he was followed by the Successors and a great one rose in the west, meaning Ptolemy. Nothing negative, then, is suggested by the prophecy. It simply concerned the rise of Ptolemy, which the Alexandrian audience would no doubt appreciate. No opponent could argue against Ptolemy's acquisition of Egypt, and so the historical sequence had been accurately foretold by "prophecy." We take note of Origen's editorial hand in reproducing Daniel. Not only does he change the very meaning of the apocalyptic prophecy to accommodate a Christian argument, but also adapts the text in a way that resonates positively with the audience that he wanted to persuade.

Origen was not the first to curtail the apocalyptic elements of Daniel. Such editorializing is also evident in Josephus' *Jewish Antiquities*. Josephus primarily reproduces Daniel 8, and not much else from the other apocalypses in Daniel 7–12 (Joseph. *AJ* 10.269–276). He identifies the last horn as Antiochus (276), but does not commit on the four Successors. In the same passage, he says that Daniel predicted the desolation of Judea, but he refuses to say more about the actual apocalypse. Like Origen, he has other concerns. He too is using Daniel's prophecies to demonstrate the truth of prophecy. It is part of a larger argument for divine Providence. He is arguing against the Epicureans, who did not believe God had a plan for the world, and he suggests that reading the Book of Daniel may convince readers of the existence of Providence. Readers themselves may discover how accurately the prophet had predicted events (277–281). Josephus and Origen thus share a common set of methods for appropriating the alarming content of Daniel available to a wider readership.

Daniel 8 held a wider appeal than the other mystic prophecies of the book. It is the least vague and needed less exegesis. Gabriel even identifies the first two combatants. On a literary level, the animal imagery also appeals to Macedonian myths (Slotki 1973: 65). Macedonian rulers were often represented as goatherders or aided by goats. A common literary motif is that the gods deployed goats to show the Macedonian kings where their principal cities were to be founded (Ogden 2011: 59). For example, Alexander founded Aegae ("Goat Town") in Cilicia (*AR* β 2.23). Clement of Alexandria held nothing but scorn for these oracular goats (*Protr.* 2.11.3). Plutarch preserves the amusing saying that Alexander's soldiers had told him the enemy would flee before them, so much did their clothes smell of goat (Plut. *Mor.* 180b; cf. Arr. *Anab.* 7.9.2; Dio Chrys. *Or.* 4.70–72). Such latent associations between goats and Macedonian royal power were ready to be adopted by the anonymous author of the Book of Daniel. Others argue that the animals referred to the zodiacal signs of Persia (Aries) and Macedon (Capricorn), and so the imagery fits well with the cosmic battle of the two forces (Bickerman 1988: 5). The imagery works on multiple literary levels. Moreover, Daniel describes the he-goat as the "he-goat of goats," ὁ τράγος τῶν αἰγῶν, a wordplay on "king of kings," βασιλεὺς βασιλέων, which was normally reserved for the reigning Persian monarch, the most powerful ruler in the world (see e.g., Ezra 7:12; Ezek. 26:7; Dan. 2:37). Jesus assumes the title in the NT (1 Tim. 6:15; Rev. 17:14, 19:16), but for the author of Daniel's book the eastern monarch held the title. By referring to the he-goat with this title, then, the author anticipates the he-goat's victory.

Early Christians imbued the he-goat with a few other characteristics. The principal aim was to map Alexander's campaign onto the actions of goat and ram. While Hippolytus and Origen gave a basic outline, Jerome takes the opportunity to provide readers with something of a history lesson:

> This [i.e. the he-goat] was Alexander, the king of the Greeks, who after the overthrow of Thebes took up arms against the Persians. Commencing the

conflict at the Granicus River, he conquered the generals of Darius and finally smashed against the ram himself [i.e., Darius] and broke in pieces his two horns, the Medes and the Persians. Casting him beneath his feet, he subjected both horns to his own authority. *And* (he had) *a large horn*. This refers to the first king, Alexander himself. When he died in Babylon at the age of thirty-two, his four generals rose up in his place and divided his empire among themselves. [...] *But they shall not rise up with his power*. No one was able to equal the greatness of Alexander himself (*nullus enim magnitudine Alexandri potuit coaequari*).

Jerome Comm. Dan. 2.8.9a (CCSL 75a: 853–854,
PL 25.536; trans. Archer)

Jerome narrates the prophecy with reference to specific historical events. Let us explore each of the episodes in turn.

First, repeated reference to Alexander's "Greekness" as opposed to "Macedonianness" may be of interest. Jerome declares elsewhere in the commentary that some readers had questioned Alexander's ethnicity. Such readers, he says, should not be disturbed that the prophet refers to Alexander as a Greek prince rather than a Macedonian (*Comm. Dan.* 10.20b, *CCSL* 75a.895–896, *PL* 25.557). The king had overthrown Greece before he turned to Persia. By emphasizing the sack of Thebes (335 BC) in the passage above, Jerome supports his own argument in that he gives an explicit example of Alexander's (re-)conquest of Greece. The exegete remains silent on Philip's prior conquest of the Greek city states, as that rule had actually passed from Philip to Alexander. Philip, as the first historical ruler of a united Greece, would pose a problem for Jerome's exegesis of Daniel and so the destruction of Thebes works well for making it seem as if Alexander was the first to conquer Greece. At any rate, Jerome knew that there were issues with identity, for otherwise he would not have needed to deploy the historical episode to anticipate critical voices.

Second, the battle at the Granicus river (Biga Çayı, Turkey; May 334 BC). In his notebook, Lucius Ampelius referred to this as the first pitched battle between Persians and Macedonians, so we must expect that everyone trained in oratory was familiar with the episode. Jerome also assumes that his reader would be familiar with much of the background information. The battle was fought near Troy and marked the first engagement with the power of Persia. It is noteworthy that he makes explicit mention of Darius through his generals, whom the Macedonians defeated. The naming of Darius makes the conflict seem as if it is one protracted battle in which Alexander constantly fights Darius' forces. In reality, it took another year before the Macedonians faced the Persian king at the Issus River (Cilicia, Asia Minor) and another two after that before Alexander finally defeated Darius at the plain of Gaugamela (near Erbil and Mosul, Iraq). In-between battles, the Macedonians besieged a number of cities and took Egypt. Darius did not surrender, but died in July 330, and it did not happen by Alexander's hand. Jerome's presentation of the war is thus made to fit Scripture's version of a single struggle between two contestants. Jerome's one-sided depiction conforms to his comment elsewhere in the commentary that, "the spirit of prophecy was not concerned about preserving historical detail but in summarizing only the most important matters" (Jerome *Comm. Dan.* 3.11.2, *CCSL* 75a.898-9). Apparently, so too was the exegete himself, insofar as he could change the interpretation to prove Scripture right.

As a brief aside, I must draw attention to a central pattern in Christian texts. In the examples above and elsewhere, the focus is fixed upon Persia as the grand enemy. Concentrating on one enemy makes all other opponents fade from sight. No interest is taken in the Indian foe, for instance. The contrast with the traditional sources is stark. For the Greek and Roman texts do much to enhance the Indians as worthy adversaries. For example, the major historical accounts represent the Indian rajah Porus as Alexander's equal (Heckel *Who's Who*, s.v. Porus [1]). As noted in relation to the Gymnosophists in Chapter 2, India was believed to be filled with the mightiest challenges. It was not the case that Christian writers did not know or care about such material, it was simply that they did not find it useful for every exposition. Since many theologians labored to insert history into the theological frame of Daniel, the image of history became skewed. We should make a mental note of this priority in writing history to which we shall return in the remainder of the present study.

A third point on Jerome's retelling relates to the death of Alexander. To give Jerome due credit, he does not distort the historical details, except the number of four Successors, which is too neat a number and one produced with historical hindsight. Not only does Jerome get Alexander's age right—a rarity, even today—but he also ignores the legendary traditions of Alexander's dividing up his empire himself. In doing so, he departs from the synoptic account of Alexander's life in the first verses of 1 Maccabees (discussed below). As we shall see, most Christians would have had access to this text, but relatively few mined it for information about Alexander.

The fourth and final point pertains to Jerome's note on Alexander's greatness, *magnitudo*. In the previous chapter, we noticed that Hippolytus assumed Plato's and Alexander's total dominance of the fourth century: the former in philosophy, the latter in kingship. Christians thus recognized the total supremacy of the king in his own time. According to another fifth-century commentator, Theodoret of

Cyrrhus, the choice of the goat imagery reflected the preeminence. Goats were faster than rams, he says, and the mighty horn symbolized its distinction and celebrity status, ἐπίσημον καὶ περίβλεπτον (Theodoret *Comm. Dan.* 8.5, *PG* 81.1441). Moreover, the horn signifies the shrewdness, intelligence, and sagacity of Alexander's thinking—high praise of a heathen, coming from a monastic community in fifth-century Syria. The king thus embodies the qualities of a philosopher-king, while acting as the instrument of God. On the breaking of the horn, Theodoret remarks, "after this greatest conquest, Alexander met the common end of humankind," μετὰ τὴν νίκην ἐκείνην τὴν μεγίστην, φησὶ, τὸ κοινὸν τῶν ἀνθρώπων ὁ Ἀλέξανδρος ἐδέξατο τέλος (Theodoret *Comm. Dan.* 8.8, *PG* 81.1444). Alexander had fulfilled his purpose: to conquer Persia.

Daniel 2

Daniel 2 represents one of the most iconic prophecies in the Old Testament. The vision is not that of the prophet, but belongs to the reigning Babylonian king Nebuchadnezzar. After his Chaldean soothsayers' failure to interpret his disturbing dream, Nebuchadnezzar turns to the Hebrew prophet for aid (2:1–16). The king does not tell Daniel what he saw. God grants Daniel the knowledge of the dream's contents, so that he can explain it to the king (17–23). Saving the other wise men of Babylon, who were unable to understand the dream, Daniel tells Nebuchadnezzar that no one can explain the dream but God (24–28). He goes on to say that the contents have been revealed to him, so that the king can know what is going to happen (29–30). Daniel describes how the king has seen an enormous statue with a head of gold, a torso of silver, a belly and thighs of bronze, and legs of iron; the sculpture had feet of iron mixed with clay. A rock was cut out of a mountain and struck the statue, completely destroying the idol. The stone then grew into a new mountain that filled the entire earth (31–35). Daniel's interpretation (from God) follows: the current kingdom is the head of gold; the silver is the subsequent lesser kingdom; the bronze is the next kingdom that will rule the earth; and the iron is the fourth that will annihilate everything (36–43). The stone will terminate the fourth kingdom and replace it with the Kingdom of God that will endure forever (44–45). Nebuchadnezzar acknowledges the truth of Daniel's words, honoring him with gifts and granting him a privileged place at court (46–49).

The literary setting matters. The Babylonian court provides a home for the exiled Daniel, and the introductory tales (Dan. 1–6) seek to establish what a pious Hebrew can accomplish in a place far away from home. Daniel 2 seems to advocate a policy of coexistence with the imperial power. It establishes a different sort of ideal to emulate for Jews in the Diaspora than military resistance and offers a "historical" example of successful cohabitation. In so doing, the story also incorporates a common motif from folktales, as the superior calls upon a lowly but wise person and makes an impossible demand; once the problem is solved, the lowly man assumes a new position of power. It is notable that the prophet does not just outwit the Babylonians, but beats them at their own game, dream interpretation, which is only possible through God's omnipotence. The theological dimension goes beyond the basic tale-type and promises a teleological end point, which is elaborated later. One can see why the author of the Book of Daniel makes such suggestions, but the political implications stretch the imagination. The king does not appear to care that his kingdom will fall; the rewards he heaps upon Daniel apply only to the action of interpreting the dream, which none of his other seers could. Comparatively, the later apocalypses, including Daniel 8, are not relayed to the king. They reveal that all earthly empires are evil and will crumble. Daniel is prudent in keeping those prophecies to himself.

The metallic statue brings together many narrative strands. The origin of the motif is Near Eastern, and a number of stories in world literature express the schema of four periods in this way. Collins (2016) discusses variations from Greece (Hesiod's ages of mankind), Rome (Aemilius Sura, a first-century BC historian), Judaism (the fourth *Sibylline Oracle*, *c*. late first century AD), Zoroastrianism (the Avesta tradition, *Bahman Yasht*), and Babylonian mythology (*Dynastic Prophecy*, Uruk prophecy). The motif thus has a wide distribution, which makes sense in a time when most cultures were monarchies. For Daniel and his readers, the "four kingdoms" prophecy has a clear-cut political dimension, as well as a theological one. God has chosen to let the rulers rise and fall in an ordered sequence. The proposed theology of history thus confers a sense of timelessness upon the line of kingdoms, while reassuring readers that the age of man-made empires will come to an end. Four kingdoms must rule before the end of idolatry. Daniel's repurposing of the literary motif serves several agendas, although the theological and political proved the most useful for later interpreters.

Since the prophecy does not label the kingdoms, anyone could speculate on their identity. The intended sequence in the original text was probably Babylon (gold), Media (silver), Persia (bronze), and Greece (iron), culminating in the age of Antiochus IV (ironically) before the stone would strike. For Porphyry, who envisioned the same end point, the chain of succession seems to have been: Babylon, Medes and Persians, Alexander, and the Successors (Jerome *Comm. Dan.* 7.7b, *CCSL* 75a.843, incorporating Porphyry *FGrH* 260 F37 = 21T Becker).

Writing before Porphyry, Hippolytus, the first extant Christian commentator, makes the prophecy to concern his own times and the future:

> And so how can we not consider that which was prophesied long ago by Daniel in Babylon is even now being fulfilled in the world? For the image which was portrayed in that time comprised the model of the kingdom of all the world. In which times the Babylonians then reigned, as being the golden head of the image. Then after them the Persians ruled for two hundred forty-five years as they are shown to be silver. After them the Greeks ruled, beginning from Alexander of Macedon, for three hundred years, as they are bronze. After them the Romans, who are the iron legs of the image, being strong as iron. Next the toes of the feet, so that in each place democracies might be shown which are destined to come[.]
>
> <div align="right">Hippolytus <i>Comm. Dan.</i> 2.12.1–7 (<i>GCS</i> NF 7.290, trans. Schmidt)</div>

Hippolytus' reference to the Romans reflects his contemporary times preceded by three previous kingdoms. The end times were thus delayed. Hippolytus makes no pretense to know the future, so he refrains from identifying "the democracies" of the ten toes (cf. the ten horns of Dan. 7:7–8, discussed below). The numbers of regnal years are a novel addition, for in his chronographical work, he uses roughly the same numbers of years for Persian and Macedonian hegemonies. In ancient numerology, as today, establishing a narrative of time through patterns of numerical units conferred another layer of authority upon the progression of history.

Now, since the Danielic prophecy suspended the sense of time with this sequence, we may find it strange that a commentator chose to replace timelessness with a fixed chronology of history. Hippolytus had another purpose in adding the numbers. He subscribed to the chiliastic view of history in which Jesus Christ would return to rule for a thousand years once the Apocalypse had occurred. In his separate treatise on Christ and the Antichrist, Hippolytus specifies that the Apocalypse would occur six thousand years after Creation, as calculated by the six days God took to create the world in Genesis 1. If the world began in 5500 BC, it would end in AD 500, roughly two hundred and fifty years from Hippolytus' own time. From this vantage point, the Second Coming was not imminent, and Hippolytus advocated patience in the expectation of Jesus' Advent, the Parousia. Hence the computations of the imperial sequence in Daniel bolster Hippolytus' eschatological vision (or lack thereof).

Josephus reigns in the apocalyptic theme in another way (Joseph. *AJ* 10.195–210). He relates the whole prophecy, mountains and all, but omits the interpretation Daniel gives. He proclaims that he does not want to speak of future events, only past and present, ἐμοὶ μὲν οὐκ ἔδοξε τοῦτο ἱστορεῖν τὰ παρελθόντα καὶ τὰ γεγενημένα συγγράφειν οὐ τὰ μέλλοντα ὀφείλοντι. Scholars have previously read Josephus' reluctance to relate the apocalyptic outcome as a sign of his dependency on Roman patronage, but one could also interpret Josephus' hesitation as a hallmark of the true Hellenistic historian who knows his genre (Gruen 2013: 264). Josephus teases interested readers by saying that they may find the true meaning of the prophecy, if they read the sacred Book of Daniel. By encouraging the reader to turn to the original text, Josephus uses the same strategy as he did for Daniel 8. If readers wanted to read history, they read Josephus; prophecy was for holy books, τοῖς ἱεροῖς γράμμασιν.

If we compare Josephus' identifications in Daniel 8 with those he makes in Daniel 2, we get the following schema: the head of gold was Babylon; two arms of silver were Persia and Media to overthrow the head; the Macedonian Empire was the third kingdom of bronze; and the last kingdom was made of the hardest metal, iron, to conquer all. We may assume that Rome is the last kingdom. Josephus notes that the third kingdom had been represented by bronze because of the armor they wore, χαλκὸν ἠμφιεσμένος (10.209), and they came from the West, ἀπὸ τῆς δύσεως.

The pattern varies in later Christian writers. Origen accepts the basic schema proposed (Euseb. *Praep. evang.* 6.11.24–25 incorporating Origen *Comm. Gen.* 1.8, *PG* 12.60). He prefers Babylonia–Persia–Macedon–Rome, thus omitting Media. He also downplays any future empire after Rome. Eusebius follows him in principle, but names the Babylonian power "Assyria" (Euseb. *Dem. evang.* 15 F1), which had some consequences for his interpretation of history (Chapter 4). On the other hand, Jerome adopts the sequence proposed in Josephus. Like Josephus' comment on the bronze armor, he cannot stop himself from offering his own reasoning why bronze defined Macedon:

> Now the Macedonian kingdom is properly termed brazen, for among all the metals bronze possesses an outstanding resonance and a clear ring, and the blast of a brazen trumpet is heard far and wide, so that it signifies not only the fame and power of the empire, but also the eloquence of the Greek language.
> Jerome *Comm. Dan.* 1.2.34 (*CCSL* 75a.794, trans. Archer)

The etiological explanation replays some common motifs. First, fame and power go well with Alexander's kingdom. Second, trumpets (Gk. *salpinx*; Lt. *tuba*; Hb. *shofar*), widely known instruments in ancient civilizations from after the fifth century BC, had associations that made them an apt metaphor for Alexander's kingdom. We possess multiple finds of metallic trumpets with copper or bronze, and ancient literature is replete with references to the instrument. For example, the epic poet Homer likens Achilles' piercing war cry to the sound of a trumpet blown at an attack on a city (Hom. *Il.* 18.219). According to a second-century lexicon (Poll. *Onom.* 4.85), the vocabulary associated with the sound of a trumpet generally had a bellicose dimension, such as "war-like," πολεμιστήριος or "hostile," ἐμπολέμιον. Moreover, the instrument also produced sounds that could be heard far and wide, although not up to fifty *stades*, or about 9 kilometers (5.6 miles), as one anecdote suggests (Poll. *Onom.* 4.88). Considering the extent, fame, and military might of Alexander's conquests, Jerome's choice of a trumpet to symbolize them works very well. Third and finally, a brief note on Jerome's praise for the Greek language. On the basis of another Biblical prophet, one of Jerome's Alexandrian contemporaries had alleged that the Greeks "were clear in their speech, as it were, not having the darkness of a barbarian language" (Cyril of Alexandria *Comm. Zech.* 2.359 Pusey). Previously, Roman writers had celebrated the beauty of the Greek language (see e.g., Quint. *Inst.* 12.10.27–37). Jerome's association of the clear language with the trumpet was evidently not too far-fetched, however inappropriate it may appear to modern minds.

The interpretations depend on the commentator's choice of placing Alexander's Macedon in the third position. In terms of symbolism, it did not matter which position Macedon occupied, for the imagery could always be reapplied, that of the iron kingdom to Macedon, for instance. One rule is that Macedon always follows Persian rule, for the Macedonian kingdom had the purpose of ending Persian power. This destructive function secured it a place in the sequence. Macedon's position only matters in terms of interest in the Apocalypse. If Macedon was towards the beginning of the sequence (second position), the Apocalypse was far off. If close to the end (fourth position), it may already have happened. At the third position, where Macedon commonly sits, the end was still reasonably distant.

The above examples come from writers that wrestle with Daniel 2 explicitly. The four kingdoms schema or *Weltreichsschema* was, however, already embedded in imperial literature, as already noted (Vell. Pat. 1.6.6, incorporating Aemilius Sura *FRH* 103). Some Christians made use of that without explicit mention of Daniel. For example, Lactantius considers multiple failed empires in sequence (Lactant. *Div. Inst.* 7.15.12–13) and even argues that Rome will fall, as the king of the Medes had foreseen long ago (7.15.19). Minucius Felix lets his main protagonist remark that Providence had arranged for the rise of Assyria, Media, Persia, Greece, and Egypt (Min. Fel. *Oct.* 25.9–12). Readers had readily understood Josephus' attempt to organize the past into a sequence of empires, even without knowing the Book of Daniel. Though Josephus drew much attention to scriptural prophecy, other writers and readers did not need to consult the prophecy. The non-Christians did not expect an Apocalypse at the coming of the fifth kingdom and so used the sequence to heap praise upon the occupant of the fifth place, typically Rome.

One scholar has collated the principal texts that use the schema, whether based on Daniel or not (Inglebert 2001: 362–364). The tabulated references result in at least four modes of interpretation:

1. an eschatological interpretation of the four kingdoms and the devastating but everlasting fifth empire, as in the Book of Daniel;
2. the Josephan model that makes use of Daniel but discards eschatology;
3. a model that concerns Providence, as in Minucius Felix;
4. the typical Greco-Roman *translatio imperii* sequence without explicit mention of Daniel (or Providence).

It follows that to make use of the Danielic imagery was a conscious choice on the writer's part. Commentators on the Biblical book had to perform exegesis of Daniel 2, of course, but in other genres the imagery was optional. We need to be aware that Christians did not always need to place the Macedonian campaign within the Danielic framework. We thus need to notice when they explicitly say that they are using the framework, for the advertisement calls attention to the religious identity in author and readers.

Hippolytus of Rome sees unity in prophecy when he juxtaposes Daniel 2 with Daniel 7 (*Antichr.* § 28). He argues that the kingdoms represented by the metals of the statue can be mapped onto the imperial identities represented by monstrous animals to which we now turn.

Daniel 7

Once the introductory court tales are over, and Daniel finds himself alone, the prophet begins to see visions of his own. Unlike the story in Daniel 2, this time he cannot understand what he sees and requires an interpreter, as he did in Daniel 8. In Daniel 7, he has a vision of a wind-blown sea from which four beasts emerge (1–3). The first appears to be a winged lion whose wings are torn off, so that it stands on the ground on two legs (4). The second seems as if a bear with three ribs in its mouth (5). The third is a leopard-like beast with four bird-like wings and four heads to whom dominion was given (6). The fourth beast, unlike any other in form and monstrosity, has ten horns and exterminates all in its path (7). A small horn appears and speaks boastful words about the end of days and the Son of Man (8–14). Daniel seeks to know the meaning of the vision, and an unidentified bystander (the archangel Gabriel again?) relates that the four beasts are the future kingdoms (15–17). The rest concerns the Apocalypse: the fourth beast and the little horn, the Ancient of Days, and one like the Son of Man (18–28).

Daniel 7 presents us with the only Biblical monsters that can match the dragon of Revelation. Monsters from the depths were not new. They were common in Ugaritic myths and appear in scattered references of the Old Testament (Collins 2016). The four beasts do not seem to have any further affinities with the sea once they leave it behind. To some extent, they can be explained by analysis of the metaphors. They appear to be opponents of the "shepherd king," the Son of Man, a figure who will fend off such wild beasts (Porter 1983). The beasts, or *Chaostiere*, correlate to similar "mantic monster" imagery in other Near Eastern texts, such as the *Šumma izbu*, a Mesopotamian handbook on birth omens. While the beasts are fascinating in themselves, they clearly serve the same literary function as Daniel 2. Daniel 7 replays the major themes of Daniel 2, namely *translatio imperii*, which anticipates the apocalyptic end at Daniel 8 (ram versus he-goat). Regarding Daniel 2, Hippolytus explicates the connection by saying, "The gold is the kingdom of the Babylonians, which is the lioness; the silver is that of the Persians, which is the bear; next the bronze is that of the Greeks, which Alexander of Macedon ruled, so that it might display the leopard" (Hippolytus *Comm. Dan.* 4.7.3, *GCS* NF 7.210). Regarding Daniel 7, Christians interpreted the four heads of the leopard as four Successors (of varying identities), just as they envisioned the four horns that emerged from the broken he-goat horn of Daniel 8 as the Successors. Forging these connections in Scripture was an important part of the Christian agenda intended to demonstrate that the prophet had in fact been right about his premonitions. If the first prophecies concerning the past were true, it followed that he would be right about what he said about the future as well. Moreover, it was important to repeat these connections between prophecies, insisting on their existence in Scripture, in order to convey the impression that the exegete provided the right reading of Scripture. In doing so, he asserted that he had understood what was divinely devised for the Apocalypse. And preparing for the Second Coming was crucial, because Christians could, "never be sure of the hour in which the Lord may be coming" (Matt. 24:42; Luke 12:40; Mark 13:35, 37; cf. *Didache* 16.1).

Again, some discrepancy in the identification of the beasts led to different roles for Alexander. In those interpretations in which Alexander's kingdom was made of bronze, Christians also consider the king the third beast, the leopard

(Dan. 7:6). In the eastern traditions that generally maintain the claim that his kingdom was signified by iron, he is the fourth beast, the super-monster (Dan. 7:7). Presumably, the latter interpretation is in accord with the intention of the author of the Book of Daniel. In the late fourth century, the Syriac exegete Pseudo-Ephrem points to the destructive nature of the fourth beast:

> This [i.e. the fourth beast] is Alexander, king of the Greeks, and the prophet says that he is similar to iron, which is the hardest among metals. He adds that the beast is armed with iron teeth, and with this symbol he indicates Alexander's powerful armies, which nearly subdued all kings. Then he adds that the beast was seen while devouring or trampling all that came its way, while destroying everything. With these words, he predicted that Alexander would have attacked the vastness of almost all provinces; would have robbed their inhabitants; and would have left their fields and estates to his soldiers for pillage and destruction. It would seem as if he had squeezed the entire world and all its precious things under a press, offering it all to his soldiers, so that they might trample upon it.
> Ps.-Ephrem *Comm. Dan.* 7.7 (trans. *ACCS* 13.226)

This passage represents one of the most vivid elaborations of the Macedonian monstrosity under Alexander's direction. No doubt prompted by the need to explain the imagery of the fourth beast, Pseudo-Ephrem offers a wicked portrait. The description lacks the usual tropes associated with the king's destructive behavior. One metaphor we also find in Greek and Roman literature is the representation of the king as a brigand (Sen. *Ben.* 1.13; Lucan 10.21; exculpated by Plut. *De Alex. Fort.* 330d). However, it is not clear whether Pseudo-Ephrem had the linguistic skills to engage with classical literature. In fact, this local interpretation follows perfectly the framework proposed by the Biblical knowledge of Alexander in 1 Maccabees (see below). The destructive power of the king and his army could then anticipate the coming of Antiochus, the small horn that appeared among the ten horns of the fourth beast (Dan. 7:8).

The absence of the standard sources for Alexander history (e.g., Diodorus) brings us to an important realization. The Biblical books provided an alternative source of knowledge of Alexander in the East before the rise of the *Alexander Romance* tradition in the seventh century (Monferrer-Sala 2011). We normally acknowledge the seventh-century Syriac translation of the *Alexander Romance* as indicative of what was known of Alexander in the East, but many Syriac-speaking Christians would have known the narratives from Daniel and 1 Maccabees. Investigating the theological reception of Alexander in Syriac texts lies outside the scope of the current story, but would present a new avenue of research.

Christians on the eastern periphery of the Roman Empire were part of it, but they always engaged with the literature on their own terms. Another Syriac exegete, Aphrahat of Persia (270–345?), offers an outstanding example. He interpreted Alexander as the winged leopard because the king was, "as strong as a leopard" (Aphrahat *Dem.* 5.18). Contrary to the western tradition, Aphrahat also says that the third and fourth beasts were one, which he understood as the Romans conquering the Macedonians (19). He offers an unbroken chronology from Alexander to Alexander Severus, though the dates reveal that he was thinking of Galerius, *d.* 311. Then he goes on to suggest that the fourth empire of pagan Rome had passed when the Christian Constantine ascended the throne. He understood Constantine as the stone of Daniel 2 and, therefore, the fifth kingdom of everlasting duration. In other words, Constantine was nothing short of the Messiah at the Second Coming. Aphrahat's interpretation must be understood within the contemporary political context of Rome and the East. As T. D. Barnes once suggested (Barnes 1985: 134), Aphrahat's aim was to persuade Constantine to come to the rescue of the Syriac Christian communities from the threat of Sassanid Persia. Aphrahat did so by implying that Constantine was divinely sanctioned to succeed in this endeavor. Unfortunately, when the homily was delivered in mid-337, that Roman emperor was already dead.

In the imperial Christian writers, negativity seems the norm. After all, the four beasts were monsters. Hippolytus provides a much more elaborate commentary than he did on Daniel 2:

> Some of the historians have recorded that these Persians ruled two hundred forty-five years until the reign of Darius, whom Alexander of Macedon deposed in the seventh year and transferred the kingdom of the Persians to the Greeks. [Dan. 7:6]. And so having named a leopard, he signals the kingdom of the Greeks, which Alexander of Macedon ruled. And he compares them to a leopard on account of them being sharp in mind and resourceful in reasoning and relentless in heart in which manner also the creature is spotted in appearance, being both quick to do evil and drink the blood of men. He says [Dan. 7:6]. For after the kingdom of Alexander was lifted up and grew in strength and was named in all the world, his kingdom was divided to his four rulers. For as he was dying, Alexander distributed it to his companions who were of his race, they were four men—Seleucus, Demetrius, Ptolemy and Philip—and these all put on crowns, just as Daniel predicts and was recorded in the book of the Maccabees (Macc. 1:1.9). And so after the Greeks ruled for three hundred years, the prophet signals to me again another kingdom.
>
> Hippolytus *Comm. Dan.* 4.3.5–4.1 (*GCS* NF 7.200–202, trans. Schmidt)

The analysis brings out some features we saw highlighted in Hippolytus' interpretation of Daniel 8: the 300 years of Greek and 245 of Persian history; the friends Alexander appointed as Successors in Daniel 8; and the growth of his power being lifted up by God. The new material is: (1) the deposition of Darius; (2) the leopard symbolism; and (3) the direct reference to 1 Maccabees. Let us take these by turn.

(1) Deposing Darius in the seventh year is correct if we count by the inclusive Greek count and agree to the idea that the Asian campaign began in 336 BC. As we saw, Christians considered the re-conquest of Greece to be the beginning of war on Persia. Darius died in July 330 BC, but not at the hands of Alexander. One of his Bactrian allies murdered him and left him by the roadside. Despite historical events, it was central for Christian commentators that king conquered king, so that the power of one kingdom could be transferred to the other—at least that was the easiest way of explaining the transition from Persian to Greek dominion. Christians also had to align Daniel 7 with the claim in Daniel 2 and 8 that Macedon and Persia would clash, and the more powerful win. In fact, Daniel 7's text says nothing of the beasts destroying each other. They rule at different points as willed by God. Only the fourth beast is slain by the Ancient of Days (Dan. 7:11), but the first three beasts had their dominion removed and lived on (Dan. 7:12).

(2) The traits Hippolytus attributes to Alexander as the leopard fits well with what was normally known about them (*RE* s.v. "Panther"). According to Aelian (*NA* 5.54), leopards were clever in setting up traps (cf. Phaedrus 3.2 = *Aesop's Fables*, Parry no. 494). Hippolytus' mention of the animal's color is also significant, for the colored version was well-known compared to the more dangerous, black panther (Jer. 13:23). In the ancient view, the leopard was always wicked, for it could not change its spots. Aristotle said that there were different panthers in Europe and Asia, but the boldest was the European one (Arist. *Hist. An.* 8.27.6-7). When one of the Apostolic Fathers was taken from Antioch to Rome for martyrdom by Greek-speaking soldiers, he called his captors "leopards" (Ign. *Rom.* § 5.1).

(3) Hippolytus makes an explicit reference to the story of 1 Maccabees that we shall consider below. It is notable that he provides the first evidence that this text from Maccabees was used for Christian purposes, because it is not normally taken into account in Christian discourse on Alexander.

Once again, Jerome summarizes previous exegesis while padding his interpretations with historical information:

> The third kingdom was that of the Macedonians, of which we read in connection with the image, *The belly and thighs were of bronze* (Dan. 2:32). The kingdom is

compared to a leopard because it is very swift and *hormetikos* [impetuous], and it charges headlong to shed blood, and with a single course rushes to its death. *And it had four wings.* There was never, after all, any victory won more quickly than Alexander's, for he traversed all the way from Illyricum and the Adriatic Sea to the Indian Ocean and the Ganges River, not merely fighting battles but winning decisive victories; and in six years he subjugated to his rule a portion of Europe and all of Asia. And by the four heads reference is made to his generals who subsequently rose up as successors to his royal power, namely Ptolemy, Seleucus, Philip, and Antigonus. *And power was given to it* shows that the empire did not result from Alexander's bravery but from the will of God, *quod… ostendit, non Alexandri fortitudinis sed domini uoluntatis fuisse.*

Jerome *Comm. Dan.* 2.7.6 (*CCSL* 75a.841–842, trans. Archer, adapted)

Jerome explains that the third position of Daniel 7 (leopard) corresponds to the third position of Daniel 2 (bronze), rather than providing the full sequence as in Hippolytus. Jerome's representation of the third beast shares some similarity with Hippolytus' interpretation, though Jerome does not concede the animal's sharpness of wit. Instead he emphasizes the rapidity and savagery of the feline beast that also forms part of Hippolytus' description. After all, like wolves, the leopard was inherently wild and violent (Arist. *Hist. An.* 1.1.12) and so was diametrically opposed to the domestic sphere. I do, however, speculate that Jerome may have made something of the irony that Alexander had seemed to be rushing towards his own death in his efforts to destroy the East, dying upon achieving his aim. In a fast-paced anecdote—just a single sentence with two participles and the main verb in past tense—Aelian mentions how Alexander's army completed a forced march of over 130 miles (1200 Roman stadia) and still defeated the enemy at the end (Ael. *VH* 10.4). For comparison, the exaggerated number equals almost three times the longest march we know of from Roman antiquity (40 miles), the flight of L. Caesennius Paetus and his troops away from Armenia in AD 62 (Thorne 2007: 226).

Although Hippolytus ignores the wings of the third beast, Jerome presents ample evidence for their symbolism. Again, velocity is the key. Jerome refers to the earliest campaigns of Alexander in the Balkans, as well as the furthest conquests in India, to stress the long flight of the monster. We know that the Macedonian army conducted several operations at the Danube river in 336 BC before quelling the Atheno-Theban rebellion in the south (see e.g., Just. *Epit.* 11.2.4), but the notion that Alexander thoroughly conquered what the Romans considered Illyria or spent time by the Adriatic Sea exceeds belief. What sort of interest did Jerome have in Alexander having seen his homeland? Jerome was himself from the city of Stridon, in northern Dalmatia (modern Croatia), on the borders of Pannonia. The notice of the Ganges River is more controversial. Strabo cites a letter the general Craterus sent his mother Aristopatra, reporting that Alexander saw the Ganges, with which Strabo disagrees (Str. 15.1.35, 702). Having discussed Alexander's letter to Olympias in the previous chapter, we too may dismiss the information as unhistorical, but the literary tradition was persistent. Even if the Hyphasis River (modern Beas) marked the furthest point the Macedonian troops went, the perceived "greatest river of the world" beckoned the greatest conqueror to cross it. In ancient history, the crossing of great rivers by monarchs was a famous literary representation of their might, and Alexander managed to cross many (Rollinger 2013: 5–16). The Egyptian Nile remains the world's longest river, but Strabo, himself a respected geographer, believed that the Nile ranked fourth behind the mighty Ganges. As we saw with the metaphysicality of the Gymnosophists, everything was bigger in the East. The issue divided readers, ancient and modern. In one of his spirited appendices, William Tarn vehemently rejected the idea of Alexander at the Ganges (Tarn 1948 ii: 275–285), but authorities like Jerome gladly accepted the tale to suit their own purposes.

The remaining details do not surprise us. Glorifying decisive victories was commonplace (see e.g., Ael. *VH* 3.23). The detail of six years of ruling comes close to the information in Hippolytus and, as we shall see, relies upon historical computations in other works (Chapter 4). The geographical area conquered by Alexander's army in Europe and Asia did indeed reflect what was known of the world and so seemed complete. Of course, Jerome takes care to say "a portion," for he does not buy into the idea that Alexander conquered Rome (and Carthage), as the author of the *AR* insists (*AR* 1.26.4–6). We will return to the extent of Alexander's conquest in Chapter 4. As for the four heads, we have already seen that commentators made them correspond to the four horns that the single horn of the he-goat breaks into in Daniel 8. Jerome repeats his four names from his interpretation of that prophecy, maintaining the factual tone of his exegesis. Finally, the last remark on the will of God makes Alexander the instrument of the Lord. Arguably, Jerome was doing no more than simply explaining what was already apparent to his readers. Given the fact that the prophet had seen the coming of Alexander in his vision, the king must seem to form part of the divine plan for eventual deliverance. Daniel 2, 7, and 8 ensured that the character of Alexander had a theological dimension, which required exegesis by religious teachers, particularly among the Christians. If we link Jerome's remark with the one he made on Alexander's unparalleled greatness, we discover that the statements would have been unproblematic for a Christian readership. Since God had guided Alexander, the greatness of the king depended on the divine. For Christians to appropriate Alexander, and the other rulers mentioned, was thus another way of glorifying God.

We may take the thought further. In the Old Testament, the basic framework of history is that God raises up rulers to do his bidding. He makes them fall if they fail or if pride or sin consume His chosen. Take, for instance, the following passage from Eusebius of Caesarea:

> It is fitting that the king [i.e. Nebuchadnezzar]—who prized the metals deemed precious among people [gold, silver, bronze and iron]—should identify these substances as the kingdoms that held sovereignty at different times in the life of humankind, whereas the prophet should describe these same kingdoms under the likeness of beasts that reflect the manner of their rule. Moreover, by the king—who was puffed up in his own conceit and prided himself on the power of his ancestors—is shown the vicissitude to which earthly affairs are subject, and the end destined for all the kingdoms of the earth. This is done in order to teach him humility and to understand that there is nothing lasting among people but only that which is appointed to the end of all things: the kingdom of God.
>
> Eusebius *Praep. evang.* 15.1.20 (trans. *ACCS* 13.169, adapted)

Eusebius expounds the Old Testament theology of history, as he reflects upon Nebuchadnezzar's pride and fall. The subtle juxtaposition of Daniel 2 and 7 shows that Eusebius also understood them together as other Christians did. As for his exposition, which takes for granted that readers knew the Danielic text well, Eusebius captures the essence of Nebuchadnezzar's fate in two chapters of Daniel. Already in Daniel 3, Babylon's monarch builds a giant idol of himself—all in gold, not just the head—and orders everyone to worship the image. When three Hebrew youths refuse him, he throws them into a furnace to burn. Though he had previously worshipped Daniel and given him gifts (Dan. 2:46–48), Nebuchadnezzar's royal arrogance, literally on display for all to see, causes his madness in Daniel 4. After another dream and Danielic interpretation, God removes Nebuchadnezzar from power (Dan. 4:31), turning him into a grazing beast outside the city (Dan. 4:33). But God later restores his mind and reason, once he has learned humility, and the fallen king returns to glory without pride (Dan. 4:36–37). In other words, the king could not see through the vanity and temporality of his position, whereas the prophet could on account of God's revelation to him. When God exerts his power, no mortal can deny Him.

Christians did not find it complicated to insert Alexander into such a framework for interpreting history. The original prophecies had already woven

Alexander into the theological fabric of history, and Christians only needed to construct a recognizable backdrop to bring out what they considered the meaning of the arcane prophecies. By superimposing images of the leopard and he-goat on to the campaign, Christians subscribed to the idea that the king had a theological purpose. He was written into the Biblical drama. Alexander was by no means viewed as one of the major players in the Old Testament, but his inclusion in it put him in a category occupied by very few characters of the "classical" world. In Christian exegesis, his purpose was straightforward. He was born to bring Persian pride low. But his fulfillment of that mission also testified to the truth of prophecy, serving another Christian agenda. Christians could claim that prophecy was fulfilled, for no one could disagree with the fact that Macedon had conquered Persia. Christians insisted that history was prophecy made manifest, over and over again, in all sorts of texts. Daniel had seen Alexander's coming, however obscure his vision was.

By interpreting the past prophecies, Christians could claim that they, and only they, understood God's divine plan in the apocalyptic literature. One striking example appears in the pages of Hippolytus. He alleges that, "the leopard had risen, the goat of goats come; it had smitten the ram, subjected its horns and trampled the animal with its feet, conquered and grown great. From the single horn another four have appeared. Rejoice, blessed Daniel, you were not mistaken; all these things have happened!" (Hippolytus *Antichr.* 32 (trans. Schmidt); cf. Theophilus *Autol.* 1.14). Commentators could thus control Christian expectations for the future by asserting that they had understood His will evident in the past. Philo of Alexandria, and the author of the Book of Daniel before him, had already noticed the usefulness of this literary device. The fulfillment of some predictions in the past validates the presentation of those that have yet to be realized (Philo *Vit. Mos.* 2.278 with Bickerman 1967: 118).

Consequence 1: Providence versus Fortune

We have now considered how Daniel 2, 7, and 8 provided Christians with alternative imagery and a "new" frame for interpreting Alexander history. Integration of these features engendered an important result: God's Providence, *pronoia*, replaced Fortune, *Fortuna* or *Tyche*, as a model of interpretation. The development carries major importance because non-Christians so often associated Fortune with Alexander's success. For instance, the rhetorical speeches of Plutarch made Alexander enter a contest with Fortune to prove that he was himself responsible for his glory, not her. Indeed, as Koulakiotis argues, the Greek discourse on the Fortune of Alexander can be traced back to the days of

Alexander himself (Koulakiotis 2006: 44–45). Fortune as a *topos* recurs across the historiography of Augustan Rome—in the historian Livy in particular—and pervades imperial texts. Every major account of Alexander mentions the theme of Fortune. Preferring the Providence of the Biblical prophecies thus shifts the balance, causing Alexander's Fortune to disappear from view.

The sudden absence of the Fortune *topos* in the early Christian tradition is striking. The *topos* is never associated with Alexander across a wide range of historiographical texts (Chapter 4), even those that seek to criticize him. Attributing his achievements to Fortune was always a way of reducing them to nothing, which is why Plutarch's defense makes for such engaging reading. Again, the *topos* never occurs in Biblical commentary or in clergical communications, such as letters and homilies. The Christian references to Alexander's Fortune are rare and sporadic, and come from periods outside the scope of this study. For example, Alcuin of York (735–804) links Alexander's death with the whims of Fortune, an uncommon trope in the Latin world (9.35–36, quoted at Cary 1956: 194 n. 93). The reference occurs in connection to the Viking raid on that famous Northumbrian center of spirituality and learning, the monastery of Lindisfarne. The earliest extant reference to Alexander's Fortune by a Christian appears in a single reference in the 370s (Ps.-Hegesippus *On the Fall of Jerusalem* 5.19, *CSEL* 66.340). Jerome and subsequent writers all but ignored it, as the majority of previous Christians had.

While the effects of the change are evident on the literary level, the substitution accomplished by Christian writers does not seem out of touch with the world around them. Philo of Alexandria asserted that the Providence of God was normally known to intellectuals as Fortune (Euseb. *Praep. evang.* 7.21, 8.14, incorporating Philo *On Providence*). Other philosophers, primarily among the Stoics, stress the role of Providence (Arr. *Epict. Diss* 1.6; M. Aur. *Med.* 2.3, 4.9, 5.8; cf. Fears 1974). Many histories of Rome insist on Fortune's significant role in history (see e.g., Polyb. 8.17.3, 10.11.9; Zos. 1.1.2). In other words, Fortune and Providence seem to have been used interchangeably. Moreover, the ambiguity emerges in Alexander's own tradition. Arrian's famous assessment of his hero's achievements revolves around the themes of Fortune and Providence, but the historian claims that Alexander was so mighty that his deeds only made sense if they were assisted by a god. Accordingly, Arrian could also claim that he had had divine assistance to write about such a divine topic. He says so explicitly. It was not without the help of a god that he himself had put the acts of Alexander into writing (Arr. *Anab.* 7.30.1–3). In the Palladian *Life of the Brahmans* (Chapter 2), Alexander believes that Providence directs him through the goddess Sophia—

wisdom, apparently a stand-in for Athene—and he prays to her. The Indian leader attempts to exorcise what he takes to be a "false demon," but it proves unsuccessful. Alexander is, however, thankful that he is now aware of its evil intent (2.30). The Indian leader wants to teach him true Providence (2.34).

Perhaps the Christian alteration of the *topos* is no more than a by-product of the insertion of Alexander into Biblical prophecy. But Christians did labor to make other texts fit the framework. The best example remains the various reworkings of the *Alexander Romance*. In the alpha recension (usually considered a non-Christian composition), Fortune plays a major role. She is often mentioned, even if Egyptian gods (Ammon, Serapis) guide Alexander (*AR* 1.8.4, 1.17.1, 1.18.6, 2.15.2, 3.33.7). However, in the beta recension—a product of Byzantine Christians in the late fifth century—all the references to Fortune are replaced with ones to Providence, *pronoia* (1.1, 1.14, 1.34, 1.38, 2.7, 2.20, 3.5, 3.25; cf. *AR* Arm. § 286 Wolohojian). Like most other ancient texts, the *Alexander Romance* had a certain amount of textual fluidity and, since no author's name was attached to the biography, it fell easy prey to revision by others. Minor Christian modifications were easily introduced. There is no reason to doubt the religious convictions of the author of the beta version. This *Alexander Romance* recension ends with an almost accurate synchronism of 320 years from Alexander's death until the word of God was made flesh by a virgin (*AR* β 3.35).

Consequence 2: Influence on wider exegesis

Another immediate effect of reading Alexander into the Book of Daniel relates to the Christian interpretation of other OT prophets. The imagery in the Book of Daniel provided Christians with a useful cross-reference enabling them to explain obscure utterances. For example, in Theodoret's commentary on one of Jeremiah's prophecies, the exegete asserts that Alexander, as the he-goat of Daniel 8, fulfilled the prophecy of destroying the Chaldeans (*Comm. Jer.* 50:8–10, *PG* 81.741). I might add that the male goat imagery feels particularly appropriate, for Jeremiah had proclaimed that the Hebrews should leave Babylon and be like he-goats before the herds (Jer. 50:8). As ever, Christian exegesis seeks to establish connections in scriptural prophecy, so Theodoret's remark is not surprising in itself. Instead the example serves as a reminder that Christians were creating a self-referential literature around the Old and New Testaments in which Alexander had been given a part, however uncharacteristically small. One may say that Jews considered the OT imagery of Alexander important too (Amitay 2010), but Christians clearly labored intensively to make it relevant elsewhere as well.

This energetic literary activity reflects an important development in early Christian literature as a whole, and of Alexander's role in that discourse. We need to remember that Alexander only had relevance for the Biblical drama through his role in Daniel and a minor historical appearance in 1 Maccabees (for some, not a canonical book), so the effort taken to integrate him into other prophecies seems disproportionate. We also need to recognize that what went on in Biblical exegesis mattered as much as for Alexander's legacy as some of the more popular receptions in the *Alexander Romance* and oratory in the pre-Constantinian phase of Christian thought. Every monastic community required instruction in Scripture, and commentaries were copied and sent to circulate in monastic communities. Indeed, we now view late antique monasteries as centers of education with regards to writing and scholarship (Larsen and Rubenson 2018).

No one makes mention of Alexander's Biblical dimension more than Jerome. While he was among the clergymen most steeped in the Greco-Roman literature in which Alexander was ubiquitous, Jerome chose specifically to employ the imagery from Daniel's prophecies. Alexander features more frequently in Jerome's Bible commentaries than in his hagiography, letters, sermons, and treatises. The king appears in most of Jerome's commentaries on the Old Testament prophets: the major prophets Isaiah, Jeremiah, Ezekiel, and Daniel; several of the minor prophets Hosea, Joel, Amos, Nahum, and Zechariah. Features of the Danielic Alexander imagery (leopard, he-goat) occur in Isaiah, Jeremiah, Ezekiel, and Zechariah. In these, and other commentaries, Jerome includes other material too: references to Alexander's building of Alexandria proliferate (Isaiah, Hosea, Nahum), along with details from 1 Maccabees (Isaiah, Amos), the time of Alexander as a historical period (Isaiah, Jeremiah, Ezekiel, Amos), and sometimes minor details, such as the cup of poison Alexander drank in Babylon or his swift victories until the campaign in India (Jeremiah).

Let us take but one example from Jerome's commentary on the major prophet Jeremiah. He is commenting on the passage (Jer. 5:6): "therefore a lion from the forest shall kill them [Jerusalem; the house of Judah], a wolf from the desert shall destroy them. A leopard is watching against their cities; everyone who goes out of them shall be torn in pieces because their transgressions are many, their apostasies are great." The verses predict a disastrous time for the people of Judah, and the historical context follows suit in light of the international conflicts with Egypt and Babylon, *c.* 600 BC, that would lead to the Babylonian exile. In context, the beasts probably refer to the dangers outside Jerusalem, that is, the Babylonian army, but Jerome comments,

The phrase "a wolf from the desert shall destroy them" signifies the Medes and the Persians, which Daniel portrays in his vision as a "bear" in whose mouth were three rows of teeth. The phrase "a leopard is watching against their cities" prefigures the onslaught of Alexander and the rapid advance from the West to India. He calls him a "leopard," because of his inconstancy and he contended against the Medes and the Persians after subjecting many nations to himself. And of this leopard it [i.e., Daniel 7:6] says, "And the beast had four heads, and dominion was given to it." But since he [i.e., Jeremiah] is not prophesying about the future or of things that are now about to take place, but is narrating the history of the past, he passes over the Roman empire in silence, although the Roman empire may be spoken of by the phrase "everyone who goes out of them shall be torn in pieces".

Jerome *Comm. Jer.* 1.95 (*CCSL* 74.53–54, trans. Graves, adapted)

Jerome makes Jeremiah's animals correspond to the four beasts of Daniel and thus extends the chronological scope considerably. In Jeremiah, the Hebrews would be in immediate danger if they left Jerusalem. The animals are not monsters (leopard with four heads and wings), but wild carnivores, certainly dangerous, but not of the apocalyptic sort. As the leopard, Alexander does not suit the chronology of a scene set in pre-exilic Judah. It follows that Jerome alters the text by re-interpreting the prophet's vision. The commentator therefore decides what Scripture means. By reproducing the same phrases of and offering cross-references to his own reading of the Book of Daniel, Jerome reinforces the reader's impression that his interpretation is correct. No doubt Jerome believed that he was right and that his wide reading of prophecy assured the accuracy of his interpretation, but he is the one deciding to bring Daniel and Jeremiah together as apocalypses, even if the latter is not strictly apocalyptic. Furthermore, it is noteworthy that Jerome emphasizes that the prophet had prophesied on events that had been fulfilled in the past. With the first part of the prophecies fulfilled, the logic followed that the rest would be fulfilled as well, which we noticed above. Prophecy not only bridges past and present with the future, but also creates a sense of timelessness in which each phase of the prophecy had an important place, like rungs on a ladder.

Given the prevalence of the concept of *translatio imperii* in understanding history (Goez 1958), Alexander frequently appeared in Christian commentary on the prophets. One of the most striking instances occurs in regard to the interpretation of the sixth chapter of Zechariah, a Hebrew prophet dating to the time of Alexander I of Macedon in the early fifth century BC. The prophet speaks of four mighty chariots drawn by horses of different colors, and the four charioteers fly out from two mountains made of bronze (Zech. 6:1–8). Cyril of Alexandria interprets each chariot as representing a different empire:

1. The first chariot was drawn by red horses and symbolized the Chaldeans or Babylonians because of their blood-thirst. The Babylonians caused bloodshed in Judea and Samaria.
2. The black steeds of the second chariot indicate the kingdom of Media and Persia under Cyrus because of the devastation they inflicted upon the Babylonians. The color suggests mourning and death.
3. The white horses symbolize Alexander's kingdom because Greeks were effeminate, *habrodiaitos*, clad in white clothing, and had clear speech unlike "barbarians".
4. The dapple-grey horses of the fourth chariot represent Rome on account of their power.

Then Cyril notes the directions in which the chariots went, modifying the Biblical text, so that it says that the black horses went towards the north, the white horses followed them, and the dapple-grey steeds went to the south. He goes on to say that the black and white horses went to the Babylonian kingdom with the words:

> Both of them [i.e. Cyrus and Alexander, the champions of the two chariots] attacked the land of the Chaldeans and took it by force. The first was Cyrus and then after him Alexander, who even overpowered Darius himself around the so-called Issus, a city in Cilicia, and an inscription was made to this effect:
>
> > *By the walls of Issus near the stormy billows of Cilicia we lie, countless hordes of Persians, following former king Darius on his last journey. This is the deed of Alexander of Macedon.*
>
> Cyril Comm. Zech. 6 (2.359-60 Pusey, PG 72.96), incorporating
Antipater of Sidon Epigrams (Greek Anthology 7.246)

Cyrus and Alexander, Cyril later explains, were God's punishment for the Babylonians' cruel deeds against Judea. The interpretation fits the scheme of *translatio imperii* and the framework of the Old Testament in which God raises up monarchs to punish others. Jerome concurs, though he argues that for the white horses "to go north" again signified Alexander's destruction of the Medes and the Persians (Jerome *Comm. Jer.* 1.6.8, CCSL 76a.793–794), that is, Cyrus' empire. For Jerome, the *translatio imperii* aspect of the passage seems stronger than to Cyril, even if Cyril accepts that the last chariot is Rome. The dapple-grey horses go south to fight Carthage.

As for Cyril's remarks on Alexander, he offers little detail, if more than on Cyrus. Noting the first battle against Darius, he makes an error. The Battle at Issus was fought at the Pinarus River, not a city, on the gulf of Issus in southern Anatolia. The city was a later foundation (Stoneman 2008: 108–109). The incorporation of Hellenistic poetry, an epigram by the second-century BC Antipater of Sidon, reminds us that the exegesis was also a literary text that had to please aesthetically and intellectually.

Consequence 3: Exegesis of Revelation

The Book of Revelation may be familiar to many readers but, given its obscure nature, the text requires a short introduction. Revelation represents one of the most remarkable compositions of Christian antiquity. It is the only prophetic book of the New Testament, in stark contrast to the plethora of prophets in the Old Testament. It may date to the late first century AD, either under the Emperor Nero or Domitian, whose persecutions are believed to have prompted its writing (the nature of those persecutions is disputed). Since antiquity, the attribution to John the Apostle, whom Jesus named "son of thunder" (Mark 3:17), has been contested, but many denominations hold that John wrote Revelation. His literary production also includes a Gospel and three letters in the New Testament canon, so he was prolific, if the attributions are true.

As previously said, some modern denominations, including the Orthodox Church, do not consider Revelation part of the New Testament canon. The concern is whether or not the text is genuinely apostolic. Early Christian readers were also divided (Euseb. *Hist. eccl.* 3.24.18). Though judgments on Revelation proliferated (Irenaeus *Haer.* 5.30.1), some Christians took the text seriously enough to produce whole works on it, such as:

- c. 180—Melito of Sardis wrote *On the Antichrist and Revelation* (lost);
- c. 203—Hippolytus, *On Christ and the Antichrist*, partially surviving;
- before 250—Origen, *Scholia on Revelation* (lost);
- 270s—Victorinus of Pettau, *Commentary on Revelation* in Latin, reworked by Jerome.

Revelation called for exposition because of its apocalyptic content. Revelation professes to contain prophesies revealed to Jesus Christ (Rev. 1:1). An address and prefatory messages occupy chapters 1–3. The main bulk, from chapter 4 to 22, pertains to coming conflicts between demonic forces and Christ's chosen. Some of the most well-known symbolic imagery of western culture appears here: dragons, fallen angels, the four horsemen of the Apocalypse, and the Whore of Babylon (17). These mystic creatures are naturally interpreted as types of earthly evil and sin. The eternal kingdom will come after Satan has waited a millennium in prison to break free and overthrow Christ, but God disposes of him and Death itself in a lake of fire (20:10, 14). The new Jerusalem will appear from heaven, thus fulfilling prophecies of Ezekiel and Isaiah (Justin *Dial.* 80).

Given that Revelation concerns a Christian future, it seems curious that Alexander should play any role in understanding the prophecy. In the text itself, the author of Revelation takes no interest in the historical past and condemns every imperial power, save Christ's kingdom. And yet, the osmosis of eschatological motifs between Daniel and Revelation helped Christians to integrate Alexander into the narrative. For example, Revelation 13:2 concerns a mix of beasts that we remember from Daniel 7: a dreadful beast rises from the ocean (Dan. 7:3), with seven heads and ten crowned horns (7:7); the monster looked like a leopard (7:6) with the feet of a bear (7:5) and the mouth of a lion (7:4). The dragon gave it dominion (7:6). Hippolytus recognized the monster of Revelation and interpreted it with reference to Daniel 7, repeating many of the conclusions he makes in the commentary on Daniel (*Antichr.* 24, 28). For him, Alexander was the leopard and so fitted into Revelation's bestiary. His treatise makes plain that the supposed Alexander of the Book of Daniel formed part of a longer narrative of history that had begun in the past with Danielic prophecy, culminated in the days of Jesus, and would eventually end with the Second Coming. Again, we remember that past fulfillments of prophecy conferred validity on those that had not yet come to pass.

Alexander and the Book of Daniel

The king's heart is a stream of water in the hand of the Lord; he turns it wherever he will.

Proverbs 21:1 NRSV

To sum up, the prophecies of Daniel had a major impact on how Alexander's history was interpreted, even before Jerome's exegesis. Daniel 2, 7, and 8 not only provided new imagery, but also a compelling framework for organizing previous history, so that it became relevant for the salvation narrative. Like many other monarchs, Alexander had unwittingly served a higher purpose, preordained by Scripture. This interpretative framework gave Alexander a role in history that Jews, such as Josephus, had already afforded him and would take in their own direction. For Christians, however, the prophecies were mainly important for theology in exegetical work rather than historiography. They could also be included in apologetic texts, though the arguments came from exegesis (e.g., Origen influencing Eusebius). In Daniel 8, the animal battle is important, but only as a prelude to the later conflict of the little horn, Antiochus. In the prophecies that deal with imperial transference, the Macedonian crown usually assumes the third position. We get the sense that the writers stretch history to solve the exegetical issues rather than maintaining a static role for Alexander. The various interpretations of which Successors followed him reflects this dynamism. Important features of the original prophecy, primarily the apocalyptic features, were eschewed and replaced with a forward-looking narrative. Indeed, the main point, as we can gauge from Hippolytus, was that the prophecy had been partially fulfilled in history. Scripture was true and so readers could look forward to seeing the rest of Scripture's promises fulfilled. The level of detail required to prove the point was not great. While Jerome embellished his interpretations to showcase his high level of learning, we can learn from Hippolytus that a mathematical proof could just as easily support the hypothesis.

J. Peltonen (2018: 499 n. 90) buries one of his best points in a footnote when he argues that the Book of Daniel was Alexander's first introduction to Christian sacred history. Of course, we have long known Alexander's importance for ancient prophecy (Pfister 1976: 301–347, citing Kampers 1901), and that is another reason why the editor of the Book of Daniel found a role for the king. Although the Danielic imagery is rich, we cannot chart the full effects on Alexander's legacy from Christian exegetical works alone. We have to look at the consequences of Alexander's inclusion. We have seen that the insistence on God's Providence in thinking about Alexander caused a shift from earlier Alexander histories that propounded the whims of Fortune. Christians simply did not engage with the Fortune *topos* any longer. Though the Danielic imagery does not immediately find its way to Christian historiography, it was put to good use in interpreting other Biblical prophets, and so Alexander and the other rulers, Nebuchadnezzar and Cyrus, entered new contexts. The fact that Alexander appears in Christian readings of Revelation, a wholly Christian composition with little to no interest in the past, showcases the theological significance attributed to the king by the third-century theologians.

I contend that Alexander's imagined role in the Book of Daniel was but one of the ways in which the king was made perpetually relevant to Christians in history. We must bear in mind that this vivid interpretation of Alexander, dependent on Biblical prophecy, coexisted with the material studied in the previous chapter. It is easily forgotten, despite the fact that the authors remain the same. It is also remarkable that this use of Alexander's legacy took place at a time when the king was worshiped as a god around the Mediterranean basin (Dreyer 2009). Christians thus laid claim to Alexander on the basis of Biblical prophecy, whereas pagans laid claim to the king by other religious means, such as temple building and cult. But Christians relied upon the ultimate authority, the written will of the Lord, and so, in their view, God had turned Alexander's heart.

Josephus and Hellenistic stories

Introduction to Josephus

We have already met the Jewish (Titus?) Flavius Josephus (c. 30–100 AD) several times in this study. We may imagine his writings on the shelves of most literate Christians. The scrolls would lie between Jewish Scripture and the New Testament. Josephus' works include the *Antiquities* and the *Against Apion*, as well as a history of the Roman wars against the Jews. These texts testified to some of the most important events, such as the demise of Jesus and the destruction of the Temple. For this reason, they held immense interest to Christian readers and, in the phrase of the historian, Josephus became, "in many respects the schoolmaster of early Christianity, which presumably made thankful use of his texts and regarded them as a gift from Heaven" (Schrekenberg 1992: 134). Indeed, Josephus offered a boundless quarry of apologetic arguments from the perspective of a Jew, readily accessible in the common Greek language. The importance and accessibility are reflected in the fact that his works were later translated into Latin twice before another re-translation in the sixth century AD. Josephus may not have intended his primer on Jewish history to be the most effective weapon *against* his own people, but that is what it became in the minds of Christian readers. In another sense, his works, which were probably meant for outside readers, were one of the most successful national histories in antiquity. For the past two thousand years people have systematically mined the texts for information on the period between 200 BC to the aftermath of AD 70.

Josephus preserves some fascinating tales about Alexander and the Jews. In what follows, we will investigate each by turn, also noting the Christian readings of such tales. While most stories were often recycled, it is important to note that the Christians used the material selectively, which should by now be unsurprising, considering previous discussions. I will focus on the stories that made it through the Christian filter in pre-Constantinian and Constantinian periods.

Just visiting: Alexander in Jerusalem

"And Alexander shall rise", Daniel says, "and will kill Darius and will take action as he pleases" (Dan. 11:3), and nobody shall rise against him. This Darius, son of Arshak, was the tenth king after Cyrus, and in his sixth year Alexander marched against him and killed him. Alexander, when he came to Jerusalem, entered the temple, worshiped God and honored the temple with many gifts.

Isho'dad of Merv *Comm. Dan.* 11:3 (*CSCO* 328:124, trans. Stevenson and Glerup)

Did Alexander really visit Jerusalem? Few questions about the king and the Jews have preoccupied scholars more since the Enlightenment (Briant 2017: 61–67). During his circuit of the Levantine Coast, the Macedonians spent seven months besieging Tyre (January to August 332 BC) and Gaza (September to October 332). Unfortunately, no Greek or Roman account takes notice of Alexander's visit to the Holy City. On the other hand, Josephus is adamant that Alexander did visit, and the legend grew in later Jewish literature. In light of the disagreement among the ancients, scholarship has marshaled arguments for and against a potential visit (Dellinger 1980; Klęczar 2012). The elaborate story, as Josephus tells it (Joseph. *AJ* 11.304–346), has been much studied, but future studies should take into account the new translation of Josephus with highly valuable commentary (Spilsbury and Seeman 2017). Never before has Josephus' detailed engagement with Alexander historiography been brought out so well. For weary readers, I offer below a short summary of the Josephan tale with a focus on the details that were of interest for the Christians.

Alexander's army was ravaging the cities of the Levantine coast when the High Priest of Jerusalem, Jaddus, refused a request for tribute from the king because of his oath to the Persian king (§§ 317–320). In his rage at their rejection, Alexander swiftly descended upon the frightened population of Jerusalem after taking Tyre and Gaza. At this crucial juncture, the Jewish God appeared to the High Priest and convinced him to lead the people outside to greet the king (326–328). The encounter between king and priest reaches its climax when Alexander genuflected before the divine name inscribed on a golden plate on the priest's headdress (329–339). He did so in front of the entire assembly of Jews and his perplexed army, declaring to his inquisitive captains that the god whose name this was had said in a dream that he would support the campaign (334–335). The High Priest invited him into the Temple and showed Alexander a prophecy from the Book of Daniel—that is, that a Greek king would defeat a

Persian ruler (Dan. 8:20–21, cf. 10:20)—which greatly increased the Macedonian hope for victory against the Achaemenid superpower (336–337). After conferring due honors upon the Jewish people, Alexander's army set out on the road to Egypt. His newly enrolled contingent of Jewish soldiers underscores the point that the king was bound for success as the divine instrument of the Jewish God and champion of His people (338–340).

Amitay points out the gist of the narrative from the Jewish perspective (Amitay 2010: 120): Jaddus could not assist Alexander because of his oath to Darius, but God intervened and removed Jaddus' need to break it. Josephus takes great care to explain that Alexander's recognition of God's name and the prophecies of Daniel confirm that God's grace had shifted from Persia to Macedon, and so the world needed to change accordingly. His appropriation of the world-changing campaign goes further. Josephus puts a short speech into Alexander's mouth to the effect that God had already informed Alexander of the plan back in Dium, and Alexander only just remembered the epiphany when he saw the High Priest in similar clothes. In so doing, Josephus does not display the king as an unwitting Messiah-type, as Cyrus had been for the prophet Isaiah (45:1). Alexander had seen the face of God and recognized that his plan formed part of God's plan.

Much more can and has been said on the Josephan canonization of the encounter (Momigliano 1979). But I will now turn to the "extra-Josephan traditions," as Ory Amitay (2017) terms them. Going beyond Josephus, Amitay provides an up-to-date account of the story in rabbinic literature, as well as other episodes that relate to our understanding of the story's context. His approach to the Jerusalem story's wider tradition dictates a shift in our scholarly focus. Instead of looking back to Josephus and his lost Hellenistic predecessors, which was until recently the norm, we turn towards the later ancient parallels that are so rewarding for exploring the story's diffusion. For example, Amitay analyzes a central passage from the eighth-century Byzantine epsilon recension of the *Alexander Romance*, namely, the passage bearing upon the foundation of Alexandria, in which Alexander similarly declares his monotheistic faith from atop a tower (*AR* ε 24.2). This version even recounts how the king prayed to God the "thrice holy", saying "O God of Gods, creator of all that is visible and invisible, be my helper now in all that I intend to do." Amitay (2017: 142–147) also reopens the debate on whether the story has a Jewish origin in the first century AD, which Pfister (1976) first argued, but was later dismissed by Amitay. For comparison, we find no such Christian material in the period under study, whereas the Jews invented fanciful legends independently of Josephus (Klęczar 2018).

The story does not appear in Christian writing until Origen's *Against Celsus* (Klein 1988: 982–985; Wirth 1993: 59 n. 188; Demandt 2009: 189). According to Whealey (2003: 6–12), Josephus' *Antiquities* was not as popular as the *Jewish War* or *Against Apion* with Christian readers until Origen, who took a strong historical interest in the origins of Christianity. The *Against Celsus* (AD 248) is not known for its authority on historical matters but, as we have seen, ancient history became a major intellectual battleground for third-century intellectuals, whether Christian or non-Christian. Origen's apologetic piece responds to a challenge the Greek philosopher Celsus posed seventy years earlier in his *True Doctrine*, or *Alethes Logos*. Origen's text takes the form of a point-by-point dismissal, revealing many of the contested, but common, ideas in the ancient discourse on religion. One recurring point is the Christian claim to the legacy of the Hebrews, which Celsus denies, but Origen maintains. Immediately prior to the pertinent passage below, Celsus had discussed three major topics: that God had assisted the Jews in any way; that angels had taken exclusive interest in the Jews; and that the Jews were the only people with access to a promised land. Origen disagreed with each of Celsus' arguments and explained that even non-Christians referred to the deity of the Jews as, "God of the Hebrews", ὑπὸ τῶν ἀλλοτρίων τῆς ἡμετέρας πίστεως Ἑβραίων καλεῖσθαι θεόν. To offer "historical" evidence of God's preferential treatment of the Hebrew nation, Origen deployed a heavily demarcated version of the Jerusalem tale (Peltonen 2018: 498):

> And because they [i.e., the Jews] were in favor with God—as long as they were not forsaken [i.e., before the coming of Jesus Christ]—they continued to be protected by divine power, even though they were few in number. Not even in the days of Alexander of Macedon did they suffer anything at his hands, despite the fact that they would not take up arms against Darius because of certain agreements and oaths. They also say that the High Priest clothed himself in his sacerdotal vestment at that time and that Alexander bowed before him, saying that he had seen a vision of a man in this very dress, who proclaimed to him that he would bring the whole of Asia under his rule.
> Origen *C. Cels.* 5.50 (SC 147.142–145; pp. 363–364 Marcovich; trans. Chadwick)

Given the passing nature of the remark, it is understandable that the passage lacks many of the features from the Josephan version. We may note that Origen recycles:

- Alexander's marching against Jerusalem in anger;
- the Jewish refusal to obey him because of their oath to their Persian overlords;

- the respectful meeting between the impressively dressed High Priest and the king;
- Alexander's dream and the prediction of his mastery of Asia.

Origen includes only those Josephan details that any religious reader would readily appreciate, such as a god's manifestation in a dream (a theophany). That Alexander sees God is, however, a risky statement from a Christian perspective. Anthropomorphism was a hotly contested issue, despite Genesis 1:27 speaking of God creating men in His image. We may note that the dream does not appear in other Christian versions of the tale, and Origen also separates himself from the statement by saying that it is something others had said, τότε φασὶ καὶ. Of course, as Josephus knew, the dream accords well with the Alexander tradition. We know of a multitude of prophecies that concerned Alexander's conquest of Asia. The most famous remains undoubtedly the cutting of the Gordian knot (333 BC), which promised him hegemony over Asia. The anger of Alexander is another case in point. Readers would recognize the literary motif of the wrathful warrior on a rampage. Origen's story assumes that the king was hell-bent on lethal punishment, which Josephus had taken pains to establish. He explicates how Alexander destroyed two central cities to enhance the sense of danger that the Jews were in. After all, the Macedonian army, antiquity's second-most successful war-machine, had come to the gates of Jerusalem. The Jews were cowed, and the implication in both texts is that, had God not stepped in, Alexander would have leveled Jerusalem, like Gaza. Both writers represent Alexander's immediate submission as a manifestation of God's dominance over human affairs.

Origen's inclusions are less significant than what he omits. He does not mention Alexander's entry into the Temple; his reading of Scripture, his acceptance of 'Jewish rights', or the Jewish soldiers in Alexander's army. In other words, Origen leaves out everything that privileges the Jews and makes the Josephan version distinctively Jewish. Instead he has filed the tale down to its basic constituents with regard to how God's will was revealed and history unfolded. For Origen, the tale is about God's power over the gentiles.

The representation of the tale bolsters the next argument Origen makes. Having used the tale as a piece of circumstantial evidence to prove that the Jews were loved by God, Origen abandons the Jews to promote the Christians. Unsurprisingly, he asserts that God transferred His grace from the Jews to the Christians at the Advent of Jesus Christ. He then posits that the transfer is the reason why the Romans had been unable to eliminate the Christians, despite many persecutions. The hand of God was fighting for the Christians and spread the Gospel from Judea to the rest of the world.

The apologetic argument is ingenious. Origen aligns the antiquity of the Jews and Alexander in an unsubtle juxtaposition with the present-day Christians and the Romans. The result not only establishes a firm connection between Jews and Christians, but also makes a claim for a historical continuity in the persecutors (Alexander, Rome) and the persecuted (Jews, Christians). But, with Alexander's submission to the High Priest, Origen seems to make a strong suggestion. Since Alexander recognized and respected the power of the Jewish religion, Origen suggests, it would be wise if the Romans followed his lead. They too should bow down to the God of the Christians, the legitimate heirs of the Hebrew heritage. In Origen's view, Alexander had done the right thing, and the Romans would also be rewarded should they choose to follow Alexander's example. The alteration of the very meaning of the tale thus depends on a distinctively Christian agenda. Its message would resonate well with contemporary Christians, as well as initiated readers, who showed interest in Christian philosophy. A further historiographical note is that selective omission provided an essential tool for how the Christians adapted Jewish stories to make them suitable for Christian argument.

At the remove of one scholarly generation from Origen, Eusebius continued his intellectual legacy in the bishopric of Palestinian Caesarea (Grafton and Williams 2006). It is well-known how Eusebius managed Origen's library with his master Pamphilius, and Constantinian patronage made their program of Christian learning less arduous. We have already noted Eusebius' historiographical abilities, which were also at work when he spoke of Alexander in Jerusalem. References to the Jerusalem tale occur twice in his corpus: one in the apologetic treatise known as the *Proof* or *Demonstration of the Gospel* (before AD 311), the other in a short review of Alexander's history in his *Chronicle* (completed AD 311; revised 325). The tale thus appears in apologetic contexts in both Origen and Eusebius.

Eusebius made a comprehensive response to critics of Christianity. No previous apologist had done so at such great length. The *Proof*, in twenty books, was preceded by his *Preparation for the Gospel* in fifteen books. Both works were addressed to Theodotus, bishop of Laodicea (modern Latakia) in Syria between 310 and 340, whom Eusebius supported in the Arian controversy. The *Proof* sought to demonstrate once and for all that the Old Testament prophets, who spoke the will of God, had foreseen the coming of Jesus as the Christ, and so Jesus himself fulfilled their prophecies. Eusebius did not use the line-by-line format of Origen, but made lengthy replies to general points. He did not compose many of the replies, but instead cited other authorities that supported his case. These texts were carefully edited and re-arranged.

That sort of editing becomes apparent in Eusebius' treatment of the Jerusalem episode. He writes, "at the time of Jaddus, Alexander the Macedonian built Alexandria, as Josephus reports, and visiting Jerusalem he worshiped God", κατὰ τοῦτον τὸν Ἰαδδοῦ ὁ Μακεδὼν Ἀλέξανδρος Ἀλεξάνδρειαν κτίζει, ὡς Ἰώσηπος ἱστορεῖ, ἀφικόμενός τε εἰς τὰ Ἱεροσόλυμα τῷ θεῷ προσκυνεῖ (*Dem. Praep.* 8.2.67). The event is dated to the priesthood of Jaddus, the same name Josephus and Origen used for the High Priest. Two interrelated features stand out: (1) the use of Josephus; and (2) the synchronism of Alexandria's foundation and the Jerusalem visit. To take the former first, nowhere in the extant works of Josephus does he narrate the foundation of Alexandria. His *Life* reports that he briefly visited the city with Vespasian (*AJ* 20.415), but he says nothing of the foundation. He talks briefly about the resettlement of the Jews in Alexandria under Alexander and Ptolemy (12.7-10). As for the latter, the geographical sequence does not add up. Alexander could not have founded Alexandria before visiting Jerusalem, unless Eusebius believes that the king visited on his way back from Egypt. Josephus is, however, adamant that Alexander came to Jerusalem after the sack of Tyre and Gaza (11.320). Josephus makes plain that Alexander was traveling by land from Macedon to Egypt via Asia Minor (345), necessitating a route through Syria, Phoenicia, and the Levantine coast to get there (cf. 305, 313). We know that the historical Alexander had dealings with North Africans while he was besieging Tyre, but no ancient authority places the foundation of Alexandria at this time.

In either case, Eusebius may have made an honest mistake, if quoting from memory. He may also have muddled several sources. For example, the *Alexander Romance* reports a different route. Alexander first went west via Sicily and Italy (Rome) and North Africa (Carthage, Siwah Oasis in Libya, Alexandria, Memphis) before he launched the campaign against the Persians in Syria and Mesopotamia, returning to Thebes for a spell (*AR* 1.26-46). Should the *Alexander Romance* be Eusebius' source, it would thus be possible for Alexander to go to Egypt before arriving at Jerusalem. Eusebius used the geography of the *Alexander Romance* in other works, as we shall see, and he may have used it here too. As we shall see, he corrected the geographical sequence in his *Chronicle*.

Another potential scenario is that Eusebius deliberately based the synchronism on someone else's authority. I speculate with little confidence that he may have employed the rhetorical figure of *hysteron proteron*, "later earlier", which reverses the actual order of events to add emphasis, if the later event is more important than one earlier in time (Smyth *Greek Gram.* § 3030). If that is the case, we need to reverse the order and read that Alexander went to Jerusalem, worshiped God, and founded Alexandria. In that case, his geography is not confused, and the mistaken reference to Josephus could easily be explained: Eusebius has swapped the sequence of the foundation and the pilgrimage, but placed Josephus' authorial authority up front, so as to make the information of the entire sentence seem legitimate. The consequences of such a reading are more immediate. It follows that Alexander had visited the Temple in Jerusalem before he founded his city in the same way that some accounts claim that Alexander visited the oracle at the Siwah Oasis before founding Alexandria. As for the trip to Jerusalem, the later foundation of Alexandria was thus an event authorized by God. If this reading is accurate, Eusebius has made a most apt appropriation of the past. However, *hysteron proteron*, as the text stands, suggests that the foundation of Alexandria was more important than Alexander worshiping God. Perhaps a simpler solution is to say that the synchronism brings two civic centers of early Christianity closer, and Alexander's and Josephus' roles are secondary to that purpose.

Jerome cited this passage in his *Commentary on Daniel* (3.9.24, CCSL 75a.872 = Euseb. Dem. evang. 8.2.67). In fact, he translates a longish extract of the *Proof* on the chronology of the Advent, proposed by the Old Testament prophet Daniel (9:24–27). This first theory he seems to cite with approval, although he cannot follow two competing theories launched elsewhere by Eusebius. Jerome mentions a full commentary on Daniel by Eusebius in the prologue, but we do not have this text available. Jerome's Latin does not change anything, except by adding that Josephus told of Alexandria's foundation (or the Jerusalem tale) in the *Antiquities*. That is certainly the place to look for verification.

Elsewhere in the Danielic commentary Jerome makes an explicit comparison between Nebuchadnezzar's worship of Daniel and Alexander's bow before the High Priest (1.2.47, CCSL 75a.796). According to Jerome, the rival philosopher Porphyry had claimed that no one would worship his own servant, but Jerome insisted that the kings had not worshiped the prophet and priest as much as they were really worshiping God, revealer of mysteries, in the persons of His servants. Having said that, Jerome saw fit to offer another explanation in case skeptical readers found the parallel unsatisfactory, saying that Daniel's miraculous interpretation overwhelmed Nebuchadnezzar and made him prostrate himself in awe.

The apologetic spin Origen had put on the tale proved useful. It is notable that neither Eusebius nor Jerome takes notice of the dream in which Alexander sees God, which Origen maintained, perhaps on the authority of Josephus. Perhaps that is the main item of interest that sets Origen apart from his heirs. To my knowledge, no later Christians accepted the dream, although they accepted Alexander's entry into the Temple, which Origen did not mention.

Our readings of the early Christian versions of the Jerusalem tale point to its canonical status (Demandt 2009: 189). While variations occur, the episode itself captured the Christian imagination. Origen first used the story, but it was Eusebius who popularized it, and Jerome brought it from the East to the West through translation. It is not a matter of a positive or negative reception, but rather the apologetic framework into which the story was fit that made it useful. As we shall see (in Chapter 4), the story also found its way to Christian historiography through Eusebius, and subsequent chroniclers incorporated it as a way of proving God's works in history, evidenced by the succession of world empires. We find the story in equal measure in the Byzantine East (Jouanno 2016) and the West (Peltonen 2018: 497–499).

At the Caspian gates

Josephus made a passing remark that would prove popular to future generations. Speaking of a raiding tribe on the periphery of the Roman Empire, he said that the king of the Hyrcanians controlled a pass that King Alexander had barred with an iron gate (*BJ* 7.244–245). The bulwark stood as a monument to Alexander's might, though few knew where it was located. The gate became a wall in later literature (Anderson 1932; cf. Sauer et al. 2013: 7–8, 9–14, 630–647), and it would enclose a host of different peoples that were considered enemies of the civilized world. In much later literature, the Syriac eschatology of the seventh century AD, the barrier became infused with an apocalyptic dimension. In this material the gate excluded the apocalyptic forces of Gog and Magog that would be unleashed at the end of the world.

Elsewhere I have sought to show that for Josephus and many other writers, the gate did not possess the aforementioned apocalyptic dimension. Instead it was simply an ordinary line of defense (Djurslev 2018a). I based my contention on a series of little-studied references, primarily the fourth-century adaptation of the *Jewish War*, known to Jerome in the 370s (*Ep.* 71.5, *CSEL* 55.6). The authors' knowledge seems to suggest that the writers were connected or were part of a literary circle of easterners with a western readership. The anonymous author, the so-called Pseudo-Hegesippus, was presumably a Greek, like Ammianus Marcellinus, for example, who thought in his native language, but wrote in Latin. He notes the existence of the gate in two instances: the first discloses details of the Alans, who lived outside the gate (*De Ex. Urb. Hier.* 5.50, *CSEL* 66.405); and the second reveals that the author did not use the legendary location for the gate. It follows that he could not have had the apocalyptic legend in mind (3.5, *CSEL* 66.193). The ethnography and geography support an un-apocalyptic reading of Josephus and the other testimonies before the rise of the *Alexander Romance* tradition in seventh-century Syria (Reinink 2005).

Mosollamus and Greek superstition

Eusebius of Caesarea parrots a short tale from Josephus, who had, in turn, extracted it from the fourth-century BC historian Hecataeus of Abdera (Euseb. *Praep. evang.* 9.4.6–9 citing Joseph. *Ap.* 1.200–205 incorporating Hecataeus of Abdera *FGrH/BNJ* 264 F21 Lang). The story went that a Jewish archer in Alexander's army by the name of Mosollamus had shot down a bird to prove a point. Bird signs could not reveal the future. If the bird was unable to foresee its own death, why should one believe in the omens it gave? The episode, tapping into the discourse on Greek superstition, represents another "Alexander-related story serving as the vehicle for a demonstration of Jewish religious superiority" (Stoneman 2008: 59). For Eusebius, the story was easily recast to present the same argument against augury or ornithomancy on behalf of the Christians. The tale did not reach a larger audience. No one repeated the story until the ninth-century George the Sinner, who called the archer "Mosomachus," but otherwise followed Eusebius, not Josephus (*Chron.* p. 32).

Moses and the Red Sea

Josephus' revision of the Old Testament pays much respect to Moses, one of the greatest Hebrew personages. One tale concerns Moses and God's parting of the Red Sea so that the Hebrews could escape the wrath of Pharaoh (Exod. 13:17–14:29; cf. Ps. 136:10–16). Josephus realizes that the story seems too good to be true, which is why he makes use of another story to corroborate the account (Joseph. *AJ* 2.348). He speaks of Alexander's passage through the Pamphylian Sea. The story of the march is famous. In the winter of 334/3, the Macedonians passed through Lycia and Pamphylia, in southern Asia Minor. On the march to Side, Alexander's soldiers traveled on the shore with the waters withdrawn, allowing them to pass. One writer says that the waves acted as if prostrating themselves before the king (Callisthenes *FGrH/BNJ* 124 F31 Rzepka via Eust. *Il.* 13.29). Arrian claims that the winds and divine providence influenced the waters (Arr. *Anab.* 1.26.1–2). Conversely, Strabo recounts how the Macedonians crossed the pass in a stormy season, but were able to march through the waters, submerged to their navels, as they trusted in the luck of the king (Str. 14.3.9, 666–667). Other writers follow Strabo in speaking of Fortune, *Tyche* (App. *B. Civ.* 2.21.149; cf. *Fragmentum Sabbaiticum FGrH/BNJ* 151 F1.2 Bearzot). For readers of Josephus then, the story of the waters' prostration was not too far-fetched. The reverse effect was what Josephus was after. Alexander's "historical" example helped to explain the Biblical account of the Hebrew crossing of the Red Sea, or at least made it seem more credible to outsiders.

Josephus appropriates the story further for his own purposes, saying that Alexander's purpose was to destroy the Persian hegemony as was God's will, τὴν δι' αὐτοῦ καταλῦσαι τὴν Περσῶν ἡγεμονίαν τοῦ θεοῦ θελήσαντος ... God granted him this miraculous march because He himself had set Alexander on the path of conquest. We noted that the message of divine retribution came across forcefully in the tale of the High Priest and Alexander; the king had seen God in a dream in which his assignment was revealed. He would later confirm his intention to carry out the task in front of numerous witnesses in Jerusalem. As Cary comments (Cary 1956: 128), this sort of "reverent" Alexander was a possible representation for Jewish writers, who could claim that their people had had dealings with the king and therefore saw him as their own hero. The Christians could hardly make such claims, and they contradicted the Jews' appropriation. As we noticed, they removed most of the details of the story that had Alexander take up Jewish customs.

No Christian made a connection between the two tales of Alexander's and Moses' crossing. It is therefore difficult to draw any strong conclusion on the basis of silence. But perhaps the Josephan juxtaposition created a blueprint for another famous reference to the Bible story. In his historiography (*Hist. Eccl.* 9.9.5–7), Eusebius made the crossing of the Red Sea function as the literary model for Constantine's victory at the Milvian Bridge. God and Constantine, Eusebius' stand-in for Moses, vanquished Maxentius, the defeated "Pharaoh." When the latter's bridge of boats collapsed, the tyrant and his army sank into the Tiber. Eusebius revisited his Biblicizing of the battle in his encomiastic biography (*Vit. Const.* 1.38). On the other hand, Lactantius' version is not so Biblical; he employs an ambiguous oracle attributed to the Sibyl (*Mort.* 44.8). Eusebius was of course not in the same situation as Josephus. He did not have to argue for the truth of the Biblical story, but took for granted that his readers would appreciate the Mosaic analogy of Constantine's victory.

As I hope to demonstrate below (Chapter 4), Eusebius seems much more well-acquainted with Alexander history than previously assumed. It may therefore be that Eusebius has found much inspiration in Alexander history for his portrait of Constantine.

Alexander, Josephus, and the Christians

Tales always accumulated around Alexander, but when it came to Christian appropriation, only some of the Josephan stories made the cut. The Jerusalem visit made a powerful impression on Christian writers, for it demonstrated God's influence on pre-Christian history. Aspects of this story and other stories were, however, omitted from the record, primarily those that referred to Jewish customs. Christians took little interest in the Jews for their own sake. Appropriating Alexander's campaign took priority, as the destruction of Persia fulfilled God's will, prophesied by Daniel. Again, we detect the same pattern we found in Chapter 2: Christians selected and edited the material that suited their own agenda. In itself, that pattern does not surprise; Jews and other non-Christians made use of the Alexander material they themselves chose to appropriate.

As a way of concluding this section, we may compare the fate of the Josephan references to Alexander with those made by Philo of Alexandria (c. 15 BC–AD 50). None of these were appropriated in the pre-Constantinian and Constantinian periods. It was not until Ambrose of Milan read Philo and referred to his version of Calanus' letter to Alexander that we have evidence for the influence of Philo's Alexander stories on Christianity. Christians, before and after Ambrose, of course appropriated much else from Philo, especially his philosophical exegesis of Scripture. After all, Philo was the main representative of Hellenistic Judaism in terms of spirituality and theology, not historiography. Nevertheless, he mentions Alexander in the way any ancient intellectual may be expected to make use of an *exemplum*. For example, in his exegesis of Genesis 3:24 on the Cherubim and the flaming sword outside Paradise, Philo refers to a prideful boast the king had once made when he wanted to take possession of Europe and Asia (*Cher.* § 63). Apparently, Alexander had stood at a good spot to see both continents and said, "that all things on this side and that side are mine." Philo dismisses the king's arrogant remarks, calling Alexander's behavior, "immature, silly, and not kingly, but ordinary of soul," μειρακιώδους καὶ νηπίας καὶ ἰδιωτικῆς τῷ ὄντι ψυχῆς, οὐ βασιλικῆς. He then compares Alexander's pride to that of Cain, whose name means "possession," and whose folly and impiety Philo goes on to expose on the basis of the first Mosaic book. The story of Alexander's boast is otherwise unattested, although his hold of both continents was often remarked upon (e.g.,

Addaeus *Anth. Pal.* 7.240). We find no such sentiment in Josephus nor did any Christian see fit to recycle the vignette.

1 Maccabees

Early Christian authors considered 1 Maccabees a "historical" text. For instance, Christian chronographers systematically mine the Maccabean books for information to write the narrative of early Hellenistic history up until the coming of Rome. They deliberately chose the apocryphal book to supplant the traditional texts that they could have used instead, such as Diodorus Siculus (whom Eusebius, for example, cites at length elsewhere). The choice of an alternative source that placed emphasis on Hebrew events reflects their change of focus. As self-conscious and "serious" historians of antiquity, Christians covered a great scope of history but with their own priorities in regard to sources and points to prove.

The first of the four Maccabean books primarily concerns the conflict between the self-proclaimed Jewish freedom-fighters, the Maccabees, and their Seleucid "oppressors." As a preamble to the political struggles, the author provides one of the earliest extant synoptic accounts of Alexander's life (*c.* 100 BC):

> After Alexander, son of Philip, the Macedonian, who came from the land of Kittim, had defeated King Darius of the Persians and the Medes, he succeeded him as king (he had previously become the king of Greece). He fought many battles, conquered strongholds and put to death the kings of the earth. He advanced to the ends of the earth, and plundered many nations. When the earth became quiet before him, he was exalted, and his heart was lifted up. He gathered a very strong army and ruled over countries, nations and princes, and they became tributary to him. After this he fell sick and perceived that he was dying. So he summoned his most honored officers, who had been brought up with him from youth, and divided his kingdom among them while he was still alive. And after Alexander had reigned for twelve years, he died.
>
> 1 Maccabees 1:1–7 NRSV

The narrative goes on to establish Alexander's connection with the principal persecutor, Antiochus IV. After the short account of Alexander, the author skips straight to the rise of Antiochus as a sinful scion of the Successors (1 Macc. 1:10). Alexander had thus begun a cycle of wicked kings that resulted in Antiochus' cruelty. Asserting Alexander to be the remote predecessor of Antiochus indicated the origin of the Seleucid king's power. He was by no means the first Seleucid monarch to make such claims to Argead kinship. It is striking that, by historical accident, Antiochus' claim for legitimacy through Alexander was maintained by the sources that sought to denigrate him (e.g., Hippolytus *Antichr.* § 49).

The author of 1 Maccabees does not compare the two kings again until Antiochus' death. At the city of "Elymais" (confused with ancient Elam, perhaps Persepolis), Antiochus learned of a temple containing the city's wealth and weaponry left there by Alexander (1 Macc. 6:1–2). Unfortunately for him, the citizens resisted him and drove him back to Babylon gravely disappointed (1 Macc. 6:3; cf. Joseph. *AJ* 12.355). His defeat is followed by bad news from Jerusalem (6:5–7), regret (8–13), and the choice of a new Successor before his death in Babylon (13–16). Klęczar (2018: 382–383) surmises that Antiochus' death follows the pattern of Alexander's within the text, as well as most standard patterns of royal succession. However, the more obvious parallel is to the death of Antiochus' father, Antiochus III. He died pillaging the temple of Bel in Elymais. Like father, like son.

Early Christians rendered the narrative of 1 Maccabees as the historical reinforcement of Daniel's prophecies. A church historian made the point clearly in 430, saying that the prophecy of Alexander's rapid rise and fall in the Book of Daniel was turned into historical narrative in 1 Maccabees (Philostorgius *Hist. Eccl.* F1.1, Phot. *Bibl.* cod. 40). Although Philostorgius pursued an Arian agenda in his history, his comment confirms the general tendency that Christians found a single message in the two para-biblical texts. For example, commenting on Daniel, Hippolytus tells his readers that they can receive further information on the history if they read the Maccabean books, καὶ ταῦτα μὲν εἴ τις βούλοιτο λεπτομερῶς ἐνιστορῆσαι, σεσήμανται ἐν τοῖς μακκαβαίοις (*Antichr.* § 49). Similarly, Theodoret directs readers to read 1 Maccabees to understand what the prophecies of Daniel meant (*Qu. Num.* 44.1 Petruccione). Accordingly, 1 Maccabees provided a general sort of reference for historical details. For instance, in his commentary on Daniel, Hippolytus says that Alexander himself divided his kingdom among his four Successors (4.41.5, *GCS* NF 7.290). From 1 Maccabees we get the idea that Alexander made the division himself and, in Daniel, we hear that there were four Successors. So, by streamlining the Biblical accounts, Hippolytus provided a coherent narrative of the divine will. To take another instance: in a chronicle contemporary with Jerome (*c.* 397), Hilarianus establishes the connection between Alexander and Antiochus through 1 Maccabees, Daniel, and mathematical computations (p. 169 Frick). As he is going through a list of Persian rulers, he arrives at Alexander, who ushered in the Greek era, signifying the end of Persia. Hilarianus then computes the time from

Alexander to Antiochus, again providing mathematical proof that Scripture was fulfilled.

Given the accessibility and availability of 1 Maccabees, as well as its straightforward account of Alexander history, one might have expected further engagement with the text itself. Surprisingly few re-use the framework proposed by the author of 1 Maccabees. For example, Jerome ignores the information of Alexander's hubris, seeing the exaltation of the king as God's magnification of the he-goat. He also claims, contrary to the Maccabean narrative, that Alexander's kingdom was divided *after* the king's demise. The king himself had no influence over who became a Successor. Jerome and others may not have considered the Maccabean books to have the status of Scripture (*PL* 27.401–402), but he did translate them into Latin. It follows that he must have made a conscious choice to depart from the Maccabean digression on Alexander in his studies of the Book of Daniel, for example, perhaps because he knew he had better information available. The same ambivalence appears in the scholarly discussions of 1 Maccabees' significance in Alexander's reception. One German historian described vividly how Christianity was the vehicle that brought the negative image of Alexander in 1 Maccabees over the Alps and into Britain, and also spread it over the continent throughout the fifth century AD (Pfister 1976: 167). Conversely, other German scholars were unwilling to afford the text and its reception any attention.

Opinions on the status of the four books of Maccabees remain divided. The first two Maccabean books are considered canonical by the Catholic Church, whereas the last two are regarded as apocryphal; the Lutheran and Anglican Churches consider all four books apocryphal; and the Orthodox Church accepts the first three as canonical, but not the fourth. It should therefore not surprise that the Maccabean books had a varied reception in the early Church, and we can see that ambiguity at work when we regard Alexander's early Christian tradition.

Coda: Rise and shine, Alexandria

Despite our interest in its Hellenistic inception, the Alexander digression in 1 Maccabees represents a tendentious piece of historiography. Jerome knew that in the fourth century, and we can easily spot details missing from the account, such as the foundation of Alexandria. Subtracting the establishment of that city from Alexander's achievements takes away much of his lasting cultural impact, as we have seen. Without it, the king becomes an instrument of destruction with a short expiry date, regardless of what force directed him. Anyone could choose to include or omit Alexandria. For instance, Hippolytus never refers to its foundation, whereas Jerome takes much interest in the city. The author of 1 Maccabees may not have made a conscious choice in omitting the city, but it is at least as indicative of his agenda as what he included.

As this chapter has made clear, Christians accepted much material from the Jewish literature, particularly that of Alexandrian origin. We may close this survey with an indicative passage. In the commentary on Daniel, Jerome cites Tertullian for the thought that Alexander had chosen Alexandria as his seat of power (Tert. *Adv. Jud.* § 8 = Jerome *Comm. Dan.* 3.9.24, *CCSL* 75a.882). The remark occurs in a parenthetical sentence within a longer computation of the Advent of Christ. On the list of monarchs and their regnal years, Tertullian says of Alexander that, "he had ruled over both the Medes and the Persians, after he had conquered them, and had established his rule in Alexandria, calling it after his own name," *qui et Medis et Persis regnaverat quos devicerat et in Alexandria regnum suum firmaverat quando et nomine suo eam appellavit*.

After Alexander's reign followed in Tertullian and Jerome's Danielic commentary a sequence of Ptolemaic rulers down to Cleopatra and the Roman conquest of Egypt under Augustus. All other Hellenistic dynasties are excluded from the list. No Seleucids or Antiochus IV. The representation of history makes Persian rule pass to Macedon (and from Alexander to "Alexandria" and the Ptolemies) and then to Rome, reflecting the widespread Christian interpretation of Daniel's *translatio imperii*. One might imagine that the Ptolemies and the Romans would have been delighted to see their political program so successfully implemented in later antiquity.

The lists' relationship between long-term monarchy and short-term world-conquest is noteworthy. Tertullian evidently accepted the idea of Alexander as a precursor to the Ptolemaic dynasty (Fraser 1996: 201). He also appreciated the tales of the foundation of the city, for which most authors held Alexander directly responsible. Alexander's empire was Alexandrian, at least to the writers like Tertullian, who lived nearby in one of the Empire's other important cities. Incidentally, the idea that Alexander lived and reigned in prosperous Alexandria is also articulated by the author of the Greek *Alexander Romance* (3.35.1). In his eulogy over Alexander, he stresses that Alexander lived in peace, freedom from care, and merriment, εἰρήνῃ καὶ ἀμεριμνίᾳ καὶ εὐφροσύνῃ, towards the end of the reign, presumably in Alexandria.

For modern minds, it may seem curious that Alexander should have been a founder of anything, whether a state or a dynasty (Ogden 2011: 79). By modern accounts, the king's campaigns signify destruction above all else. Killing is the key point of the original Danielic prophecies. Alexander's life was a brief period of oppression, which the chronicler of 1 Maccabees knew. In this chapter, we have witnessed how Christians renegotiated that balance between Alexander's short- and long-term impact.

4

History and Rhetoric

Introduction

In *The Triumph of Time*, Mogens Herman Hansen sums up the Christian vision of history: "Christian chronology sees the world as going from a starting-point, the Creation, through a high-point, Christ's life and resurrection, to a finish-point, Doomsday. [...] It is intended as universal and not limited to any particular society" (Hansen 2002: 45).

The first statement may remind readers of the adage that the Hebrews saw time as a straight line, whereas the Greeks had a cyclical view of history. While scholars have moderated that view (Momigliano 1977: 182), Hansen is right to emphasize those high points of history. Christians were much concerned with history, because it mattered to them that the world was created at a certain point in time, that Jesus had entered the world at a specific moment, and that the world would someday come to an end. For example, Christians argued that the imperial peace of Rome, the *Pax Romana*, had only come about in the reign of Augustus because the advent of Jesus Christ coincided with Augustus' tenure on the throne. Indeed, some Christians said that Augustus had abolished the Roman Republic, the rule of many, inspired by Christian monotheism (Origen *C. Cels.* 2.30; Euseb. *Hist. eccl.* 4.26; *Praep. evang.* 1.4.2–4). Historical events were connected on a deeper level. Scholars refer to this as "historical typology," a method with which one could establish meaningful correspondences between events (Williams 2011: 280). As we saw in the previous chapter, through the prophets the Christians had assurance in God's own word that these events either had happened or would come to pass. By divine ordinance, Alexander's empire was singled out as one of those high points in the *Weltreichsschema*.

Hansen's second point on universality reflects one of the great successes of Christian historiography, namely, its claim to impartiality. Presenting universalism as a counterpoint to a classical historiography that was concerned with national or local histories, Christians could argue that they were better informed about the world than the opposition. The claim requires some qualification. In the fifth century BC, the Ionian Herodotus would have opposed the idea that his account of the Persian Wars was limited to a single society and, already in the fourth, Ephorus of Cyme appears to have invented a universalist approach to history. But Christians regarded God's providence to apply to all societies, although the most we hear of are those that were thought important for Hebrew and Christian origins. The *Weltreichsschema* offers a good example with its set of kingdoms that matter. Great and well-known civilizations like Egypt do not feature; priority is given to other cultures which were world-changing on a grand scale.

As a result of the synchronism, Alexander filled a role in Christian assertions of cultural priority and, indeed, primacy. To take a better-known example, the church—and the Hellenistic synagogue before it—argued for the priority of Old Testament Scripture over the philosophy contained in Greek prose and poetry. The result is a tenuous argument, elegantly expressed by Henry Chadwick, "Moses and the prophets could be proved to be earlier than the Greek philosophers and poets, and therefore must have been the sources of their learning, so that all the mysteries of Greek philosophy are to be found expressed, even if obscurely, in the Pentateuch" (Chadwick 1965: ix). Proving such precedence required computations with fixed points in history. Alexander may not have mattered as much as Moses but, as we have already seen, the method of dating events from the time of Alexander was a feature of much cultural discourse, as in the Septuagint legend. This method of dating was taken over from classical models. According to Quintilian, a first-century AD teacher of rhetoric in Rome, one could refer to different periods by general statements, such as "now," "formerly," "under Alexander," or "during the siege of Troy" (Quint. *Inst.* 5.10.42). The mention of Alexander shows that his era was readily familiar. The times of Philip, Alexander, and the Successors constitute distinct periods for Diodorus in his *Library of History* (Diod. Sic. 1.3.3). Unlike Alexander's father, who gave his name to Pompeius Trogus' *Philippic History*, Alexander did not receive his own world history. Arrian wrote an *Events after Alexander*, based on previous models of Greek historiography concerning Persian kings, such as Darius I.

References to Alexander in a chronological context are a common occurrence. They appear in apologetic literature with such frequency that it would be impractical and repetitive to account for every single occurrence. We may separate the references into three distinct groups:

1. **Periodization.** One example occurs in Methodius of Olympus, who claims, on the authority of Josephus, that the Temple had been sacked six times

(Methodius *Res.* § 28). In his summary of the past periods, he makes reference to Babylon, Persia, Macedon, and Rome. He thus follows the *Weltreichsschema* and its organization of history.

2. **Specific time** (as in Quintilian). For example, Tatian dates the flourishing of Berossus, a Babylonian historian, to the reign of Alexander (Tatian *Ad. Gr.* § 36). Moreover, the first book of the *Miscellany* of Clement of Alexandria provides innumerable references of the same kind.
3. **Lists of rulers.** For instance, Clement of Alexandria preserves a list of post-Persian rulers (*Strom.* 1.21.128.3). Alexander features first, though Clement is wrong to note that he ruled for 18 years, δεκαοκτώ. Later in the same work, he provides the more widely accepted number of regnal years, 12, with a reference to Eratosthenes' chronologies (*FGrH/BNJ* 241 F1a Pownall via Clement *Strom.* 1.21.138.1–3), and we note that 1 Maccabees maintains the same number.

Examples of these groupings appear frequently in Christian discussions of chronology. Apologists found themselves using chronological arguments in many genres, such as "letters, dialogs, appeals to the emperor, protreptic tracts, point-by-point refutations and epideictic orations incorporated under the apologetic rubric" (Johnson 2006: 5). Communicating a Christianized version of the past was essential for converting outsiders and maintaining that the Christian view of the world was the correct one. Christian chronographic efforts not only supported the underlying plot of the Biblical drama, but also accommodated the Christian hopes for the future. The stakes were high when reconstructing history.

The following case studies display the diversity of Christian experiments with history. They show that Alexander's integration into the Christian past was by no means a straightforward or static process, because Christians had to make a choice of what material to use for their exposition. Since Alexander-related material came from both classical and Jewish backgrounds, the possibilities for combination were practically endless. Moreover, the histories had to complement the exegetical activity and strengthen the apologetic arguments that Christians were making. Christians took different approaches, and the results are intriguing. Christian historiography offers us an even clearer picture of what we have seen in Chapters 2 and 3. We shall review some of the same patterns we have seen before, but in new and subtle forms. The historiography presented here is important because it was the one that most Christians would encounter. We often stress the importance of the *Alexander Romance* in its Christian guise from the beta recension onward (*c.* AD 500), but Christians were much more concerned with chronicling. That conclusion presents itself, not only in terms of sheer number of chronicles, but also in the greater number of manuscripts of each such works. While large-scale monographs on Alexander ceased to be produced, save for the reworkings of the *Alexander Romance*, epitomizing his history continued precisely because that was the fashion in which Christians and non-Christians worked in later antiquity. The complete integration of the past into a Christian historical stream thus had a profound, if hitherto unappreciated, effect on the Alexander tradition. In the same breath, we may say that the culminating method of writing history from Eusebius onward also impacted all subsequent chronicling until the modern age.

Adventures in apologetic historiography

Julius Africanus

In the Severan period, under either Elagabalus or Alexander Severus, Julius Africanus wrote two historiographical works in which Alexander occasionally appears. Both works are fragmentary, preserved by later writers who cited them. Because of Africanus' popularity with later chroniclers, we tend to forget his importance as the first Christian historian to engage with previous non-Christian histories. What remains of his writings offers important testimonies to Alexander's role in the Christian revision of history in the early third century. The fragments betray an Alexandrian influence, naming Alexander as the "founder", *ktistēs*, in multiple instances, although it is not clear whether that term comes from Africanus himself or the text preserving the fragment. We have already noticed how successfully Ptolemaic literature influenced the North African church, and so it is no surprise that another Christian intellectual with a North African connection used the material to great effect.

Africanus' *Chronography* presents us with numerous lists of important people and places. Alexander features on the list of Macedonian kings (Jul. Afr. *Chron.* F 82, *GCS* NF 15.245–249). Africanus provides more detail on him than on any other Macedonian king, saying that Alexander reigned for thirteen years (cf. *Chron. Oxy. FGrH/BNJ* 255 F9 Rzepka), controlled every kingdom and ruled as the *ktistēs* of Alexandria. Upon his death the kingdom fell into the hands of his governors, while Alexander's brother Philip III emerged as the Macedonian king. We find no mention of other events on this list, just a list of the line of Macedonian kings. In his view, Macedon's timeline began with the reign of the mythological Caranus (r. c. 808–778 BC) and ended with Perseus, the 39th ruler of Macedon.

More strikingly, Alexander appears in the king-lists of other peoples. For example, he features at the end of the list of Persian kings. The Macedonian king (once again referred to as *ktistēs*) slew Darius and transferred the Persian royal power to Macedon (F 73, *GCS* NF 15.225–229). The remark reinforces the notion of *translatio imperii*. Elsewhere, on a list of Olympiad victors, Africanus states that Alexander captured Babylon and killed Darius. After Alexander's death his empire was divided and Ptolemy became king of Egypt and Alexandria (F 65, *GCS* NF 15.206–207). The association between Alexander and Ptolemy runs strong throughout the work, emphasizing the link between the founder and his successor in the Ptolemaic dynasty. In another fragment, the author stresses that the Jews enjoyed a period of peace under Alexander and subsequent Ptolemies until the days of the wicked High Priest Onias in the mid-second century BC under Ptolemy VI Philometor and Ptolemy VII Euergetes II (F 84, *GCS* NF 15.252–253). The last fragment depends on the narrative in Josephus, whom Africanus mentions that he is using. The Jewish peace comes from the narrative of the *Jewish Antiquities* that records exactly how the Jews fell out of favor with the Hellenistic kings, a decline culminating in the rise of Antiochus IV (12.154–241).

While the work offers a great compilation of authoritative lists, annotated selectively with the facts that Julius Africanus found important, we must remember his ultimate aim. He made synchronisms of the Greco-Roman and Biblical events to ascertain the time of the Apocalypse. To this end, he incorporated the theory taken from Genesis 1:31–2:4 that it had taken God six days to create the world and it would therefore last 6000 years. By computation with other Old Testament material, such as the seventy weeks before the first arrival of the Messiah in Daniel 9:24–27, he dated the age of the world to be 5500 years old when Jesus was born. Since we know that Julius Africanus wrote his work in 220/221 during the reign of Elagabalus—the last Roman emperor on his list—there were only 279 years left before the Second Coming. The end was only relatively nigh. In this framework, Alexander marks an important high point as a marker of change for the Greeks and the Jews.

Pseudo-Hippolytus

The so-called *Collection of Chronologies*, *Synagōge chronōn*, exists in fragments. Completed in AD 235 under Alexander Severus, the text has been attributed to Hippolytus of Rome, by no means a certain attribution. The text survives partially in Greek, but completely in Latin and Armenian translations. There were later revisions of the work, for example, the *Greek Chronicle of 334* (pp. 80–129 Frick).

According to a major study of ancient chronicle writing, the *Chronologies* served as a pedagogical handbook for the study of the Old Testament, especially the ethnographic and geographic dispersion of the nations after Noah and the Flood (Gen. 10 with Burgess and Kulikowski 2013: 117–119). The catechism-like nature of the text sets it apart from the works addressing matters relating to the Old Testament, for it had a specific audience and purpose in providing instruction. We know of many other memory lists, such as the *Liber Memorialis* of Lucius Ampelius, and the rhetorical schools also made students write lists of important data to remember. The *Collection of Chronologies* thus fills a need for understanding the Biblical world. Being a Biblical chronology, it contained an assorted variety of material that concerned the Hebrews, the duration of the world (also 6000 years as in Africanus) and shorter histories of different peoples with which the Hebrews came into contact. The text does not make for pleasant reading, but provides useful information structured around lists of important events.

Pseudo-Hippolytus lists non-Hebrew kingdoms matter-of-factly in the table of contents: Persian kings from Cyrus and how long they reigned; Macedonian kings from Alexander; and Roman emperors from Caesar Augustus (Ps.-Hippolytus *Chron.* §§ 9, 17, 18, *GCS* NF 46.6–7). Again, we note that the Persians were taken over by Alexander, and the Macedonians by the Romans. The reader had to know these empires from the Old Testament and New Testament (Luke 2:1). After the table of contents, Alexander first appears when the author computes the chronology of the Persian kings. The entry for Darius says that he reigned seven years until Alexander crushed him at the battle of Arbela (Ps.-Hippolytus *Chron.* § 715, *GCS* NF 46.122–123). In such a concise entry, the geographical detail demands the attention of the Alexander historian. Arbela was an important Achaemenid city in what is today northern Iraq near the river Khazir, to which Darius fled after his defeat (Curt. 5.1.3). Arbela was, however, not the site of the actual battle, as Strabo, Plutarch, and Arrian take pains to tell us (Str. 16.1.3; Plut. *Alex.* 31.6; Arr. *Anab.* 6.11.5 citing Aristobulus *FGrH/BNJ* 139 F6 Pownall and Ptolemy *FGrH/BNJ* 138 F10 Howe). They insist that the Macedonians fought the decisive battle on the nearby plain of Gaugamela (Tell Gomel), and they are probably correct. The misconception of the battle's location began already with Callisthenes (*FGrH/BNJ* 124 F14a via Str. 17.1.43), but both Strabo and Plutarch blame the Macedonians themselves for the confusion, since the army historians had associated the battle with the central city rather than the unimportant hamlet at Gaugamela. When the Christian chronicler mentions "Arbela" then, he makes use of popular tradition, not the corrected view. We need not chastise him too much for doing so, because most of our other sources did the same, including the military handbooks (Frontin. *Str.* 2.3.19; cf. Polyaenus *Strat.* 4.3.6; Ael. *VH.* 3.23).

Pseudo-Hippolytus does not provide any further details, but inserts a longer synchronism in which he omits Persia. He computes the further high points by using the Greek system of dating by Olympiads, a cycle that began with the first Olympic games. The biggest event in the Greek world was instituted by Iphitus, king of Elis in the Peloponnese, when he restored the games at the sanctuary of Olympia after the Dorian invasion (legendary date: 776 BC). The chronicler notes that there were 114 Olympiads, that is 456 years, from Iphitus to Alexander; from Alexander to the birth of Jesus Christ, 80 Olympiads, that is 320 years; from Christ to Alexander Severus, 58 Olympiads, that is 232 years (Ps.-Hippolytus *Chron.* § 717, *GCS* NF 46.123). The author thus stresses different high points in the past than a non-Christian would, but the regular Greek dating system gives the impression that we are reading any other work on historical chronology. The synchronism makes the Christian claim that Jesus marked a high point as Alexander and the current Roman emperor had done. After the Greek computation, many others follow. They concern Hebrew affairs (the names of Hebrew patriarchs, the prophets, female prophets, Hebrew kings, and the High Priests) after which the author lists the "Macedonian" kings (§§ 742–756, *GCS* NF 46.136–138). They begin with Alexander and end with Ptolemy XII Auletes (*d.* 51 BC). The author abbreviated the list of Macedonian kings considerably compared to his predecessor Julius Africanus. For Julius, Caranus was the first ruler of Macedon, whereas for Pseudo-Hippolytus, Alexander was the first Macedonian king. Pseudo-Hippolytus did not need to worry about the previous rulers of Macedon, for Macedon did apparently not matter to the Biblical Hebrews until Alexander.

After Alexander, the Macedonian list focuses exclusively on the Ptolemaic kings and Alexandria. The list jumps directly from Alexandria to the Roman emperors from Caesar Augustus onward. Either some information has fallen out or the author may have wished to posit that there was imperial equilibrium between the two great centers of Christianity. Again, we notice the Alexandrian pattern prioritizing the Ptolemies at the expense of all the other Successor dynasties. While Julius Africanus used the chronological system, he still gave priority to Alexandrian sources. It follows that Christian chronographers appreciated the imperial connections between the two cities from early on. This tendency did not stop in the third century. We turn next to early Christian Antioch for a different perspective on the Alexandrography of Rome and Alexandria.

Antiochene chronography

Founded by Seleucus I, Antioch on the Orontes River was presented by a local as the first city in the Roman Empire upon which the rays of the sun fell (Lib. *Or.* 11.16). The vibrant city housed many religious communities. For instance, we first hear of "Christians" in this city (Acts 11:26; cf. Ign. *Magn.* 10.1–4, *Rom.* 3.3; *Phld.* 6.1), perhaps defined to distinguish them from the great community of Antiochene Jews. Religious interaction seems to have been the norm. The Apostles Paul, Peter, and Barnabas spent significant time in missionary activity at the city. The seventh bishop of Antioch, Theophilus, wrote three books of apologetic argument to the pagan Autolycus in the time of Marcus Aurelius. We do not know whether Autolycus converted to Christianity as a result of reading the work, but the Christian community did grow rapidly, as many converted. Early Christian Antioch thus takes a spot in the triptych of great imperial cities, along with Alexandria and Rome, in which Christianity took shape.

We find important comparanda for the "Alexandrian" histories in Antiochene literature. For example, Theophilus' work holds much of interest for the chronographer, especially in Book 3. From Chapter 17, Theophilus engages in a regular war of words on the topic of chronography with non-Christians. He claims the following: only Christians know the truth from the prophets (§ 17); the Greeks had erroneously dated the fables of great floods, Moses gave the only historical example when he spoke of Noah's ark (§§ 18–19); Moses was more ancient than the Egyptians (§ 20); Manetho, the fourth-century chronicler from Egypt, was wrong in assuming the antiquity of the Egyptians (§ 21); the date of Solomon's Temple in Jerusalem was before the mythic kings of Argos (§ 22); even the prophets were more ancient than Greek writers (§ 23); the chronology of the Hebrews from Adam, the first man, proves that they are the most ancient people (§§ 24–25); Hebrew Scripture was truer than the Greek historians (§ 26); and Hebrew antiquity surpassed Roman antiquity (§ 27). The arguments Theophilus rehearses read as standard apologetic of the age. When he summarizes the epochs of history, he does so on the basis of previously mentioned high points, ending with the years from Cyrus of Persia to Emperor Lucius Verus. None of the eras he has mentioned feature Alexander. But then Theophilus does not mention Jesus as a high point of history either, for his argument deals with the Hebrew patriarchs' relation to the Greeks and the Romans. Theophilus is not concerned with something so late as Hellenistic history, nor is he writing history for the sake of it. Therefore, we need not read too much into the absence of Alexander, though it does stand out when we consider the other apologetic writings of the period.

Alexander does return in Antiochene chronography proper, although we are faced with problematic testimonies. The *CHAP* database of ancient historians reveals that at least three different Antiochene chroniclers wrote works relevant to our purposes: (1) Clement of Antioch, a second century chronicler; (2) Bottius, also possibly active as early as the second century, but probably later; and (3) Domninus, writing under Diocletian. The first and third are thought to have written accounts, now lost, recounting history from Creation to their own times, and so they must have made reference to Alexander in some form. Domninus seems to have written approvingly of Diocletian, the greatest persecutor of the church, and so he was probably not a Christian. John Malalas, a sixth-century chronicler of questionable reliability, refers to Bottius in his account of Alexander history. It is unclear how long the fragment of Bottius is but even in the shortest form, it contains much of interest. Malalas says of Alexander that:

> ... he defeated Darius emperor of the Persians, the son of Assalam, and captured him, all his empire, all the land of the Assyrians, Medes, Parthians, Babylonians and Persians and all the empires on earth, as the most learned Bottius has written. Alexander freed the cities and territories and all the land of the Romans, Hellenes and Egyptians from subjection and slavery to Assyrians, Persians, Parthians and Medes; he restored to the Romans all that they had lost.
> Malalas *Chron.* 8.1, 193 (citing Bottius *FRH* 98 F1, trans. Jeffreys et al.)

This treatment of Alexander corresponds to that of an anonymous chronographer from Alexandria. His text survives in a later Latin translation known to us as *Excerpta Latini Barbari* since the great Renaissance philologist J. J. Scaliger (1606) gave it that moniker (Garstad 2011). The original Greek text of the *Excerpta Latina Barbari* was collated in late fifth-century Alexandria or, perhaps, slightly later. It was originally a lavish compendium with many images of the historical episodes. These illustrations are now lost. The compiler of the work brought together material from as early as the Severan Julius Africanus (Burgess 2013). He arranged the data to recount a Christianized version of world history. Beginning with the Biblical figures (Adam, Abraham, Moses) and the dispersion of people around the world after Noah's flood, the text turns briefly to the rise of the early Roman kings. After them, God granted universal rule to the Assyrians embodied by the Chaldeans and, later, the Persians and the Medes. Their rule passed to Alexander when God raised him up to fight against them (*Excerpta Latina Barbari* 1.6.6 Garstad with Garstad 2016b). Alexander acts as God's instrument as he proceeds to conquer Assyria, Persia, and Media. The king frees the lands of Rome, Greece, and Egypt from Chaldean slavery and bestows laws upon the entire world.

Bottius' remarks correspond not only with what we found in Christian readings of Daniel (Chapter 3), but also with the story of Alexander's circuit of the Mediterranean in the *Alexander Romance*. Alexander spends much time in the western Mediterranean before he goes east to face Darius and then briefly doubles back to sack Thebes in Greece (*AR* 1.26–46). Garstad (2018) argues that the liberation of Greeks, Romans, and Egyptians fits well with how an imperial Alexandrian author would have conceived of Alexander's history. He makes a case for the third century AD for such a route-making, which is not implausible. If we accept the dating, it is intriguing to observe the immediate influence of the *Alexander Romance* on Christian historiography. But Bottius and the *Excerpta Latina Barbari* represent problems. For instance, the former is a shadowy historian, variously dated between the early third and the late fourth centuries AD (comm. *FRH ad loc*). Scholars rely solely on Malalas—he is the only testimony to Bottius' work—and they currently consider that attribution dubious, noting that the name of "Bottius" seems inspired by Zeus Bottius, the principal deity of Antioch (Garstad 2016a). As far as we can tell, none of the other authors under scrutiny follows the route Bottius attributes to Alexander, although they may be influenced by the *Alexander Romance* in other ways.

Arnobius of Sicca and Orosius

From Antioch, we skip to North Africa and Sicca (modern El Kef), a town in the vicinity of Carthage. Here, we find a different strategy of apologetic chronology in the polemic of Arnobius Afer. A recent convert, he wrote seven books of apologetic to distance himself from his previous convictions of paganism and to declare himself a true Christian. One purpose of the work was to respond to an important criticism. Christians were accused of bringing about great misery and misfortune for the Roman Empire because they refused to worship the Roman gods. Non-Christian critics believed that their gods had abandoned Rome because of the "atheist" Christians. The premise of the Christian counterargument rested upon the fact that calamities on an equal, or greater, scale had troubled Rome even before the Christian religion came about. This notion, in turn, supported the argument that Christians could not be held directly responsible for the present sufferings. Arnobius' disregard for the "distant" past may surprise readers because, in previous apologetic arguments, Christians such as Theophilus of Antioch took pains to assert that Christianity was not new but ancient in its

Hebrew roots. God and the proto-Christian religion had influenced everything since Creation.

Arnobius, however, took issue with that past to represent the present as an improvement brought about by the coming of Christ. In the pertinent passage at the beginning of the work, he makes reference to the terrible fates of previous societies. He alludes to the fall of Atlantis (Plato); the battles between the Assyrians and Bactrians (Ninus versus Zoroaster); the Trojan war; Xerxes' invasion of Greece; Alexander's conquest of the Orient; and the Romans' fight for world domination (Arnobius *Or.* 1.5). Arnobius' bundling together of wars from myth and history conveys the immensity of past havoc. To suit his purpose of representing a bleak past, he projects Alexander's campaign as an evil. He posits that the conquest of Persia was a quest to enslave the East, prompted by the ambitions of an unnamed young king of Macedon, *ut ex Macedoniae finibus unus exortus adolescens Orientis regna et populos captivitate ac servitio subiugaret, nos fecimus atque excitavimus causas?* Arnobius asks rhetorically whether it is fair that the Christians should take responsibility for Alexander's short-lived enterprise. It would be an egregious anachronism to say that the Christians had blood on their hands from Alexander's conquests. And so, we must assume that Arnobius came away with a cheap point on the scoreboard.

Although scholarship has been aware of the passage since at least the late nineteenth century (Carraroli 1892: 145), the passing remark on Alexander has not generated much interest. It may appear too succinct for great exposition. One scholar noted that Arnobius represents Alexander in this way because the Christians despised his world empire (Wirth 1993: 60 n. 189), but the local context surely determines how we need to read Alexander's campaign. The representation of an atrocious past, not an exemplary one, prompted Arnobius to present Alexander, and the other events, unfavorably. Perhaps a better approach is to see Arnobius' work in light of the other apologetic histories under review in this chapter. In this company, he is an outlier who, by his negative example, confirms the general tendency to generate less pessimistic impressions of the remote past. After all, others believed that God had orchestrated that past for a purpose.

Scholars usually date Arnobius' polemic to the Diocletianic persecution of the early fourth century, but the argument Arnobius makes remains relevant for the entire pre-Constantinian period. More surprisingly, the context of the work, and the line of argument pursued by Arnobius, exhibit a striking resemblance to *The Seven Books of History Against the Pagans* by Paulus Orosius (*c.* 416/7). For example, both works fill seven books. Both writers responded directly to contemporary criticism of Christianity. They tried to connect the fate of Rome with Christianity. They both sought to represent pre-Christian times negatively in order to emphasize the security and stability of the Roman present. As opposed to their critics, they claimed that the present world had not (yet) been destroyed, thanks to Christian prayer. While Arnobius defended Christianity in the face of persecution, Orosius acquitted Christians of the charge of responsibility for Alaric's devastating sack of Rome in 410. In both cases, the author responds to pagan intellectuals who had charged the Christians with the crime of introducing a new god to Rome that had forced the old gods to abandon the city. Rome was supposed to have collapsed without its deities, and the citizens suffered the consequences. The pagans' strategy was to emphasize the glory and greatness of an exemplary past free of Christianity; to this end, treasured classical characters, such as Alexander, served as figures of power and of virtue. Orosius sought to overturn that view to vindicate Christianity. Instead, he highlighted the atrocities of human history, such as natural disasters and military conflict. Given the magnitude of Rome's catastrophic defeat, Orosius had to turn Alexander into one of the most destructive and monstrous monarchs from the pre-Constantinian period (3.16–20). Alexander's Successors were but lion cubs compared to him (3.23.6).

Orosius' long digression on Alexander invites us to reconsider the short remark in Arnobius. The latter emphasizes two traditional *topoi*: youth (cf. Curt. 10.5.26) and enslavement (cf. Sen. *Ep.* 94.62). The first does not appear as a criticism in Orosius. The *topos* of youth was ambiguous. One Roman historian could claim that Alexander's youth was a weakness in comparison to Rome's ostensible "800 years of military experience" (Livy 9.18.9); another referred to Alexander's youth and beauty in a eulogy of the deceased general, Germanicus, who had died before he was thirty years old (Tac. *Ann.* 2.73; cf. *It. Alex.* § 6). The second *topos*, enslavement, crops up throughout Orosius' account of Alexander's campaign, in regard to Thebes (3.16.1–2), Persia (3.17.4), Asia Minor and Egypt (3.17.9), and Greece (3.18.1). *Topoi* like these could be liberally applied to narratives as building-blocks, which could be imbued with specific meaning and deployed to help construct a certain representation of the past that the author sought to create. That Arnobius and Orosius shaped the building-blocks of *exempla* in the way they did cannot surprise us when we recall that their aim was to vindicate the Christian present at the expense of the past their opponents held to be exemplary. For that, the Christian authors chose to undermine the Roman literary tradition by turning it against itself.

Orosius' weighty claims upon our attention need to detain us for some space. It would be too tedious to summarize every detail of his account, but it is beneficial to chart the key *exempla*, divided into positive and negative features. My purpose in doing so is to show how Orosius utilizes *loci* to create a certain image of the king. We begin with a few highlights of Alexander's military glory:

- The Macedonians show spirit and courage in war.
- 3.16.4. Alexander shows martial skill and courage (cf. Curt. 3.6.17–20).
- 3.16.5. The army has an amazing swiftness.
- 4.1.13. Because so few of Alexander's soldiers died in battle, the admiration and fear of his prowess grew.
- 6.21.19–20. The glory of Alexander was reborn in Julius Caesar, as suppliants came to the Roman ruler from everywhere.

Orosius bundles the seemingly favorable remarks together at the beginning of the narrative, representing Alexander as a great warrior in command of his justly famous army. The reference to Julius Caesar makes Alexander seem a precursor of Roman military might. But this was not meant as a compliment. Indeed, Orosius gives the impression that warfare was all Alexander was good at. Orosius stresses the military aspect in the beginning of the digression because it reinforces and anticipates what the historian is eventually going to criticize, namely the king's warmongering. The Christian historian condemns the king's atrocities:

- 3.7.5. Alexander, whom Orosius mockingly calls "the Great," was born in the year of Rome's first treaty with Carthage (348 BC). His coming foreshadowed a maelstrom of suffering and an ill wind for the East.
- 3.15.1. Philip and Alexander brought great afflictions upon the world.
- 3.16.3. Alexander killed all his male relations in order to claim the throne of Macedon.
- 3.16.8. Both Alexander and Darius were wounded in the battle of Issus. Normally, historians record that Alexander suffered no injuries in this battle.
- 3.16.12–13. Alexander had an insatiable lust for conquest. At the oracle of Ammon, the priests were forced to tell him what he wanted.
- 3.16.14. On the way back from the oracle, Alexander founded Alexandria on the way to battle with Darius' forces.
- 3.17.5. Alexander spent 34 days cataloging the spoils of war, after which he plundered Persepolis for more wealth.
- 3.17.7. Contrary to all other sources on the subject, Orosius considers the burial of Darius an empty gesture of pity. Alexander kept the Persian royal family in cruel captivity.

- 3.17.8–9. Orosius finds it difficult to speak of so much evil. During Alexander's campaigns, so many men died, so many cities were sacked, and their inhabitants were enslaved.
- 3.18.8–10. Orosius recounts the deaths of central Macedonian personnel (Amyntas, Parmenio, Philotas, and Clitus the Black). Alexander murdered Clitus at a banquet for no reason.
- 3.18.11. Besides these men many more suffered death because they would not honor Alexander as a god, including Callisthenes. Alexander's lust for blood knew no limits (cf. Sen. *Clem.* 1.25).
- 3.20.3. The world feared Alexander so much that suppliants came to him from places that could hardly have known his name.
- 3.20.4. A poisonous draught finally quenched the king's thirst (for blood).
- 3.20.9. Alexander was nothing but a fugitive thief. He plundered a corner of the world (Asia).
- 3.20.12–13. Orosius compares the evils of Alexander and the Romans. Unsurprisingly, he finds Alexander's actions worse than Orosius' present suffering.
- 3.23.6. Like a lion, Alexander crushed a world that cowered in fear. His Successors were mere lion cubs next to him.
- 3.23.14. Alexander's Exiles Decree caused the Successor wars of the Hellenistic age.

In short, Alexander's life and legacy was comprised of nothing but war. To create this impression, Orosius reworked Justin's *Epitome* of Pompeius Trogus' *Philippic History*. Verbatim citations of Justin's text inform us that Orosius abridged the epitome rather than the original text from the Augustan age. His reworking eliminates many of Justin's positive remarks on Alexander, which Justin, in turn, had taken from Pompeius Trogus. For instance, in Orosius, the kind treatment of Darius' family is reversed (cf. Just. 11.9.11–16), and the story of Philip the Doctor, who miraculously cured the king, is omitted (Oros. 3.16.5). The latter symbolizes Alexander's trust in his friends, which Orosius did not stress. Silences are also indicative of method. In both Justin and Orosius, Alexander's excessive consumption of alcohol is absent, despite the remarks on Clitus' death. Alexander's heavy drinking would be an obvious vice to attack, but both writers remain silent on the matter. Another underused *topos* in Justin is Fortune, which does not feature in Orosius either. Orosius does not follow Justin in all respects, then. The English translator of Orosius makes the observation that Orosius does not always seize the opportunity to attack Alexander when Justin's account would have allowed him to (Fears 2010: 134 n. 120). For instance, Fears points out that Orosius does not mention Alexander's developing arrogance that came about after the visit to Siwah, which Justin does. But this is to misunderstand the key difference between Justin and Orosius in terms of Alexander's character development. Justin's Alexander represents an all-powerful world ruler, who developed into a tyrant when he came into contact with the luxury of the East. Orosius' Alexander did not change, however, but was wholly evil from beginning to end. His reign of terror proved consistently terrible because Orosius had to make it fit with the overarching representation of the pre-Christian past. That past had to appear much worse than the present and so it did.

In my view, *exemplum* literature and literary context give us the best model for explaining Orosius' sustained criticism of Alexander. Orosius was a moralizing Christian and was, therefore, selective in his historiography, as Van Nuffelen has argued (Van Nuffelen 2012: 9–15). I voice these views because Alexander-related scholarship that ventures so deep into later antiquity has previously proposed other models of interpretation. For more than a century (Eicke 1909: 88–89), Orosius' Alexander has been conceived of as the fulfillment of Stoic criticisms of the king. Scholars have pointed to the similarity of Orosius' work with those of Seneca (*Ben.* 1.13) and Lucan (10.21), who take Alexander for a pirate or a brigand (Cic. *Rep.* 3.24; cf. Curt. 7.8.19; August. *De Civ. D.* 4.4). For instance, Eicke found four linguistic parallels between Orosius and Seneca. However, given the number of citations from Justin, it is fitting that Orosius excerpted material from other Roman writers as well, certainly those that formed the rhetorical curriculum in the urban schools. Moreover, it should be noted that Seneca's Alexander is also based on *exempla*, and inconsistently so. Like Cicero (Ortmann 1988), who was not completely immune to Stoicism, Seneca deploys Alexander in a variety of diverging contexts, sometimes even favorably (e.g., *Ep.* 53.10). That divergence also points to the idea that there was no fixed "Stoic" school of thought on Alexander, as is commonly accepted now (Asirvatham 2012). I would prefer to think differently of Orosius' handling of the Roman writers. He cited them selectively and with great care. His aim was not to construct a Stoic Alexander, if such a thing ever existed, but rather to create a hostile literary portrait by fusing together multiple existing Roman *exempla*. As an analogous example, we should not consider Curtius Rufus' *History of Alexander* part of an ostensible "Stoic" tradition just because the author criticizes Alexander's heavy drinking, which is also in Seneca, but not in the poet Lucan, who had a Stoic education.

Wirth, a proponent of the Stoic Alexander theory, makes two further arguments about the Christian nature of Orosius' work (Wirth 1993: 67 n. 221).

First, he refers to Orosius' history as "unique," *sui generis*, and, secondly, he claims that Orosius found much of import from Ambrose of Milan and Augustine of Hippo. Ambrose of Milan had passed "an opinion of condemnation," or *Verdammungsurteil*, of Alexander on to his student Augustine. From him, it passed to Orosius, who regularly interacted with Augustine while the latter was writing the *City of God* (published *c.* 426). Wirth's view seems to be in conflict with his overarching argument that there was no "Christian" Alexander tradition or continuity between texts. I do not believe that either standpoint is very compelling, nor do I agree with the "Stoic" reading of Orosius' Alexander. To take the *sui generis* argument first, Arnobius' *Against the Nations* attempts the same tactic as Orosius in representing the past, albeit briefly. As for the second point, I accept that there were common points of interest between Augustine and Orosius, the self-proclaimed "stray dog" of Augustine (Van Nuffelen 2012: 197–205). As far as Alexander historiography is concerned, however, the pair only has one story in common, namely the story about Alexander and the pirate, which they share with many previous Roman writers. Orosius had a free hand to rework his own selection of *exempla* to create a continuous account of Alexander history.

I have chosen to include Orosius, although he lies outside the chronological parameters of this study, for the sake of showing the continuity and discontinuity between periods. I have approached his work from a late antique perspective, even if Orosius has drawn more interest from scholars with an interest in the medieval period. Orosius made a huge impact on medieval historiography in the Latin West, as his work became the basic school-text of universal history. More than 240 manuscripts attest to that fact. For comparison, Arnobius' text is preserved in one manuscript (BnF Lat. 1661). Cary is one scholar who approached Orosius from the medieval direction. He too accepted the Stoic influence on Orosius and claimed that medieval Christians read Orosius' work as the historical supplement to the Biblical imagery of Daniel 7, which announces Alexander as the four-headed flying leopard monster. He argues that Orosius' Stoic plus Biblical "conception of Alexander was the first in the field. Already developed in Fulgentius and in St. Jerome, it established a prejudice that bore down all evidence favorable to Alexander and brought about his general condemnation" (Cary 1956: 141). I do not wish to enter a new minefield of medieval views on Alexander, but I do have a few reservations about Cary's statement. I do not think that the sentiment applies to Jerome or Orosius' predecessors for the following reasons:

1. There is no evidence for a collective condemnation of Alexander in early Christianity. The rhetoric of invective and panegyric licensed Christians to

pass various judgments on Alexander as they saw fit, and they did so without firm reference to the Bible. In fact, it is often not clear what the general attitude was within in a single author. Local context determined representations of Alexander, as we have seen, and will see, repeatedly.

2. In early Christian literature, there seems to be no clear connection between the historiographers and the commentators on the Biblical passages that ignited discussion of Alexander's achievements. In Chapter 3, we noticed that information about Alexander from historians' works was never used to help explicate Biblical passages, such as those in the Book of Daniel. In this chapter so far, we have noticed that no Christian historiographer has used the Danielic framework or imagery for explaining Alexander's place in the past. Orosius does not allude to any of the Old Testament prophecies about Alexander. Moreover, we noted that the commentators primarily interpreted the key passages in the Book of Daniel as positive toward Alexander, which does not cohere with the depiction in Orosius.

3. As already said, Jerome is not clear on how we should understand Alexander's deeds in the grand scheme of God's plan for the world. Jerome's commentaries frequently feature Alexander, more so than in any other Christian writer, but they do not give any indication of how we should view Alexander as a character. Jerome's aim was to clarify what the Bible could tell his readership of Alexander's purpose in the history of Providence, not to write a biography. By tracing a negative "prejudice" back to Jerome, Cary seems to be misled by his reading of the medieval authors who commented upon the same passages that Jerome did.

Lactantius' Sibyls

A Chaldean or a Hebrew prophetess (Clem. Al. *Protr.* 6.77.4; Paus. 10.12.9), the first Sibyl is said to have survived the flood in Noah's Ark (Nicanor *FGrH/BNJ* 146 F1a via Schol. *Phaedrus* 244b). Married to a son of Noah, her offspring dispersed across the globe. A list of ten Sibylline seers emerged from as early as the Roman polymath Marcus Terentius Varro (116–27 BC), though the number was not uncontested (1 in Heraclitus F92 = Plut. *de Pyth. Or.* 6, 397a; 3 at Paus. 10.12; 4 in Ael. *VH* 12.35). In her various guises, she embodied the best of both the Greek and Jewish worlds, as both recognized her divine inspiration. Christians took an early interest in the figure. She frequents Christian literature from as early as the second-century *Shepherd of Hermas*. Unfortunately, the corpus of Sibylline Oracles was long lost until its rediscovery by Renaissance scholars in the sixteenth century (Buitenwerf 2003: 6–64). Scholars have since invested much energy in editing the enigmatic utterances (e.g., Potter 1994; Lightfoot 2007). The fourteen books, a collection of her prophecies delivered in epic hexameter, contain material written between the second century BC and the seventh AD. The imprecise dating indicates just how uncertain we remain about the nature of the compositions in the collection.

The Sibyl is said to have prophesied the coming of Alexander and Jesus (*Suda*, s.v. Σ 361 Adler). The former is no surprise, given Alexander's association with various prophetic oracles, such as those at Delphi and Didyma. The Sibyl also plays a minor role in Alexander-related literature. For example, Strabo paraphrases Callisthenes when he says that Athenaïs of Erythrai had proclaimed Alexander's divine descent (Callisthenes *FGrH/BNJ* 124 F14a Rzepka via Str. 17.1.43). Strabo quotes Callisthenes in the fitting context of Alexander's visit to Siwah during which the priests hailed the king as the son of Zeus (Ammon). Strabo notes, however, that Callisthenes had exaggerated in dramatic fashion, προστραγῳδεῖ, by adding the utterances of oracles elsewhere, including that of the Sibyl. Although Strabo does not appreciate Callisthenes' flattery of the king, he provides important testimony to the Sibyl's association with Alexander from the very outset of Alexander historiography, indeed, from the king's very lifetime.

In the fourth century AD, Lactantius also connects the Sibyl with Alexander on the basis of a first-hand account by Nicanor (Lactant. *Div. Inst.* 1.6.8 citing Nicanor *FGrH/BNJ* 146 F1b Müller). Using Varro's famous list of ten Sibylline prophetesses in the *Divine Antiquities* (*c.* 40 BC), Lactantius posits that the first Sibyl was Persian. Varro, Lactantius asserts, had read that in the *Deeds of Alexander* by Nicanor (*res gestas Alexandri Macedonis*). Unfortunately, Nicanor's name was common in Macedon: we know at least twelve instances of it from Alexander's era (Heckel *Who's Who*: 176–178). Müller's *FGrH/BNJ* commentary summarizes most of the scholarship, tentatively suggesting that Nicanor the historian should be identified with the one from Stageira, who proclaimed Alexander's Exiles Decree at the Olympic Games of 324 BC. Whoever Nicanor was, three independent writers of later antiquity cited his work, and so we should not dismiss his existence outright. Lactantius' passing notice of Nicanor's work once again attests to the use of Alexander's time as a way of dating an event. In this case, it is the "earliest" mention of the first Sibyl, according to Varro and Lactantius.

Lactantius does not tell us much about what the Sibyl had said about Alexander. If we compare the fragment of Nicanor on the Sibyl's notice of Alexander with the fragment on the Sibyl surviving the Flood, we may presume that Lactantius too knew that Nicanor's history made notice of an oriental Sibyl, who had predicted the coming of Alexander at the time of the Biblical Noah (FF1a+b). Of course, from the Hellenistic perspective, there may not have been much difference between a Hebrew prophetess and a Chaldean/Persian seer (cf. the mythic confusion in Paus. 10.12). After all, the Sibyl was emblematic of "alien wisdom," as one scholar famously called it (Momigliano 1975). One seminal study of Alexander in the Sibylline Oracles (Gunderson 1977: 64–66), not mentioned in Müller's commentary, attempted to make the case that Nicanor was the source of the negative Persian prophecies in Books 3 and 11, discussed below (cf. Fraser 1972 i: 708–716). While Gunderson's observations seem sound at first glance, he himself admits that the hypothesis rests on the shaky evidence of two passing testimonies and his Alexander-centric readings of the prophecies. More recent scholarship on Books 3 and 11 does not make the link to Nicanor, but argue that Book 3 had roots in Hellenistic Judaism of second-century Near East, perhaps Egypt. Whether or not the Jewish author of the third book had read Nicanor, as Varro seems to have done, remains speculation.

Besides Gunderson's study, scholars of Alexander have paid little attention to the rich representations of the king in the Sibylline Oracles (Pfister 1979: 314; Stoneman 2008: 51). This is a shame because they tell us much about the negative use of the figure not only in Helleno-Jewish contexts outside the Alexandrian tradition, but also in the wider literary contexts of the Hellenistic world. In the third Sibylline Oracle, the author predicts the impending doom of Europe and Asia: the race of Cronus, bastards and slaves, will conquer Babylon and master every land under the sun. They shall perish because of their evil deeds, but their name shall survive among the much-wandering later generations, ὀψιγόνοισι πολυπλάγκτοισιν (3.381–387). The purple-clad man of no faith will come to pillage affluent Asia, a savage stranger to justice and fiery because the light of a thunderbolt had raised him up (388–391). Bearing a heavy yoke, the Asian lands shall imbibe much blood. But Hades will ensure that the man will disappear completely, πανάιστον (392–393). Biblical allegories of plants and horns embellish the historical content: the root left behind will be cut down (Alexander IV?) and ten horns will rise (the Successors?) from which the killer of the root (Cassander?) will plant a new shoot. He will, however, be killed by his own men before a new horn grows up (394–400 with Buitenwerf 2003: 227–229). Of course, it is our choice to read Alexander into this vague prophecy, but not many other suggestions have been made (Flusser 1972). That is not too surprising. As we have previously seen, the Macedonian conquest of Asia was an essential feature of Jewish prophecy. Alexander is also believed to appear elsewhere in

Sibylline prophecy (4.88–94, 5.6–7, 11.102–108, 11.195–219 Geffcken), and we will return to these oracles below.

Eusebius and Jerome

Eusebius' *Chronicle* grew out of the context of apologetic histories. The full title is *Epitome of Universal History of the Greeks and the Barbarians with Chronological Tables*. Eusebius completed the work around 311, but edited and republished it in its final form in 325, with minor modifications made in the following year (*CHAP* s.v. Eusebius; cf. Burgess and Kulikowski 2013: 123 n. 89). Unfortunately, the work suffered the same fate as Julius Africanus' historiography. The work was so often reworked that the original Greek version no longer survives, except in later quotations. Fortunately, however, Jerome translated and updated a part of it (*GCS* NF 47 Greek/Latin), and another adaptation survives in two eastern languages, Armenian (*GCS* NF 20) and Syriac (*CSCO* 5.5.77–105). Reconstructions of Eusebius' own copy, one that also was reworked multiple times, are therefore problematic.

Normally regarded as the background research for his celebrated *Church History* (Euseb. *Hist. eccl.* 1.1.7 with Johnson 2014: 89), the work offers much more than the average epitome. Eusebius divided it into two books: the first, the *Epitome*, consisted of long lists of kings, including the chronology of their reigns. The second, the *Chronological Tables*, offered a chronological overview of their exploits and related cultural events, such as the flourishing of certain authors; Demosthenes and Cicero, for instance. The innovative aspect of the second part was the organization of history into a coordinated system. The horizontal axis showed lists of kings and countries, and the vertical axis counted the number of years. The immediately comparable columns would have proved useful to ancient readers, and scholars have argued that Origen's six-columned scripture, the *Hexapla*, inspired this sort of formatting for Eusebius' history (Grafton and Williams 2006: 133–143). For instance, one glance at the text made clear to readers that Alexander had been born 1660 years after Abraham, the first Biblical patriarch. When faced with such numbers, one could not argue for the priority of Alexander over the Hebrews, which some non-Christians had done. The synchronism of Greek kings and Roman emperors with Old Testament and New Testament events makes a grand apologetic statement and represents a defining Christian trait of Eusebian historiography.

The innovative layout of the *Tables* charts an impressive universal chronology of empires (Chaldeans, Assyrians, Babylonians, Hebrews, Egyptians, Greeks and Macedonians, and, finally, Romans). This organization of the past departs significantly from Eusebius' idea of the four or five successive world empires articulated in other works, such as his exegesis. According to Johnson (2014: 88), the *Tables* had at least three major effects on the representation of ancient history. First, the separate national histories were synthesized into "a single, massive world-historical stream" (Johnson *id*.), that foregrounded the Hebrew patriarchs by using a dating system beginning with the birth of Abraham. Secondly, the many columns were gradually consolidated into one that focused on Rome (omitting the Goths, Ethiopians, Indians, Persians, and Parthians). Thirdly, the close proximity of Rome to Eusebius' Christian column says something important about his imperial vision. The implicit claim of the chronological tabulation in Eusebius' *Chronicle* is that God's Providence has steadily guided the history of humankind from the Hebrew patriarchs up until the apex that was Eusebius' contemporary Rome. The eternal city had grown with Christianity, as Jerusalem had for the Jews.

Not all Christians shared Eusebius' vision of Rome but, as a powerful apologetic tool, the *Chronicle* spread widely into early Christian historiography. I noted that Jerome was thought to have modernized the *Tables* in Constantinople in 380 (Williams 2006: 277). It is uncertain whether Jerome's friend, the Spanish proconsul Nummius Aemilianus Dexter, translated king-lists in the first part of the *Chronicle* into Latin (*CHAP* s.v. Dexter). We also know of many attempts to "correct" the *Chronicle* by rewriting it to begin from Adam, the first human, such as that of the theologian Diodorus of Tarsus (*d*. 390, *CHAP* s.v. Diodorus). This work then taught Christians the basics of ancient history. The format helped the Christians write histories based on the efforts of their predecessors. The popularity of chronicles provides an important insight into the Christians' primary point of reference regarding many historical periods and, for our purposes, Alexander.

In Book 1 of the *Chronicle* Alexander features on more lists than any other monarch. Eusebius identifies him by standard sobriquets, such as "the son of Philip," or even "the Great." The Armenian version has him bring the list of Persian kings to an end by killing Darius III (*GCS NF* 20.152), as number twenty-four on the list of Macedonian kings (20.109), and as the first ruler on the list of Ptolemaic, as well as Seleucid, monarchs (20.152–153). Eusebius' list of Macedonian kings corresponds to that of Julius Africanus because both writers mark Alexander as the twenty-fourth king of Macedon (*Chronography* F 82, *GCS* NF 15.248–249). However, Eusebius' list of Successor dynasties in Macedon, Egypt, and Asia does not dovetail with the *four* projected dynasties proposed by his exegesis of Daniel. Recall from Chapter 3 that the four Successor houses were supposed to be symbolized by either the four horns or the four winds (Daniel 8).

In Book 2, the story becomes more complicated. I will provide an outline and commentary of Eusebius' Alexander-history below, but first a quick note on the text. We need to take into account the Latin, Greek, Syrian, and Armenian testimonies. As a result we get a somewhat coherent narrative in each version, but variations do occur. These primarily occur in regard to names and numbers. Divergences will be pointed out below, with numbers in parentheses to be discussed further. Commentary will be provided point-by-point. Some agreement exists between Jerome and the great Byzantine chronographer George Syncellus (d. after 813, *CHAP* s.v. George Syncellus), which points to continuity in some Christian version across the centuries. On the basis of, primarily, Jerome (*GCS* NF 47.121–124; *PL* 27.399–400), we may say that Eusebius gave the following account of Alexander in his *Chronicle*:

1. **Philip and Olympias gave birth to Alexander.** A notable divergence from previous histories that never record the birth of Alexander. Only "romantic" biographies make note of the birth or, even youth, of the king (Plut. *Alex*. 2.1; *AR* 1.12–24). Eusebius records this fact a little before the actual digression on Alexander begins.
2. **Alexander took Thrace and Illyria.** These campaigns in the Macedonian hinterland mark the starting point of the standard histories, such as Arr. *Anab*. 1.1–6; cf. Plut. *Alex*. 11.4–6. It is notable that, from points 2 to 6, Eusebius follows the historiographical outline from the Parian Marble inscription (*FGrH* 239 B-C2 Jacoby text = *FGrH/BNJ* 239 Sickinger comm.) and the so-called Oxyrhynchus historian from Egypt (*FGrH/BNJ* 255 F6 Rzepka).
3. **He sacked Thebes in Greece.** All major historians preserve details of the Theban disaster, e.g., Diod. Sic. 17.8.2–14.4; Plut. *Alex*. 11.6–13.15; Arr. *Anab*. 1.7–9; Just. *Epit*. 11.3.6–4.8; *AR* 1.46–47 (the episode does not appear in Curtius because his first two books are lost). Jerome notes that this city is the one in Greece, perhaps to distinguish it from the one in Upper Egypt. It was important for Jerome to emphasize that the Greeks, represented by the city of Thebes, were conquered early on. That fact was crucial when he made the careful clarification that the Greek king of Daniel 10:20 was an allusion to Alexander because he had conquered Greece before setting out on the Asian campaign.
4. **He took the city of Sardis.** The order of 4 and 5 is confused. The historical Alexander defeated Darius' generals before he traveled 200 miles to Sardis, Lydia's capital, and claimed the Persian treasury, for which see Diod. Sic. 17.21.7; Curt. 3.12.6; Plut. *Alex*. 17.1; Arr. *Anab*. 1.17.3.

5. **He defeated Darius' generals at the Granicus River.** A battle that features in every major account: Diod. Sic. 17.19–21; Plut. *Alex.* 16; Arr. *Anab.* 1.13–16; Just. *Epit.* 11.6.8–13.
6. **He besieged and sacked Tyre.** A siege that figures in every major account: Diod. Sic. 17.40.2–46.5; Curt. 4.2–4; Plut. *Alex.* 24–25; Arr. *Anab.* 2.16.1–24.5; Just. *Epit.* 11.10.10–14; Polyaen. *Strat.* 4.3.3–4, 13; *AR* 1.35.
7. **He came to Judea, sacrificed to God, and honored the High Priest.** The knowledge could come from Josephus, Origen, or Eusebius' other works. After all, he had noted the story in the *Proof* (Chapter 3).
8. **He appointed Andromachus to govern Judea, but the Samaritans killed him. Alexander retaliated by killing the Samaritans and repopulating their city with Macedonians.** This piece of information only appears in Curt. 4.7.10–11.
9. **He took Babylon thereby dissolving the Persian empire.** In Jerome's version, Darius' death, not the capture of Babylon, marks the fall of the Persian empire. Cf. Oxyrhynchus Chronicle *FGrH/BNJ* 255 F7; Just. *Epit.* 10.3.7.
10. **He conquered the Hyrcanians and Mardians.** This detail corresponds to material in Diod. Sic. 17.75–76; Just. *Epit.* 12.3.4; Oros. 3.18.5. To this, Jerome confusedly adds that returning from the temple of Ammon, Alexander built the city of Paraetonium in Libya. The Armenian Eusebius has corrupted the names of the cities here. George Syncellus omits Ammon and Paraetonium. I note that Jerome's inclusion of Paraetonium is almost identical to the description of Alexander going to the Siwah Oasis and the foundation of Paraetonium in the second-century Oxyrhynchus Chronicle *FGrH/BNJ* 255 F7. The *AR* tradition reports the foundation, see e.g., *AR* 1.31.1; *AR* Arm. § 78; *AR* β 1.31; Julius Valerius 1.31. According to most authorities, the city is already there when Alexander travels to the Siwah Oasis, see e.g., Arr. *Anab.* 3.3.3 incorporating Aristobulus *FGrH/BNJ* 139 F13 Pownall; cf. Str. 17.1.14 (799).
11. **He built Alexandria in Egypt in his seventh year.** Jerome notes that Alexander reigned in Asia for seven years and twelve in total. For the twelve years, see e.g., Diod. Sic. 17.117.5; Arr. *Anab.* 7.28.1; *AR* 3.35. Afterward Jerome inserts a unique detail that Harpalus fled Asia and Alexander's court.
12. **He captured the Aornus Rock and crossed the Indus.** Jerome records, however, that Alexander waged war against Porus and Taxiles instead.

13. **He died in Babylon when he was 32 years of age.** Jerome's postscript runs thus, "After his death the power was handed over to many. It was the beginning of the kingdom of Alexandria by Egypt, and different kings reigned in the various nations Alexander had conquered". The Armenian version and George Syncellus record the twelve years of Alexander's reign at this point.

We may take note of some immediate reactions. The Eusebian narrative, as reported by Jerome, is idiosyncratic, to say the least. Despite the inclusion of many historical events that Eusebius could only have known from certain sources, there are some glaring absences in his account. Eusebius omits the decisive Macedonian victories against the Persians at Issus (333 BC) and Gaugamela (331 BC). By comparison, the sole battle at Granicus seems underwhelming. Given the prevalence of sieges and war in his account of Alexander, it is noteworthy that Eusebius hardly took notice of the India campaign. Previous chroniclers, such as Julius Africanus, had also omitted the battle at the Hydaspes River against the Indian Rajah Porus (326 BC), which naturally was less essential to the retelling of Alexander's specifically *Persian* campaign.

Some of the numbered points call for further exegesis on a case-by-case basis.

(1) A possible purpose in recording the birth of Alexander may be the need to stress the human nature of Alexander and, thus, to reject the rumor that Alexander had been the son of Zeus Ammon (Ogden 2011: 7–78). For example, if one compares Eusebius' notice on Alexander's birth with the elaborate narrative of Olympias' seduction by the Egyptian astrologer Nectanebus in the *AR* (1.4–14), one may see the logic in emphasizing Philip's paternity of Alexander. At least focus on the father exists in multiple sources available to Eusebius. For instance, Plutarch stresses Alexander's genealogy at the outset of his biography by naming his parents and their mythological ancestors (Plut. *Alex.* 2.1). One of the Sibylline Oracles makes the same point by saying that Alexander was neither the bastard son, *nothos*, of Zeus, Ammon, nor anyone else (11.197-198). Eusebius may ultimately have preferred to specify the sire of Alexander for the same reason. Subsequent Christian chroniclers, such as Orosius, followed his lead, as we have seen (3.7.5). We have also seen that divine birth myths about Alexander were not popular in the Christian textual tradition (Chapter 2).

(2–6) These battles and sieges establish Alexander's military might and provide an unimpeachably historical context into which Eusebius can insert the fictional tale of the Jerusalem visit.

(7–8) This version of the Jerusalem tale confers a different meaning upon the visit than in the *Proof*. In the *Proof*, Eusebius discussed the visit to Jerusalem with reference to the foundation of Alexandria, so as to link two important cities of Christendom. Removing any association with Alexandria from the episode and organizing it in the context of the Samaritan conflict, Eusebius may be driving at two different possible points. He may be trying to present a literary portrait of a warlord who is careening along a path of rampage. In my view, that representation does not seem to agree with the respect shown for the Jerusalemite community and the appointment of the governor Andromachus (Heckel *Who's Who* s.v. Andromachus [1] and [2]). The Macedonians only react because the Samaritans rebel and burn Andromachus alive. The second possibility is that the king is viewed as a dispenser of justice in the region of Samaria, which had a notoriously bad reputation in early Christianity, because of the so-called heretics, Simon Magus and Menander.

Eusebius also creates a context in which Alexander actually solves a religious dispute alluded to in Josephus' *Antiquities* (11.340-345). Josephus notes that the Samaritans came to Alexander and declared themselves to be "true Jews," so that they could share in the rights Alexander had just conferred upon the Jews of Jerusalem. The Samaritans were adherents of the Abrahamic religion, but that believed in the holiness of Mount Gerizim over Jerusalem, and, at the beginning of the story, Alexander himself had granted Sanballat the privilege of building a new Temple there (11.323), thus instituting a schism between the communities in Jerusalem and Schechem (later Neapolis and Nablus) near Mt. Gerizim. But when the Samaritans tried to lay claim to Jewish heritage but were not able to support their claim, Alexander responded that he had only granted privileges to the Jews. He would, however, return later to hear their petition. Though the Macedonian king left for Egypt and would have to come back through the region to face Darius, he never returns to Samaria before his death. The Jewish author ends with a complaint about the Temple on Mt. Gerizim as a plaintive reminder of the schism.

Eusebius does not give us that much of a backstory, and it is too ambitious to expect ancient readers to know Josephus by heart. But Eusebius' brief mention does suggest that the Macedonians did not respect the Samaritans but only the Judean Jews. Of course, it is a harsh solution to have Alexander's army destroy the opponents of the Jews of Jerusalem and Judea, and then to replace them with Macedonians. And yet, the difference between Josephus and Eusebius is simply that Alexander leaves the door open for the Samaritans in the former, whereas his hand is forced to action in the latter. Given the fact that Eusebius next refers to the fall of Persia, I find it probable that we should interpret his representation of Alexander not only as doing God's will wittingly, but also as an unwitting purifier of heresy. Of course, the region did not stop producing heretics, but Christian orthodoxy produced other heroes to combat them later on.

(9–10) The close proximity of the fall of Babylon with the conquest of the Hyrcanians and the Mardians seems to suggest the Biblical imagery of Daniel 8 in which the Greek he-goat charged the two-horned Persian ram and made its two horns subject to him. Commentators considered the horns to be symbols of Persia and Media, and it would enrich Eusebius' narrative if he implied that the ram was a representation of Babylon with its two horns in Hyrcania and Mardia.

(11) Placing Alexandria so late on the list and in Alexander's reign seems to grant the city a special pride of place. It is no longer juxtaposed with Jerusalem, as it was in his *Proof* (Chapter 3). Given the foundation in the seventh year, Eusebius' date (330/329 BC) is slightly inaccurate compared with the historical accounts of Arrian and others (331/330 BC). The city receives a climactic spot in the creation of Alexander's empire, namely after the conquest of Persia. In the Parian Marble inscription, the anonymous author also juxtaposes the building of Alexandria with the capture of Babylon (Parian Marble *FGrH* 239 B5), which hints at a transfer of power. Eusebius may aim for the same representation because he goes on to write of the Alexandrian empire under the Ptolemies. If we briefly return to the Sibylline Oracles, Book 11 of this text also grants Alexandria a special place closer to Alexander's death (*Sib. Or.* 11.199–200 with Gunderson 1977: 62–63). The text represents the conquest of the known world, the conquest of Babylon, and Alexander's victory over Darius at Gaugamela as events happening *before* the foundation of Alexandria. Alexander founds the city just before he is treacherously poisoned by his own men in Babylon. The Sibylline prophetess then relates how the majestic metropolis will be the Egyptian bride of the great hero (Ptolemy I), a nourisher of cities, and there will be peace throughout the whole world for generations (11.232–235). Peace will last until the reign of Cleopatra VII, and Alexandria will be in peril during her rule. Finally, Egypt will be punished and her power will be transferred to Rome by the will of the Lord.

Alexandria becomes a sort of civic heir to Babylon and the empire of Persia, which is corroborated by Eusebius' computations of the rise of the Alexandrian empire that commences upon the death of the king. This representation thus confers authority upon the notion that Alexander's conquests were truly world changing. The new Greek empire sprang from Alexandria. Other Christian chronographers maintain the Alexandrian empire as the most important successor state to the king and, in Pseudo-Hippolytus' *Chronologies* it is the only successor. Most Classicizing pagan histories of Alexander amplify the meaning of Alexander's city too. This says something important about Alexandria as emblematic of Alexander's legacy and imperial power across the literatures of the ancient world.

(12) Eusebius' references to the Sogdinian rock of Aornus and the Indus River seems to suggest the Herculean might of Alexander. The places were the famous markers of Alexander's conquest of India, a feat only a handful of gods and legendary heroes were believed to have achieved. The Alexander historians recount that these places were specifically associated with the heroes of old. For instance, Arrian points out that Alexander and Dionysus were the only ones ever to have crossed the Indus (Arr. *Anab.* 7.10.6). Justin claims that only Alexander and Semiramis, the Babylonian queen, conquered India (Just. *Epit.* 1.2.9). Aornus certainly had the status of a *topos* in ancient historiography (see e.g., Diod. Sic. 17.85, 96; Curt. 8.11.2-25; Plut. *Mor.* 181c, 181d; Arr. *Anab.* 5.16.5; *AR* 3.4; Polyaen. *Strat.* 4.3.29; *It. Alex.* §§ 107-108; *Metz Epit.* §34).

(13) I speculate that the brief summary of Alexander's deeds is inspired by eulogies elsewhere (Arr. *Anab.* 7.28.1-2; *AR* 3.35). This sort of epitaph is at any rate common. It presents a fitting end to the story that has taken several pages to tell. In fact, the spotlight has only been on Alexander; the only other event recorded in the same space is the flourishing of the philosophers Anaximenes and Epicurus. Jerome adds three events from Roman history in this period: (1) Manlius Torquatus' execution of his own son for disobeying orders; (2) the Roman conquest of the Latins; and (3) the Roman subjugation of the Samnites. The synchronism indicates that Rome conquered the West while Alexander conquered the East.

Jerome makes some changes to what may have been in the Greek original. He adds the trip to the Siwah Oasis, the foundation of Paraetonium, and the Harpalus affair in which Alexander's treasurer fled Babylon with the wealth he won there. We may consider these events to present more embarrassing details that reveal a few of Alexander's faults, such as his longing for deification. More incriminating, Jerome highlights the defeat of historical figures: (9) Alexander defeated Darius rather than Babylon, the symbolic heart of Asia, and (12) Alexander vanquished the Indian Rajahs Taxiles and Porus rather than taking Aornus and the Indus River, deeds reminiscent of Hercules and Dionysus. In short, Alexander conquers nature in Eusebius; he defeats human beings in Jerome. If we are to consider Jerome's representation of Alexander's history slightly negative or less encomiastic than Eusebius', we can compare the account in the *Chronicle* (AD 380) with what he wrote in his exegesis of Daniel (AD 407):

> But there shall rise up a strong king and he shall rule with great power, and he shall do whatever he pleases. And when he shall have arisen, his kingdom shall be broken. Daniel clearly refers to Alexander the Great, king of the Macedonians, and son of Philip. For after he had overcome the Illyrians and Thracians, and had conquered Greece and destroyed Thebes, he crossed

over into Asia. And when he had routed Darius' generals and taken the city of Sardis, he afterward captured India and founded the city of Alexandria. And then, when he had attained the age of thirty-two and the twelfth year of his reign, he died of poison.

Jerome *Comm. Dan.* 3.11.3–4 (*CCSL* 75a.898–899, trans. Archer)

We note that Jerome's source is Jerome's own version of the *Chronicle*. All the pieces of information correspond to what was in the *Chronicle*. The only new detail is that Alexander died of poison, no doubt the more popular explanation for the cause of the king's death in antiquity. Again, although Alexander's end is hardly a happy one, it does not depart from previous, positive models that also spoke of poison, such as the *Alexander Romance*. We best leave the representation ambiguous.

Facts and factoids

There are a number of scattered pieces of historical information about Alexander in more texts than the historiographical accounts. Such references often occur in the many miscellanies produced in antiquity. The genre was popular: numerous Christians and non-Christians compiled them, Aelian, Ptolemy Chennus, Aulus Gellius, Clement of Alexandria, and Julius Africanus, to name a few. The genre is distinguished by curious names for the works, such as Gellius' *Attic Nights* or Africanus' *Embroideries*. The miscellanies do not order content in a systematic organization of factual information, but some authors maintain overarching themes and patterns of interest. The contents may vary a great deal, and it is useful that the works preserve a great deal of information that otherwise would be lost. For example, Julius Africanus attests to two stories of Alexander's chemical warfare against the Scythian Alans (Julius Africanus *Miscellany* F 12.2, *GCS* NF 18.43; D[ubia] 17, *GCS* NF 18.107). None of them appear in the major accounts, as it is a minor stratagem. The king ordered his Macedonians to spread hellebore over the Alan fields, and the crops were quickly ruined by the plant's chemical substance. The Alans surrendered immediately.

Julius Africanus probably got the story from another source. One potential source is Arrian, who is said to have written two treatises on the Alans, *Against the Alans* and *History of the Alans*, of which the former survives, whereas the latter does not. The story echoes the chemical warfare directed at Kirrha's water supply in the First Sacred War (595–585 BC) in which the Amphictyonic League of Delphi also used hellebore against their Phocean enemies to end the war (Aeschin. *In Ctes.* §§ 107–112; Ps.-Scyllax *Periplus* § 37; Paus. 10.37.5–6).

While the Scythian tale itself may not shed much light on the Alexander tradition, the circulation of such anecdotal information must be noted and appreciated in its local literary contexts. Sometimes such a piece of information represents the last piece of a puzzle, as I have argued elsewhere (Djurslev 2018b). That piece engages with another tale preserved in Julius Africanus' *Miscellany*, worth citing in full:

> They assign this use and practice to the soldier king. For Alexander himself was the one who ordered his soldiers to shave off their beards. When someone protested that he was cutting off his facial adornment, he replied, "do you not know, ignorant civilian, that in battle there is nothing easier to grab hold off than a beard?". Therefore, face to face with such equipment (the combination of Roman and Macedonian), no barbarian would be able to stand firm, however he should have been fitted out.
>
> Julius Africanus *Miscellany* F 12.1 (*GCS* NF 18.39, trans. Wallraff, adapted)

We shall return to the context of Africanus' story after a brief discussion of the anecdote's origins. A study of Alexander's portraiture in the Hellenistic courts has now situated the origin of the story in the context of the disputes between Alexander's men (Ptolemy, Seleucus, Hephaistion, Craterus), who would imitate the king's beardless chin and those from Philip's old guard (Parmenio, Antipater), who would not (Alonso Troncoso 2010: 21). The argument of youth versus veterans finds support in the writings of Plutarch. Plutarch relates this story twice: once, in the *Life of Theseus* (5.4), he explains how Theseus made the Athenians cut their hair for religious and martial reasons. Plutarch's other reference appears in a collection of sayings attributed to Alexander, which forms part of an essay. In the, perhaps spurious, *Sayings of Kings and Commanders* (172b–208a), Alexander makes the remark to his assembled generals, including Parmenio, rather than a soldier (*Mor.* 180b).

The anecdote of the beards is elsewhere attested. Writers before Julius Africanus made use of the story, underlining varying details. The second-century AD Macedonian Polyaenus places the saying at the second entry in his handbook on military strategy under the heading of Alexander (*Strat.* 4.3.2). In other words, a strategic shave before battle was the second lesson to be learned from Alexander's success in warfare. The most important attestation occurs long after Julius Africanus wrote, in the fourth-century work of Synesius of Cyrene, but the source ostensibly cites Ptolemy's first-generation *History of Alexander* (Synesius *Enc. Cal.* §§ 15–16, incorporating Ptolemy *FGrH/BNJ* 136 F11 Howe). Whether or not the fragment belongs to Ptolemy's work has spawned extensive debate

(Pearson 1960: 189; Howe comm. *ad loc*) but, as I argue, we need to pay due attention to the orator's method of citation to determine the genuineness of the fragment. When we do that, it quickly becomes apparent that Synesius, who says that he is quoting Ptolemy, has not seen the actual text. His elaboration of the anecdote—by far the longest and most engaging version of the battle of "Arbela" in antiquity, which he terms the "Battle of Hair," *trichomachia*—was composed to counter an argument made by Dio Chrysostom. Dio had apparently written a now lost *Encomium of Hair* in the first century AD. Dio had argued that the battle of Thermopylae in the Persian Wars (480/479 BC) was the greatest, for the three hundred Spartans had combed their hair before it. In Synesius' *Encomium of Baldness*, Synesius lampoons Dio for omitting the most glorious battles against Persia, namely those by Alexander, who had won because his Macedonians shaved before battle. If modern minds find the cause of conflict between the two orators ludicrous, they need only reflect upon the energy invested in discussing men's facial hair today. There is, of course, a lot more going on in the literary exercises of Dio and Synesius, who wrote three centuries apart, but suffice it to say that Synesius has put the anecdote to good use for his own purposes.

Let us return to the specific context of the anecdote in Julius Africanus' text. The anecdote appears as part of a longer argument about the contemporary military. The author attempts to explain how the Romans could conquer the Macedonians (148 BC at Pydna) and Greeks (146 BC at Corinth), but not the contemporary Sassanid "Persia" in the Severan age (AD 230s), even though the Persians had been previously defeated by the Greeks and Macedonians under Alexander. Ignoring the fact that Alexander had fought more than 500 years ago, Julius Africanus suggests that the armament of Greeks and Macedonians enabled them to be very effective against light-armored Persians, but not against the heavy-armored Romans. Conversely, Roman military gear did not prove effective against the agile Persians. He concludes with the solution that Romans could wear a combination of Greek and Roman gear to defeat the contemporary Persians.

Some readers may balk at Africanus' advice. But it was not the first in the field. Under Trajan, Aelian Tacticus had proposed similar solutions to Rome's problems on the eastern frontier. His *Tactica* repeatedly refers to the Macedonian phalanx as a tactical model (e.g., Pref. 6). It was thus fairly commonplace to lock Greeks, Romans, Macedonians, and Persians in a historical sequence that made the past directly relevant to the conduct of warfare in the imperial present. We might have seen that already from Polyaenus' collections of stratagems, dedicated to Emperors Marcus Aurelius and Lucius Verus. Works of this kind were written for the edification of elite males and entertained readers or acted as useful tools for understanding the machinations of war.

Of the Christian authors considered in this study, Julius Africanus does not stand out in preserving such military material. Many of the early Christians preserved such *varia* across multiple genres, as we have seen. Like Julius Africanus, they fully participated in the contemporary discourse on Alexander. Ultimately, Christian participation in contemporary society is much easier to accept than the Christians claims to the contrary. Some of the factoids used may be no more than simple platitudes, and their appearance attests to their rhetorical context. For example, we find two attestations of the saying "for a king the law is unwritten," βασιλεῖ γὰρ νόμος ἄγραφος, one in the Greek *Alexander Romance* and the other in Clement of Alexandria (*AR* 3.17.37; cf. Clem. Al. *Strom.* 3.4.30.2). The former attributes the saying to an Indian priest guarding the oracular trees of India, whereas the latter prefers a group of Gnostics. In the case of Clement, no mention is made of Alexander, and it is a hard task to argue for any kind of interaction between the two texts. It seems much easier to assume a common intellectual backdrop of an Alexandrian milieu.

Felix Jacoby (1856–1959) prudently provided an extra entry in the *FGrH* for miscellaneous information on Alexander in his great collection of the fragments of the Greek historians (*FGrH/BNJ* 153 Bearzot). The assorted testimonials and random fragments of Alexander history do not make a homogeneous gathering, but give an impression of how much we are missing when we study Alexander through only the major surviving historians. The devil may indeed be in the details of which *topoi* continued and which did not. If we compare some of the titles in Jacoby's entry, we notice that the greatest difference between Christians and non-Christians has remained undetected. No Christian produced texts with Alexander as the sole focus. No major histories or prose treatises remain extant or are referred to in the literature. Everything from the written record suggests that Christian interest in Alexander did not stretch so far as to make him the subject of an entire work. Conversely, many non-Christians composed full-scale histories and biographies, continuing a general trend from the inception of the imperial period. For example, the writer Soterichus of Oasis from the time of Diocletian (*fl.* 300) composed a history on Alexander's destruction of Thebes, called *Python* or *Alexandriakos* (*FGrH/BNJ* 153 F14a Bearzot via *Suda* Σ 877 Adler; I prefer her reading to that of Soterichus 641 T1 Schubert). Although the *Suda* records that Soterichus was an epic poet, ἐποποιός, the titles of his works indicate that many of them were prose, such as his *Encomium of Diocletian* and *Life of Apollonius of Tyana*. We know of authors with similar interests under

Constantine. Praxagoras of Athens penned a history of Constantine in two books and a six-book work on Alexander (*FGrH/BNJ* 219 T1 via Phot. *Bibl.* 62.20b29–21b17). Since these works only survive as notices in much later lexica or compilations of literature, we can only speculate on their content and contemporary success. We can say, though, that Christians seem to have differed from their non-Christian colleagues in their unwillingness to devote whole works to Alexander.

Some modern scholars take the distinction too far, though. One scholar has even suggested that the Christians "lost" to the pagans and so had to create a new historiography that was far removed from the contemporary political and local histories (Janiszewski 2006: 464). While I agree that the time and transmission of texts have skewed our impression of the decline in non-Christian historiography, I find it misleading to assume that the discrepancy was because Christians lacked the ability to write traditional historiography or that they tried hard to disrupt pagan historiography. Christians were not trying to duplicate pagan efforts. Indeed, their interest in ancient history was focused on different material, at least for the most part. They created a whole chronicle literature to accommodate the new needs of Christian history (Burgess 2018). Their scope was wider than that of writers who only needed to know what happened from the Trojan War to Alexander's campaigns. Christian teachers knew such history for the purposes of teaching the standard curriculum. For example, Synesius certainly shows the appropriate level of learning. As Janiszewski concedes, most historiographers worked as rhetoricians too, and the shared culture of the schools of rhetoric made the same demands on Christian and non-Christian teachers and students. Moreover, we must also consider the fact that only so many Christians chose to articulate their "Christianness" in the texts they wrote, so much so that scholars have long considered some Christian writers to be non-Christians, such as the Alexandrian poet Claudian. Such examples mostly come from the fourth and fifth centuries. Some genres simply did not activate a religious identity.

Christian comparisons

This wondrous man, Alexander of Macedon, was the archetype and image of our heavenly king Jesus Christ.

Vark Agheksandri, *History of Alexander*, preface
Khachatur Kecharetsi (*c.*1260–1331) (ed. Simonyan 1989: 360–362, trans. Topchyan)

Eastern Christians, such as the above man of letters from Kecharuyk, Armenia, seem to have been quite ready to associate Alexander with Jesus. As previously noted, one great Byzantine lexicon claimed that the "Chaldean" Sibyl had prophesied about both Alexander and Jesus, and *only* those two (*Suda*, s.v. Σ 361 Adler). Philostorgius, in an early fifth-century church history by the Arian writer, recorded a tale that told of three Delphic oracles predicting the coming of Alexander and then Christ, which a contemporary church historian tried to emend (Socrates *Hist. Eccl.* 3.23.54–56).

Khachatur's *synkrisis* may also strike us as sacrilegious. It was certainly a bold statement for the time. Historians have read the remark in the context of the Tatar-Mongolian oppression of Armenia; the Armenians hoped for the prototype of their national hero to return as liberator (Hacikyan 2002 ii: 568). Alexander enjoyed a vivid afterlife in the Armenian tradition: the Greek *Alexander Romance* was one of the first pieces of non-ecclesiastical literature translated into Armenian in the late fifth century AD (Wolohojian 1969: 8), and intellectuals assigned it a high literary status, surpassed only by Scripture (Thomson 1994 xv: 43). It is not surprising then that Khachatur should place Alexander on a pedestal he had rarely mounted in previous Christian texts.

The theme of comparison will be familiar from imperial literature. Most readers will know some case of comparisons between Alexander and the political leaders of Greece and Rome. After all, a large part of Plutarch's *Parallel Lives* depends on that very theme. But active comparisons between Alexander and living people—from local governors to the highest-ranking members of court—proliferated. The tendency did not go unnoticed in the higher political echelons of the Roman Empire. None other than Marcus Aurelius made a note of it in his *Meditations* (6.18). For him, it was a curious trend at court that so many sought to compare themselves with people that were long dead rather than the living (cf. 10.27). In other places, Marcus Aurelius took no issue with making such comparisons himself, as long as the objects compared were of equivalent status. For example, one passage asks what Alexander, Caesar, and Pompey have in comparison with Diogenes, Heraclitus, and Socrates (8.3). Elsewhere, the emperor makes a poignant comparison between Alexander and the king's muleteer (6.24). He saw no difference between the two, for they were both dead and gone. Death gave them equal status. To maintain the memory of one over the other was nothing but vanity. His criticism is nothing personal. He also targets Romans. There was no good reason to bring forth the examples of ancient Roman nobles (4.33). Although these passages differ from one another in their purpose, we may note Marcus' testimony to the rhetoric-driven culture of his times.

The kinds of comparisons above represent a juxtaposition of two persons by an ancient writer. British historian Peter Green once proposed three different modes of comparison in Rome: (1) *imitatio*, referring to someone's imitation of Alexander's actions; (2) *aemulatio*, meaning a desire to rival and surpass Alexander, primarily in politics or war; and (3) *comparatio*, referring to the idea that author/artist could compare someone to Alexander (Green 1978, revisited by Welch and Mitchell 2013). An overwhelming amount of material comes from written evidence, but some artifacts pertain to numbers 1 and 2. We may especially interpret numismatic evidence as echoes of Alexander's iconography (Kühnen 2008). As far as we know, Christians never attempted *imitatio* or *aemulatio* in antiquity.

From a treatise of the late third century AD, we learn that Alexander *comparationes* were standard procedure in epideictic oratory. This form of rhetoric for ceremonial activities focuses on passing praise or blame, panegyric or invective (Pernot 2015). In the treatise, Menander of Laodicea, or Menander Rhetor, teaches his students the following about praising the imperial representative in a city:

> And you will then talk about the governor's virtues. If this is to be his first visit, you should follow the personal encomium by a brief description of the country, and then of the city, as has been said. Finally, you should invite him to come to all this: "Come then and behold these things, come to add to our glories, to be our second Alexander (ἄλλος Ἀλέξανδρος). You will find nothing lacking for a governor's welcome: not pleasant climate, nor well-mannered people, nor moderate behavior, nor dignity in general. Our city is a shrine of virtues."
>
> Men. Rhet. p. 426 Spengel (trans. Russell and Wilson)

We do not know if the budding orator's flattery of the governor hit home, but the city sounds worth a visit. Of course, students of Menander and teachers like him were to employ the lesson learned in their work across the empire. That kind of training was rudimentary for anyone that had passed through the urban school system. We have to imagine its proliferation across the cities of the eastern empire, at the very least, although rhetoricians also performed in the West. Given how common this sort of praise was, it follows that there were many *second Alexanders*, or *another Alexanders* roaming the Roman world. Unfortunately, we have lost the thousands of panegyrics that would make such high-blown adulation, perhaps because of chance or the literary tastes of later times. But Menander's words evidence a widespread phenomenon on the non-Christian side.

Clement of Alexandria makes the earliest comparison of Alexander and Jesus in the pre-Constantinian tradition (*Strom.* 1.24.158.3–159.6). At least scholarship has not detected earlier, explicit instances (Ehrhardt 1945; De Focara 2013; Broad 2015). The *synkrisis* occurs in a discussion of Moses' competencies. Clement declares the Hebrew patriarch a prophet, προφητικός; lawgiver, νομοθετικός; tactician, τακτικός; general, στρατηγικός; politician, πολιτικός; and a philosopher, φιλόσοφος (cf. Philo *Vit. Mos.* 2.3). Clement represents Moses using Greek terminology, for the whole of the first book concerns Greek culture as opposed to Judaism, and the priority of the latter over the former. The professions noted contribute to kingship, and Clement ranks four types of kingship: (1) the divine king, God and Christ, who supply all good things; (2) the mighty king, such as Hercules and Alexander, who alone ruled by the high spirit of their souls, τὸ μόνῳ τῷ θυμοειδεῖ τῆς ψυχῆς; (3) the destructive king, such as the Persian kings, who ruled by right of conquest; and (4) the despot, the sort of king ruled by his passions, exemplified by Sardanapalus, the proverbial decadent monarch of Assyria. Clement ends the digression with a praise of Christ the King, citing the ultimate authority of the New Testament that, "Jesus Christ is Lord," κύριος Ἰησοῦς Χριστὸς (Phil. 2:10–11).

The list reveals several fundamental features of Clement's agenda. Clement inserts Jesus and Moses into a framework that readers, Christian and non-Christian, would readily appreciate without much introduction. He takes the stock examples of Greek and barbarian rulers from school-examples of what constitutes a proper ruler (Arr. *Epic. Diss.* 3.23.38 with Eshleman 2012: 74). This ranking of kingship makes it immediately convincing that Moses' authority, just as Christ's, must take priority over the typical rulers of Greeks and "barbarians." As far as the historical character of Alexander is concerned, we expect he would not have appreciated second place, although he may have contented himself with sharing that position with Hercules, the founder of the Argead royal line. At first glance, Clement seems to regard Alexander with great esteem, as, indeed, most of those in his Alexandrian audience would have done. However, the word Clement uses to describe Hercules and Alexander, *thumoeidês*, does not have positive connotations when we find the word attested elsewhere in the *Miscellany* (7.10.59.3). In this passage, the word is taken to refer to men, who do not have knowledge, but still manage to succeed, e.g., by physical and mental traits, such as fortitude and bravery, ἀνδρεία. Clement contrasts this type of person with the knowledgeable man, who always performs the correct action. The clever man overpowers the bold and brave. If we compare the two passages, we may interpret Clement's remarks as a veiled criticism of Alexander's (and Hercules') *andreia*. In this sense, Clement's list reminds us that "second place is for the first loser."

Another aspect of the kingship of Alexander and Jesus that Christians saw fit to compare was what we may term the "extent of empire" (Klein 1988: 951–955; Wirth 1993: 60 n. 193). In a religious treatise addressed to the Jews, Tertullian rose to the task of discussing whether the Messiah had come in the figure of Jesus or not. The issue was one of fundamental importance for early Christians. To substantiate that Jesus was the prophesied Messiah, Tertullian establishes the condition that Jesus had already arrived because Christians worshipped him in all parts of the world. Another argument follows immediately on from that, namely, that Jesus Christ was the only king to have reigned over all nations. Conversely, the kingdoms of Solomon, Darius I, the Pharaohs, Nebuchadnezzar, and Alexander, as well as the lands of the Germans, the Britons, and the Romans were confined to their own, self-imposed boundaries. Tertullian states, "Although Alexander had reigned, it was only in Asia and other places" (Tertullian *Adv. Jud.* § 7.7, *CCSL* 2.1355).

It is important to take note of the *dramatis personae*. Tertullian includes Alexander in a group of monarchs from Scripture (Solomon, Pharaoh, Nebuchadnezzar) because he is arguing against Jews. It was they who had incorporated the Macedonian king into the Scriptural canon in the first place. Tertullian is integrating Alexander into a sequence that seems to make a point of transition from Biblical material (Solomon to Nebuchadnezzar) to contemporary peoples (Germanic tribes to Romans). Although it is difficult to speak of his audience, Jewish and Christian readers would immediately recognize the names. Elsewhere, in a speech against the heretic Marcion, Tertullian places Alexander alongside vain monarchs from the Old Testament, Darius and Holophernes. The three kings present key examples of rulers cast down because of pride (Tert. *Marc.* 1.7.2, *CCSL* 1.448). In Tertullian's great corpus of Latin writing, the liminal space between the Biblical drama and the Roman present came together as one unified stratum through Alexander's legacy.

Tertullian's comparison of territory echoes a *topos* of empire in Arrian. According to the historian, Alexander used to say that Persian monarchs were wrong to refer to themselves as "Kings of Asia," because they had ruled a comparatively small portion of it (Arr. *Anab.* 7.1.3). Alexander's empire at the peak of his power, Arrian argued, was bigger than that of any Persian king before him. Indeed, Arrian claims that it seemed to Alexander and his followers that he was lord of all lands and sea, Ἀλέξανδρον καὶ τοῖς ἀμφ' αὐτὸν φανῆναι γῆς τε ἁπάσης καὶ θαλάσσης κύριον (Arr. *Anab.* 7.15.5). In the same way, Tertullian can argue that Jesus' universal reign was larger than that of Alexander's Asia (and the lands of many other nations too). In other words, just as Alexander's realm surpasses Persian Asia in Arrian, Jesus and the Gospel message capture the whole world in Tertullian.

The Apostle Paul

Jerome makes the following comparison of conqueror and apostle in one of his translations of Origen:

> After that, Paul says, from Rome he intended to set out for Spain. Behold Paul, the Persecutor of Judea, preaches among the Gentiles! Where are those who preach about Alexander the Great, the Macedonian general, because he conquered so many peoples within a short span of time? He had an army, he had great multitudes; and yet he was not able to accomplish anything as great, only something slight. This man, Paul, however, once a persecutor—he who used to say, "although unlearned in speech, but not in knowledge," and so making solecisms in speaking—carries the cross of Christ and, as one triumphant, he captures all people. He subdued the whole world from the Ocean to the Red Sea.
> Jerome *Tract. Ps.* 14 (*CCSL* 78.81, trans. Ewald, adapted)

Jerome did not invent this powerful *comparatio*. Recent research has established that Jerome's work on the Psalms introduced only slight variations on Origen's homilies about (or selections of) the Psalms, some of which were rediscovered in a Byzantine manuscript in Munich (*Codex Monacensis Graecus* no. 314, *GCS* NF 19). The comparison was presumably therefore more than a hundred years old at the time Jerome translated Origen, without any attribution. As we have seen, Origen certainly could have deployed such a *synkrisis* because his older contemporary, Tertullian, made a very similar assertion about the extent of empire with regard to Alexander and Jesus. Jerome's translation thus ensured not only a chronological continuity between Christians of the third century and those of the fifth, but also a shortening of the intellectual distance between the East and the West. Jerome may have finished the translation as late as the time when he was himself entangled in the "Origenist controversy." The conflict culminated in a synod in which Christians, led by Theophilus of Alexandria, would condemn Origen formally as a heretic in Alexandria (*c.* 400/1). Now a "hydra of all heresies," *hydram omnium haereseon* (*Ep.* 98.9), Origen and his works lost their appeal but, up to that point, Jerome had carefully produced texts that made Origen's thought survive in the West (*Ep.* 33). Tyrannius Rufinus, at first the friend and later adversary of Jerome, pointed out this inconsistency in Jerome's use of Origen, much to Jerome's displeasure (Rufinus *Orig. Princ.* pref. 2).

The direct comparison represents a single instance of Alexander and an Apostle, which, by proxy, indicates a comparison to Jesus. John Chrysostom would compare the Apostles to Alexander, if only indirectly, by talking about the tomb of Alexander and the sepulchers of the saints (*Hom.* 2 Cor. 26, *PG* 61.581–582). John also emphasizes Alexander's dependency on an army for his success. For both Jerome and John, the speed of the conquest and the extent of the empire were impressive but momentary. Since none of their contemporaries preached the Gospel of Alexander, his legacy was as dead as he was himself. Furthermore, word versus deed represents a latent theme across ancient literature, but the significance seems marked by the fact that Paul did not speak well and so needed support from above. Paul's achievement, despite all his faults, revealed that everything was possible with Christ.

For his literary portrait of Paul, Jerome reproduces much material we know from the New Testament (e.g., Acts 9:20, 13:5, 13, 14:1, 17, 18:4, 18:19, 18:26–28, 19:8, 28:17–29). After Paul's conversion on the road to Damascus, his missionary activities took him around Syria, into the Roman province of Achaia and, lastly, to Rome. The indication that Paul planned a trip to Spain comes from Paul himself in one of the New Testament epistles (Rom. 15; 24; 28). What Jerome means by the extent of territory Paul actually conquered is unclear, but the Red Sea could mean the Indian Ocean. If so, the phrase "from the Ocean to the Red Sea" could be a way of expressing the entirety of the known world. Paul did not travel so far east, of course, but the Apostle Thomas and other missionaries undertook the mission to India, at least in Christian legend. In that way, Jerome's reader could see Paul's work continued and completed in the Christian mission from Gibraltar to the Indus.

By contrast, Alexander did not accomplish much with his military might. The sentiment matches that of Livy, who also said that Alexander conquered from Illyria and Thrace to India and the Red Sea (Livy *Per.* 45.9). But the Wars of the Successors brought Alexander's imperial legacy from the pinnacle to the pit, its zenith passed. There is an appropriate context for the statement. Livy spoke of Alexander when he was recounting the Roman conquest of Macedon, and he had just mentioned how the last of the Antigonid line, Perseus, was captured at the battle of Pydna, 168 BC.

From other texts, we find more positive uses of the "extent of empire" *topos*. We have noted that some writers were willing to say that Alexander had conquered from the Pillars of Hercules, that is, Gibraltar, to India (*AR* 3.33.3). Such extensive conquest was "history as it should have been" (Lewis cited at Garstad 2018: 129 n. 2). Many writers inform us that Alexander had plans for further conquests in the west. For imperial writers, whether Christian or non-Christian, were prone to adjusting Alexander's cultural achievement. For example, in light of the positive comments that Origen, Jerome, and John Chrysostom make on Alexander elsewhere, such as in their exegesis of the Book of Daniel, it is ironic that they so vehemently reduce the king's achievement in comparison to an Apostle. Elsewhere Jerome makes much of Alexandria's high status in his world. All three Christians agree that Alexander's campaign was ordained by God. But new literary contexts made new demands of the preachers. In the church, Alexander could never be elevated to match the power of the Gospel message, at least not until Kachatur of Kecharuyk. As we shall see below, Alexander's campaign could justify the spread of the Gospel, according to John Chrysostom.

We must take notice of the pattern that the Christian use of the king depends on the argument and juxtaposition of characters that the Christians were discussing rather than the abilities or motives they project onto Alexander. Christians chose to amplify key features (e.g., preaching) and characters (e.g., Paul), not to add anything new to or affect the figure of Alexander (general, army, empire-builder). His representation needed to stay somewhat static for the Christians to surpass him. By saying that nothing new is invented, I mean that Alexander himself does not acquire any other traits than what we know from contemporary non-Christian *synkriseis*. For instance, sophists and orators used the *topos* of Alexander's conquest against contemporary emperors from Augustus to Constantine and beyond. These two homilies by Origen and Jerome, delivered in speech or parchment to Christian congregations of two very different times, must be supplemented by an analysis of the Christian use of Alexander in the rhetoric at court. The richest example of imperial Christian rhetoric is Eusebius' *Life of Constantine*, which is our next stop.

Constantine

> Ancient history records that Cyrus was more illustrious than those before him among the Persians. But one should not think highly of just that fact, but look to the end of his long life. Of this, they say that the king suffered an unfitting death, vile and shameful at a woman's hand. The sons of Greece sing praise about how Alexander subdued countless tribes from different peoples but, before he reached full manhood, he departed to an early death, (1) carted off by revelry and drunken orgies among the Macedonians. He reached but two years past thirty and reigned for one-third of his life. (2) A man zapping like a thunderbolt (ἀνὴρ

σκηπτοῦ), (3) he waded through blood and, without mercy, (4) enslaved entire nations and cities, young and old alike. But as he was close to blossoming and (5) lamented the loss of his favorite, (6) fate dispatched him childless, rootless, homeless (ἄτεκνον ἄρριζον ἀνέστιον) in a foreign and hostile land. (7) Fate removed him, so that he might not harm the human race any longer (ὡς ἂν μὴ εἰς μακρὸν λυμαίνοιτο τὸ θνητὸν γένος). The kingdom was torn apart in an instant since his attendants each cut off a portion and seized the territory as a prize for himself. And yet, he is celebrated in song by choirs for such deeds.

Euseb. Vit. Const. 1.7 (GCS NF 7.18, trans. Cameron and Hall, adapted)

Considering the previous portraits of Alexander by Eusebius in the apologetic writings, one hardly recognizes the demon presented to us here in the *Life of Constantine*. The digression reads as one of the most vituperative remarks on Alexander's conquest in antiquity. Neither Lucan nor Seneca at their most critical came close, though they have long been regarded as part of the literary precedent for Eusebius' condemnation (Klein 1988: 960-961; Wirth 1993: 62-63; Demandt 2009: 426). But Eusebius refers twice to the "sons of Greece" as his opposition. He develops Alexander's portrait against the topics that the admirers of Alexander would have used to praise the king. Eusebius' ironic tone strikes a chord with Tatian's false praise of Alexander's education from Aristotle (Chapter 2). Eusebius makes use of the same *topos* of alcoholism, but does not mention Clitus or Callisthenes. However, he seems to have forgotten the praise he had previously showered on Alexandria and Alexander's visit to Jerusalem. We are thus in the same situation as we have been before: a Christian using a select set of *topoi* to construct a literary portrait that fits the specific context of what he is trying to say, in this case a praise of the newly deceased Constantine (337). Eusebius himself died before the publication of this work in 340, and it was lightly edited by others (Cameron 1997: 142). The *Life* did not enjoy wide circulation, despite the fact that it would have provided readers with the best source for Constantine's career. Nevertheless, the lack of attention paid to the *Life* in antiquity should not prevent us from investigating the digression above, especially since we have studied the other Eusebian digressions on Alexander. I must say at the outset that the negative digression was not prompted by learning that Eusebius may have acquired between 325 and 340, but rather by the special demands the *Life* made on its author. Great praise required great contrasts with the exemplary past.

I begin with some general remarks on the *synkrisis* before I turn to the numbered points inserted into the digression. From the perspective of *Quellenforschung*, my key suggestion below is that the Sibylline Oracles are as likely to have been a literary influence on Eusebius as Stoic writers may have been. My overarching argument remains that the Christian Alexander discourse was extremely multivalent and influenced by a broad range of *topoi* from often indeterminable places. I wish to show that Eusebius' remarks, while powerful, were clearly not made in a vacuum.

Comparison of a subject with Cyrus and Alexander was a traditional form of *progymnasma*, a written training exercise, and one teacher of rhetoric advised such *synkrisis* in formal writing, as we saw above (cf. Men. Rhet. p. 327 Spengel with Averil Cameron 1997: 152; Flower 2013: 73 n. 195). The *Life* does not follow slavishly the prescriptions of the "royal life story," *basilikos logos*, but at least this kind of requirement is met. The *synkrisis* prompts Eusebius to praise Constantine's achievements (*Vit. Const.* 1.8). The emperor began to rule at the age Alexander died; he doubled his length of life; he tripled the extent of his empire; he commanded his army with mildness and sobriety; he conquered the North (Britain, Scythia), the South (Africa), and the East (India) with beams of light from the true religion; and he proclaimed his God to every "barbarian" nation under his rule.

Arguably, Eusebius uses the negative digression on Alexander to model his features of the idealized Constantine. He stresses the extent of empire and a few typical moral features, such as mildness (*clementia*) and soberness (*prudentia*), but he does not linger over other virtues, such as piety or divine support. I note in this context that the conquest of Britain had previously been used to set Roman military might over that of Alexander, for which Arrian had to excuse him (Arr. *Anab.* 7.1.4; cf. Julian *Caesars* 321a; *De Ex. Urb. Hier.* 2.9, CSEL 66.149–150). Conversely, Lucan said that Macedon had conquered further than Rome in the East (Lucan 10.48–52), which Eusebius counters with references to Scythians (4.5), Blemmyes and Ethiopians (4.7), and India (4.50). The rhetoric falls flat when the peoples either have been conquered by Alexander or were part of the standard rhetorical places to conquer (Blemmyes, Egyptians, Erembians = Men. Rhet. p. 387 Spengel). Despite claims to the contrary (1.11), Eusebius glorifies the violence of Constantine's wars as a means to advance Christian missions to foreign nations, not Rome (Demacopoulos 2016). It is worthy of note how well Christianity fits with imperialism.

Eusebius' primary focus on age is consistent with a very Roman conception of youth versus maturity, as is expressed, for example, in Curtius Rufus' assessment of Alexander (10.5.34–36). Curtius argues that experience might have cured the king of his youthful irascibility, had Fortune not intervened and directed him to his ruin at the hands of the fates (*fata*). Curtius' focus on Fate, Fortune, and

Nature as agents that disrupted Alexander's campaigns resonate well with Eusebius' digression.

Let us now consider the numbered points inserted into the digression. I will pay significant attention to two of the Sibylline Books, 3 and 11, of which Eusebius shows awareness (*Praep. Evang.* 9.15.1, 10.11.27, 13.13.15, 13.13.42; *Onom.* p. 40).

1. Eusebius claims that Alexander died an early death because of alcohol. According to Amitay's appendix, "Alexander Alcoholicus," this theme is present from the earliest Alexander histories onward (Amitay 2010: 163–165). For example, the first-generation historian Ephippus of Olynthus claims that Alexander died as the result of a bout with the legendary drinker Proteas (*FGrH/BNJ* 126 F3 Prandi via Athen. 10.44, 434a-b). The histories discuss revelries in various contexts, but Alexander's death certainly features the strongest focus on heavy Macedonian drinking, even the *Alexander Romance* (3.31.6-8). Keeping in mind that previous scholarship has connected this passage with Seneca and Lucan, while Seneca mentions Alexander's intemperance in the context of the king's death (Sen. *Ep.* 83.23), no mention is made of Alexander's drinking in Lucan nor in the Sibylline Oracles.

2. Being a thunderbolt was a compliment to the contemporaries of the historical Alexander. His painter Apelles painted him wielding one (Plin. *HN* 35.92–93) and the Neseios gem depicts him in the same fashion. As the figurative son of Zeus, the thunderbolt was a fitting attribute. We know of at least one medallion that may depict him with that attribute (Holt 2003). Ptolemy of Macedon (r. 281–279 BC) famously acquired the epithet "Keraunos." For Eusebius, the thunderbolt does not carry positive connotations because he associates it with merciless killing. For Lucan too, the thunderbolt imagery is associated with "earthly evil," *terrarum malum*, and a "harmful star," *sidus iniquum* (Lucan 10.34). In the eleventh Sibylline Oracle the reader is ordered to "flee the man who is like a thunderbolt," φεῦγε κεραύνιον ἄνδρα (*Sib. Or.* 11.217 with *Sib. Or.* 3.390–391, ἤγειρε γὰρ αὐτοῦ πρόσθε κεραυνὸς φῶτα).

3. *Wading through blood* is a more graphic way of saying that Alexander killed many people. Lucan stresses the conqueror's mass-killing by having blood defile the rivers Euphrates and Indus (Lucan 10.32–33), whereas the *Sib. Or.* say that the "drenched earth would imbibe much gore," πολὺν δὲ χθὼν πίεται φόνον ὀμβρηθεῖσα (*Sib. Or.* 3.392; cf. *Sib. Or.* 11.118).

4. As previously observed in the case of Arnobius and Orosius, references to Alexander's enslavement of the East were common. Lucan deplores at length the thought of one man ruling the world (Lucan 10.25–28), whereas the *Sib. Or.* devote half a hexameter to this matter (*Sib. Or.* 3.391–392, 11.217).

5. Averil Cameron and Stuart Hall translate τὰ παιδικὰ πενθοῦντι with "he still mourned his lost childhood," which I render, "lamenting the loss of his favorite" (Cameron and Hall 1999: 70, comm. 118). According to the LSJ, s.v. τὸ παιδικόν was often used in the plural to denote a single person, a "darling." To me, and the German translator Paul Dräger (2007: 48–49), Eusebius is making a pointed allusion to the death of Hephaistion, whom Alexander mourned more than anybody else. This would add extra pathos to the narrative, because Hephaistion died shortly before Alexander himself. We find none of this Eusebian emphasis in Lucan or the Sibylline books.

6. Fate or death, τὸ χρεών, does not appear as an agent in Lucan's digression (10.41). He mentions the occurrence of Alexander's final day, and that Nature alone, *naturaque solum*, withstood the king. Strikingly, the Sibylline author also makes the Lord of the Underworld the key agent: "Hades will see to it that everything becomes as if unseen," ὡς πανάιστον ἅπαντ' Ἀίδης θεραπεύσει (3.393; cf. 11.221). Moreover, Eusebius uses a brilliant alliterative asyndeton of the three predicates to the object αὐτόν, ἄτεκνον ἄρριζον ἀνέστιον, which resonates well with a similar figure of speech in the *Sibylline Oracles*: Alexander is conceived as "savage, foreign to justice, fiery," ἄγριος ἀλλοδίκης φλογόεις (3.390; cf. 11.216: ἄγριος ἀλλοδίκης λώπην ἀμφειμένος ὤμοις). Eusebius' meaning is slightly different in his focus on Alexander being childless, rootless, and homeless. We do find the sentiment expressed elsewhere. According to Curtius Rufus (10.5.12–14), however, a major complaint among Alexander's soldiers was that they were left homeless in a foreign land with no obvious heir. Eusebius has superimposed such a notion upon Alexander himself.

7. That fate terminated Alexander to preserve human life makes for quite a powerful statement. I have not found a convincing parallel in other texts, whether Christian or non-Christian, not even in Orosius' hostile history. It might be thought that Eusebius laid the emphasis on life because the Holy Ghost was known as the giver of life, ζωοποιόν, in the Nicene Creed. But Eusebius did not support Nicene orthodoxy at first, and we do not know about his posthumous editor. A much more attractive solution is to focus on

the contrast with Constantine's long life. The whole circuit of a ruler's life needed consideration, which is Eusebius' point in mentioning that Cyrus died humiliated by the hand of a woman. In Alexander's case, his impiety, immoderation, and inhumanity made God bring his life to an end. The contrast is clear: God had granted his chosen emperor a lengthy life on account of his piety (1.3–5), but cut Alexander's short. Constantine lived the full duration of his life in glory and honor. Eusebius points to Constantine's vitality at multiple points in the emperor's campaigns (2.10; 2.13), even noting the youthful vigor of Constantine when he has lived twice the length of Alexander's life (4.53). At the funeral of Constantine, Eusebius uses images of life, arguing that Constantine ruled from beyond the grave. He makes clear that this imagery does not have to do with the self-immolation of the phoenix, but rather resembled the Resurrection. Everlasting life for Constantine among the saints (1.9) was an honor that neither Cyrus nor Alexander could enjoy. Two centuries earlier, Lucian, one of Eusebius' predecessors in criticizing the pair, had pointedly spoken of how Alexander had to sit throne-by-throne with Cyrus in Hades (Luc. *Ver. Hist.* 2.9).

If the above discussion is valid, we can dismiss outright Cameron and Hall's suggestion that Plutarch's *Life of Alexander* provided the source for the Alexander digression. Heavy drinking is the only *topos* we can connect to Plutarch, who creatively blamed Alexander's body-heat for causing him to drink and be easily angered (Plut. *Alex.* 4.5–7). Yet, I can think of no other striking parallels between Plutarch and Eusebius. One might be the death of Hephaistion, but his death is hardly an obscure *topos* either. Another proposal about Eusebius' sources for the digression suggests that we need to explain the passage with the apocalyptic imagery of the third beast of Daniel 7 (Wirth 1993: 63). This idea is oddly reminiscent of Cary's argument about Daniel and Orosius' Alexander. None of that Danielic material, however, features in Eusebius' digression. Alexander's lust for blood was a standard *topos* in imperial oratory. For example, the third-century historian Cassius Dio tells the anecdotal story that the emperor Caracalla was once listening to an orator who kept saying, "the bloodthirsty Alexander, the enemy of the gods," ὁ μιαιφόνος Ἀλέξανδρος, ὁ θεοῖς ἐχθρὸς (77.8.5). The repeated remarks so enraged Caracalla, who loved Alexander, that he promised the orator that he would kill him if he did not stop. Eusebius did not necessarily rely on our knowledge of Daniel 7 for that image.

Discussing Eusebius' use of Cyrus in the *Life*, Cameron and Hall argue that the literary portrait does not correspond to the one Eusebius constructs for

Cyrus in his *Commentary on Isaiah* (Cameron and Hall 1999: 188). Cyrus is the same historical character, but Eusebius has used two different traditions to inform his two distinct narratives on Cyrus. One is the Messiah of Isaiah's God, whereas the latter is Herodotus' hubristic king who died shamefully. I would argue that we need to consider Eusebius' use of Alexander in the same way. The negative portrait of Alexander in the *Life*—one of the harshest criticisms of the king in antiquity—is best understood within the context of imperial invective, whereas Eusebius created other representations of Alexander in his other works.

Eusebius begins the *Life* reflecting upon the death of Constantine, underlining that the *Life* will provide an immortal monument to his piety. The deceased emperor may have ruled from beyond the grave, but his memory required control by the bishop. Even if Eusebius did not live to see the *Life* to its completion, he had at least invented a new, wholly Christian, component to the discourse in seeing Alexander's death as opposed to Christian life. Unfortunately, the text did not immediately make the impact Eusebius had hoped for.

Coda: Alexander, Rome, and the Gospel

One very interesting passage that combines historiography, *paradeigma*, and *synkrisis* appears in the homilies of John Chrysostom (Wirth 1993: 65 n. 210). It occurs in a sermon on 1 Thessalonians, which he delivered in Antioch at the close of the fourth century (before 397). Chrysostom proclaims:

> Before the Advent of Christ, the Macedonian people dominated and were more widely known than the Romans. The conquest of Macedon was what made Rome famous. For the stories about the Macedonian king, who set out from a village to vanquish the world, surpass every tale. This is also why the prophet envisaged him as a winged leopard that symbolized his speed (τὸ τάχος), strength (τὸ σφοδρὸν), fiery spirit (τὸ πυρῶδες), and the sudden flight over the world with trophies of victory. They say that, when he was told by some philosopher that there were countless worlds, he sighed heavily knowing that he had not yet conquered one among many. He was of such a high mind (μεγαλόφρων), greatness of soul (μεγαλόψυχος) and celebrated everywhere. The glory of the people went forth with the name of the king. For his name was: "Alexander the Macedonian". Because he was commonly celebrated, the things that took place then have rightly been admired everywhere. For nothing can cover fame. Hence the achievements of the Macedonians were no less distinguished than those of the Romans.
> John Chrysostom *Hom.* 1 Thess. 1.8–10 (*PG* 62.399).

In order to understand properly the strong emphasis John places on Alexander's fame, it is necessary to begin with the context of the homily. The passage occurs at the very beginning of the text: the preacher expounds the following line in Paul's letter, "For the word of the Lord has sounded forth from you not only in Macedonia and Achaia, but in every place where your faith in God has become known, so that we have no need to speak about it" (1 Thess. 1:9). John argues that the Gospel, unlike local praises of virtuous men, has been spread to the furthest corners of the earth. Its message has been understood equally well everywhere it went. To demonstrate that the Apostle's (and his own) words were not empty boasts, he brings in the Macedonian fame under Alexander as a point of comparison. Alexander's glorious enterprise licenses John to posit that the Gospel also spread far and wide at a rapid pace. The result was self-evident for anyone living in the imperial East of the late fourth century. John uses the fact that the memory of Alexander remained strong to illustrate the way in which the Gospel's fame had also lingered long. This is the single most striking argument on behalf of the religion: by analogy, the greatness of Alexander confirms the purported glory of the Gospel. If, for Byzantine Christians, Alexander could be used to corroborate the religious mission of what had originally been a small sectarian movement, he could clearly be deployed in every type of Christian argument. As if that assessment was not enough to warrant interest, the passage also ranks Alexander and Rome at exactly the same level. Alexander, Rome, and the Gospel go hand in hand in Christian Antioch.

John's exposition brings out many of the themes under consideration in this chapter. John arranges Biblical imagery (the leopard of Daniel 7) with the famous *paradeigma* of endless conquest (e.g., Val. Max. 8.14.ext2; Plut. *Mor.* 446d–e; Ael. *VA* 4.29), giving them both a positive spin for the sake of argument. The former displays his virtues, not his bloodlust or wickedness, and the latter—Alexander's insatiable longing for more, typically used as criticism for his hunger after power and, therefore, not a very Christian character trait—is adapted to mean that conquest is desirable. A powerful individual with high mind and soul could have a negative connotation if placed in the context of Christian humility but, in this case, the local context of the passage makes other demands on the Christian preacher. Elsewhere in John Chrysostom's work, we find no evidence that we should treat the specific terms used here, μεγαλόφρων and μεγαλόψυχος, as inherently negative. In this instance, John's projection of Alexander was thus underpinned by his belonging to the imperial East, as much as his personal Christianity.

Conclusion

Palladius, a fifth-century bishop of Helenopolis, wrote that "Alexander rose like the sun in Macedon and rode across the whole world before he set in Babylon" (Palladius *Life of the Brahmans* 2.1, trans. Stoneman). The king reversed the course of the sun. He sped across the world, *kosmos*, like a shooting star. The vivid imagery recalls similar symbolism in pagan Classicizing authors, who spoke of Alexander as a sun over Asia (Diod. Sic. 17.54.5; Val. Max. 6.4.ext3). In this study, we have witnessed that Christians and non-Christians shared many other thoughts and stories about Alexander. But the Alexander tradition is one thing, and the Christian thought world is another. In it, what has Alexander to do with Jesus Christ? Alexandria with Jerusalem? Alexander's visions with Biblical prophecies? The conquest of Persia with the spread of the Gospel? Alexander's death with the Resurrection?

The short answer is more than one might expect. The preceding pages have proved that Alexander played a significant role in Christian discourse from the reign of Marcus Aurelius to that of Constantine I. It may seem strange to apply such an imperial context to ancient Christianity, but we must remember that the religion was tied to Rome since New Testament times (Luke 2:1). Although Christian discourse on Alexander continued far beyond the reign of Constantine, we have witnessed how the principal components came into shape in this early period. Much of the material was already available in other texts, and the Christians made their own selections and subtle alterations to accommodate their views and arguments. In fact, the process of selection established Alexander's importance in the Christian church and developed the king's legacy in profound ways that would influence readers from antiquity until the present day. One may still encounter Alexander in the church, especially in the Orthodox Church, and generally in sermons and iconography.

Chapter 1 introduced the principal sources, their contexts and agendas. The scattered references to Alexander revealed what kind of discourse we are dealing with. Although the list of writers is uneven, it betrayed other key patterns in the learning and social standing of the sources. One central observation was that the intellectuals under review worked in imperial milieus across the cities of the Mediterranean basin, not as outsiders but as integral parts of the textual communities. They had much in common with the rhetorically trained writers that we normally depend on for our knowledge of Alexander. In other ways, their version of the story of Alexander would seem very strange, if we only had early Christian authors to consult. It was observed that multiple authors not only appropriated Classicizing material, but also Jewish material for exegetical, apologetic, and historiographical purposes.

Chapter 2 scrutinized the Classicizing Alexandrology with a focus on three overarching themes: education, epistolography, and deification. At a general level we saw that the Christians were at least as adept as their pagan peers in manipulating the material, and they often made use of the same stories as their contemporaries across the religious divide. With regard to education, Christians criticized the teachers of Alexander on the basis of examples of the king's bad behavior. The student's lack of self-control reflected the failure of his teacher. This sort of strategy was typical for critics of Greek philosophies, even non-Christians, such as Lucian, and we should not over-interpret that hostile tendency, although the Christians were of course criticizing pagans. But they did so in the manner of traditional rhetoric. Other encounters between Alexander and philosophers interested Christians. They devote close attention to the Indian philosophers. The most striking difference from the Classicizing pattern is the complete absence of Diogenes the Cynic, which was explained by the Christian emphasis on the Brahmans. In terms of epistolography, Christians seized upon one pseudo-letter in particular, Alexander's letter to his mother associated with the name of Leon of Pella, and we saw how Christians emphasized a single aspect of it, namely Alexander's revelation that the Egyptian gods were men. Alexander's witness to the supposed folly of their beliefs was more frequently revisited in apologetic literature than most other themes pertaining to the Alexander tradition. Finally, in terms of deification, we saw that Christians missed a great opportunity to find fault with Alexander's own deification. They rarely engaged with the *topos* of birth myths and the king's death, and thus it appears that Christians collectively regarded Alexander as more useful for other apologetic arguments.

Chapter 3 turned to the alternative tales of Alexander from Jewish literature. Christians differed from their pagan peers in taking this material seriously. It was observed how the Hellenistic aspect of Judaism made Jewish discourse available to Christians and, in many respects, they simply took over material without alteration. But Christians also exploited Jewish stories in the same eclectic fashion as they did Classicizing material, focusing on three nodes of story: Alexandria, the Bible, and Josephus' story of Alexander's visit to Jerusalem. Alexandria, a central city of the Jewish diaspora, supplied some tales that resonated well with Christians, such as the Septuagint legend, that hardly needed modification. It was usually more important how the story was arranged in historical time, because Christians could confer upon it an apologetic dimension if they wanted to dismiss pagan claims to having a philosophy of superior antiquity. The Bible, primarily the Old Testament Book of Daniel, provided Christians with God's announcement of Alexander's world-changing conquest, and they labored hard to explain how Alexander fit into God's providential plan. The Danielic prophecies, more than anything else, re-framed ancient religious discourse on Alexander. The text supplied Christians with a different frame of historical reference with its own set of imagery that every exegete was required to comment on or use in exegesis of other Christian texts, such as the NT Revelation. The inclusion of Alexander in the Biblical drama also removed features often found in the common Alexander tradition, such as the *topos* of Fortune. Lastly, Josephus' historiography had already incorporated the Danielic material into Alexander's history, and once Christians discovered the method, the Christians took Josephan Alexandrology in a different direction. While they appropriated Josephus' most famous tale, they removed from it many features and Josephan emphases, so that the Jerusalem tale was reduced to its most basic import: God's influence on historical events, and Alexander's submission to divine power. In this form, parted from its Jewish roots, the story could be used to support other apologetic agendas in various genres. Christians did not appropriate many other stories from Josephus, since several of them concerned Alexander's—or other monarchs'—granting of privileges to Jewish culture.

Chapter 4 explored the largest melting pot of story, namely historiography and rhetoric. J. R. R. Tolkien once wrote of a "Cauldron of Story" (Tolkien 2006: 125) in which the soup, a blend of stories, kept boiling, and to which anyone could add new bits, dainty or gross. In the same way, early Christians needed to mix classical and Jewish bits into one single soup of history, which yielded rich results. Christians had to experiment, and no particular flavor was preferred until the early fourth century. Some experiments were successful, and others were not. We cannot pin a given story's success to a single point. Some additional pieces of story were present, but were only paraded on occasion, and they almost always come directly from *exemplum* literature. Classicizing rhetoric ensured a smooth transition between types of story, and historical comparisons became an important part of the discourse. Comparison with Christian characters was a contest Alexander could not win. Nevertheless, the comparative use of the king indicates how closely linked Alexander became with Christian discourse on power and fame, to the effect that most Christian leaders were compared to Alexander. This method reveals a strong continuity between imperial rhetoric and Christian discourse.

These chapters have worked towards the general two-pronged conclusion that Alexander mattered for Christian self-definitions, and that Christianity mattered for Alexander's tradition. Let us take these by turn.

In a time before Peter Brown's concept of Late Antiquity, Brown's supervisor Arnaldo Momigliano (1907–1987) had done much to enrich our understanding of ancient historiography in Judaism and early Christianity. In his contribution to *Paganism and Christianity in the Fourth Century* (1963), Momigliano argued that hagiography became more important, and so "the ordinary biography of kings and politicians became insignificant" (Momigliano 1963: 93). While this is true with some qualification, we have seen that Alexander's life was certainly made relevant. Christian versions of the *Alexander Romance* were not produced until the fifth century in Armenia and Byzantium, but the process of incorporating him into Christian literature in other ways had begun already in the second century.

Ultimately, Alexander's place in this enculturation process reflects the fact that the Christians were themselves part of the Roman Empire and its culture (Averil Cameron 1991; Brown 1992). They lived in a world in which the legacy of Alexander was ubiquitous (Lane Fox 1986). Given this imperial canvas for Christian activity, it seems wrong to me to impose the binary "East and West" relationship on the discourse (Klein 1988); we have seen how Alexander motifs and stories travelled freely all across the Roman Empire and even deeper into Eurasia. Intriguingly, the greatest geographical difference actually lay in the choice of texts for Biblical exegesis. The only reason why Alexander was employed relatively less in western exegesis of Scripture was because the Latin Christians were concerned with expounding Revelation rather than the Book of Daniel. Since the Byzantine East did not accept Revelation as canonical, they turned to the Old Testament prophets to stimulate their eschatological expectations. It is a facile point that, without the same focus on Daniel, Latin Christians would simply not encounter Alexander as much in their exegesis. Despite Jerome's composition of a *Commentary on Daniel*, the Latin West did not take the same interest in the text until the age of the Venerable Bede.

Outside the world of exegesis, civic discourse on Alexander represents another connecting factor for Christians. That is why great imperial cities have held such a high place in this study, since they are emblematic of cultural exchange and the migration of tales. Looking at these cultural centers, I believe that it is wrong to think of distinct Alexander traditions in terms of language. For instance, it is incorrect to assume that the "Senecan hostility known from the Latin tradition is completely absent from the Greek" (Stoneman 2008: 218), because the same "hostile" *topoi* regularly appear in Greek texts as well. In fact, as far as the Christians were concerned, most of the material pertaining to Alexander seems imported from Greek discourse at an early stage. The Christian unity of the East and the West was explained with reference to the fact that the same sort of Alexander *exempla* were extensively used in both halves of the empire. While the Christians certainly debated fiercely among themselves, they at least seem to have made the same assumptions about Alexander-related themes, wherever the authors were physically based in the empire.

Of course, once imperial Christians had established Alexander in Christian thought, other parts of the Church felt the influence in other regions. The present study has touched upon the eastern figures of Aphrahat and Pseudo-Ephrem, who do not draw upon any of the Roman *exempla*, but focus solely on the material derived from the Book of Daniel. The chronological parameters of this study prohibit us from venturing into the Coptic Church and a fragmentary fifth-century version of the *Alexander Romance* in the famous White Monastery of Shenoute of Atripe (Demandt 2009: 22–23). We saw that the Armenian Church brought the Greek *Alexander Romance* to Armenia sometime during the fifth century. Recall that the text was the only non-theological text translated from Greek into Armenian at the time, and Christians granted it a high status surpassed only by Scripture (Wolohojian 1969: 8). But Armenian Christians also wrote their own Alexander tales, such as the *Conversion of the Greeks* (fourth century?), which focused on Constantine's conversion (Rapp 2014: 196). Another Armenian text, *The Life of the Kings*, purports to rely upon a host of other written sources: a book of the Greeks on Alexander; a conversion of the Greeks; and a history of Armenia featuring Gregory the Illuminator, Armenia's patron saint, and the conversion of King Trdat (Tiridates III), the first Christian king of Armenia. Moreover, in the Syriac Church and the literature it produced (Gero 1993; Reinink 2005), there are even longer prose and poetic narratives of interest. For instance, the seventh-century Syriac Marionite Chronicle strikingly begins its world history with Alexander, just as 1 Maccabees did. Alexander could thus help to define Christianness elsewhere.

To take the other point that Christianity mattered for Alexander's tradition. I have argued that Christian use of the Alexander tradition left its mark. I am thinking more about important effects than a singular attitude towards the king. It has long been typical of scholarship to question whether Alexander was a good or a bad guy (Niese 1897), but this approach is only productive when we look at isolated passages in which an ancient author is trying to construct a certain image. As for a singular Christian attitude, I cite the recent observation that "one certainly cannot postulate a uniquely or uniformly critical 'Christian' attitude to Alexander in late antiquity" (Smith 2011: 84; cf. Wirth 1993: 68). Such an observation needed to be made, but the fact that it needed to be made reveals a bias in the scholarship. After all, there was no single attitude to Alexander in the non-Christian Greek and Roman worlds either. The best we can do from our perspective is to detect how the literary patterns make the Christian Alexander stand out, and I hope to have shown on the preceding pages that pre-Constantinian Christians at least did agree on some overarching matters, despite being a heterogeneous group.

We noticed that Christians departed from previous traditions in some major ways. The following list consists of what I consider the most important:

- No Christian wrote a full-scale life of Alexander, or a history of his reign, from the second to the fourth century. A revision of the *Alexander Romance* came to fill that need in the fifth century.
- The Christian emphasis on Providence over Fortune may seem a minor if subtle change, but the shift deletes a canonical *topos* from the repertoire of Alexander.
- Christians systematically removed the sympathetic connections that Jewish tales sought to make with Alexander, the creator of the Hellenistic world in which the Greeks had encountered Jews at an equal footing.
- The Alexander imagery of Daniel (2, 7, 8) and of 1 Maccabees 1.1–8 was used to expound other scriptural passages. For instance, Christians recycled their interpretation of these passages in the commentaries on the Psalms, Isaiah, Jeremiah, Ezekiel, in the commentaries on some of the minor prophets (Hosea, Amos, Nahum, Habakkuk, Zephaniah, Haggai, Zechariah) and, importantly, Revelation. Previous scholarship has not realized the full extent of Alexander's importance for the early Christian interpretation of Scripture.
- The association of Alexander and his great city was of constant concern for the early Christians because Alexandria was a Christian city. Its civic history was rewritten repeatedly, and the quasi-divine Founder was adapted to a Christian framework. As a civilizing and peace-keeping founder, Alexander was projected in an imperial role to the point of being a virtuous conqueror

and pious ruler. His victories and rule in peaceful harmony were licensed by God. The Christians promoted this projection to corroborate their belief in Providence. Although this representation depends on Hellenistic sources, Christians took the stories in their own direction.

But such divergences with previous tradition betray the emphasis I have placed on the seeming coherence of the non-Christian and Christian Alexander discourse. If we raise the question of how distinctively *Christian* the Christian side of the discourse actually was, we find few obvious points of divergence. To take one example, the vehement insistence upon the power of Jesus in comparison to Alexander is a Christian trait, but it is done on a well-established model that anyone with rudimentary rhetorical training would recognize. We cannot then study Christians in isolation. We not only have to look at what had gone before, but also what was going on in the contemporary intellectual culture in which the Christians were participants.

Looking at the legacy of Alexander in early Christian texts also raises questions about the general Alexander discourse in antiquity. Serious work has naturally been devoted to the establishment of a more complete picture of the non-Christian traditions, but often without adequate collation of references or the proper comparative framework for understanding them in their various contexts. Scholars make very few cross-references to the contemporary Christians, and our understanding of the pagan sources themselves must clearly suffer as a consequence. Take, for instance, the orator Maximus of Tyre. Maximus also deploys Alexander frequently (Max. Tyr. 2.6, 8.4, 14.8, 23.7, 28.1, 29.2, 32.9, 36.6, 41.1), but his name does not appear in studies of Alexander and his tradition, not even those on the Antonine age (Zecchini 1984). Many of Maximus' references offer important testimony to what people were doing with the legacy of Alexander in the time of Marcus Aurelius, the emperor who himself commented on Alexander. From a modern perspective, Maximus' fault was that he did not cite a primary first-generation historian, which would have included him in Jacoby's *Die Fragmente der griechischen Historiker* (*Fragments of the Greek Historians*). But, as we saw in Chapter 4, Jacoby reserved a space for such writers. His collection of many noteworthy passages shows how much potential there is for the study of post-Arrian literature on Alexander. I believe that the *exemplum* literature framework will help us to discover a more complete picture of the ancient reception of Alexander in the later parts of antiquity.

No matter what we do with the data, we cannot accuse the Christians of single-handedly causing the complete distortion of Alexander's image. That process had begun long before, even while Alexander strode the earth. To me, it seems misguided to apply the adage of "decline" to later Alexander discourse (Wirth 1993), and I hope to have shown how there was both continuity and change in Alexander's tradition from his entry into the Roman world. If we must speak "in the interest of historical accuracy," it does not make sense to look for the historical Alexander in early Christianity, any more than it makes sense to look for the historical character among the writings of imperial non-Christians. But we can say with historical interest that we now know more about the methods with which Alexandrology was filtered through to Christians, pagans, and Jews.

More broadly, I believe that Christians and non-Christians all shared in and contributed to the overarching discourse of the period as a whole. If we give priority to one group, we must always be mindful of the patterns in the discourse of other groups. Comparisons must be made in order to establish a more holistic picture of the tradition of Alexander in ancient literature. And, since it may not be possible to recover every single aspect of the Alexander tradition, one must always strive to make the most of the opportunities that give a better impression of it. I think that a guiding principle in future studies of Alexander receptions should be Briant's contention that we must not only seek to recover the legacy of Alexander in the period, culture, or text we study, but also strive to learn more about the objects of study by means of the representations of Alexander that the writers choose to employ (Briant 2012: 12). In my case, I have applied this principle to early Christianity. I am convinced that this approach is fundamental for understanding Alexandrology in the ancient and modern worlds.

Epilogue: Writing Alexander, Writing Constantine

We have seen many examples of Alexander's afterlife in imperial rhetoric. For example, Eusebius' *Life of Constantine* featured one of the most damning literary portraits of Alexander in antiquity (Chapter 4). We witnessed how Eusebius created the image from traditional rhetorical material that was taught in urban schools. The only "new" *topos* included was Constantine's preservation of life contrasted to Alexander's mass-killing. Eusebius uses the *synkrisis* to transform Alexander into the ultimate antithesis of Constantine, and scholarship has normally not looked beyond this particular interpretation. But the text also emphasizes Constantine's martial might and his great conquests. Some of the areas conquered were the same as in the Alexander tradition, such as India (4.50). The Indian embassy to Constantine reminds us of the ones that came to previous Roman rulers, such as Augustus and Trajan, so the literary traditions of other Roman monarchs may supersede any connection to the Macedonian king. Nevertheless, given the focus on war and Eusebius' extensive knowledge of the Alexander tradition, it remains worth testing whether any echoes of Alexander reverberate elsewhere in the Eusebian hagiography of the first Christian emperor. By this, I mean correspondences in their respective literary traditions that Eusebius drew upon, not actual historical episodes that played out in the ways they did. I am interested in the literary representation conveyed by Eusebius' composition, that is the literary monument for Constantine, the emperor's memory controlled by his bishop.

I tabulate the literary parallels that I believe are pertinent below.

1.10.2, 4.75.	No one is equal to Constantine.	No one is equal to Alexander, Diod. Sic. 17.1.3.
1.19.2–20.1	Physiognomy of Constantine.	Physiognomy of Alexander, Plut. *Alex.* 4.1–7.
1.13–21.	On Constantius, father of Constantine.	On Philip, Alexander's father, e.g., Plut. *Alex.* 2–10, *AR* 1.5–24.

1.22.1–2	Succession between Constantius and Constantine well ordered.	Ascension of Alexander after Philip, typically disordered, see e.g., Just. *Epit.* 9.7.1–6.
1.25.1	Consolidation of the western frontier on the Rhine.	Consolidation of the western frontier on the Danube (Istros), see e.g., Arr. *Anab.* 1.1–6.
1.25.2	Constantine in Britain.	Alexander never came to Britain, see Arr. *Anab.* 7.1.4.
1.29.	Constantine's vision revealed in a dream. Promise of victory.	Alexander's vision of Jerusalem and God's name revealed in a dream. Promise of victory. E.g., Joseph. *AJ* 11.333–335; Origen *C. Cels.* 5.50.
1.37–41.	Constantine destroys Maxentius' armies and reorganizes Rome.	Alexander sacks Thebes of the Greeks, but later rebuilds, see e.g., *AR* 1.45–46; cf. Diod. Sic. 17.8.2–14.4; Just. *Epit.* 11.3.6–4.8; Plut. *Alex.* 11.6–13.5; Arr. *Anab.* 1.7–9.
1.43.	Constantine's charity, gives to the poor.	Alexander's charity, gives treasure to his friends and soldiers, see e.g., Arr. *Anab.* 7.28.2–3, Amm. Marc. 25.4.15
1.47.	Plots again Constantine revealed by divine premonitions.	Plots against Alexander revealed by divine intervention, see e.g., *AR* 3.31, Curt. 8.6.16.
2.1–22.	Constantine defeats Licinius twice on the field of battle.	Alexander defeats Darius twice, at Issus and Gaugamela.
2.14.1.	Constantine's traveling tent and court, cf. 4.56.	Alexander's traveling tent and court, see Arr. *Anab.* 5.1.2; Plut. *Eum.* 13.3–4; Ael. *VA* 9.3; Polyaen. *Strat.* 4.3.24.
2.30–31.	Constantine's Exiles Decree.	Alexander's Exiles Decree. See e.g., Diod. Sic. 17.109.1; Curt. 10.2.4; Just. *Epit.* 13.5.3–4
3.13–14.	Constantine speaks Greek and Latin.	Alexander speaks Macedonian and Greek, e.g., Plut. *Alex.* 51.6.
3.24.1.	Constantine's letters, cf. 3.24.1: "I can do a special collection of letters later."	Alexander's letters, see Montaigne 2014.
3.25–40.	Constantine's building program of churches, sanctifying Jerusalem. Seeing the Tomb of Jesus.	Alexander's foundation of Alexandria and construction of its religious precincts. Visits the cave of Serapis. See *AR* 1.30–34.
4.15.	Constantine's eyes gaze upon heaven on his coins.	Alexander's iconography similar, Dahmen 2007: 96–97 n. 337, Wienand 2016.

4.30.	Constantine asks one of his courtiers how far they should desire to conquer. He draws a small spot on the ground with a spear, and explains that, regardless of wealth and world conquest, a man only takes as much land with him in death as he had drawn up on the ground.	The same advice given to Alexander by the Indian Gymnosophists. See e.g., Arr. *Anab.* 7.1.6.
4.36.	Constantine requests books.	Alexander requests books, see Plut. *Alex.* 8.
4.48.	Flatterers praise Constantine for being a new Jesus. The emperor cannot accept this blasphemy.	Alexander actively opposed flatteries and deification, e.g., in the ichor anecdote, Bosworth 2011.
4.63-71.	Constantine's last days.	Alexander's last days.

I have illustrated each episode in the *Life of Constantine* with an analogous episode in the Alexander tradition, but saved the most convincing for last. Eusebius' narrative of Constantine's last days reads as if it has been extracted directly from the ending of the *Alexander Romance* (*AR* 3.30-35). Eusebius writes that Constantine welcomes death after his late baptism; he states that he is ready for the immortal life in heaven; he writes his will; and he dies on the greatest day during the celebration of Pentecost. There is lamentation everywhere in the city. Constantine's body is put on display in a golden coffin. The soldiers and ruling class filed past Constantine's coffin and greatly lamented his death. The order of succession is sorted out slowly, and the news of his death reaches Rome. The emperor is laid to rest in the Shrine of the Apostles accompanied by continuous weeping. For comparison, the *Alexander Romance* relates how Alexander is poisoned and dies during a grand celebration (for Dionysus?); when he realizes that death is imminent, he asks to be received in heaven as the third mortal made god (Hercules and Dionysus being the other two); he writes his Will; just before death, his men file past him to see that he is still alive; and upon death he is deified (cf. *Vit. Const.* 4.73). A contest of mourning between Persians and Macedonians ensues. The division of the empire is made clear from the Will. Alexander's body is brought to the Egyptian Memphis, then Alexandria, to be put on display in a shrine as is appropriate for his majesty (cf. Diod. Sic. 17.117-118, Curt. 10.5-10, Just. *Epit.* 12.15-16, Arr. *Anab.* 7.24-30).

On the basis of the analysis above, I contend that we can make a case for a common pattern in the narratives on the two rulers. In my view at least, Eusebius seems heavily inspired by the Alexander tradition. Some passages seem antithetical or corresponding to specific episodes, going much further than the directions of the *basilikos logos* template. We know of many contemporary writers from this period who also wrote works on both Alexander and Constantine, such as the pagan Praxagoras of Athens (*FGrH/BNJ* 219 Ager; cf. Bemarchius *FGrH/BNJ* 220 Banchich), so it is not implausible—indeed, it seems likely—that Eusebius may have been inspired by what his contemporaries were doing. Perhaps the author inserted an openly hostile digression on Alexander at the beginning of the *Life* to misdirect readers away from the fact that Alexander's tradition fueled Eusebius' portrait of Constantine. In any case, Eusebius' use of Alexander to praise Constantine adheres to the models of imperial rhetoric that we have discussed in this study.

For now, a final observation on Alexander and his literary tradition: Richard Stoneman (2003: 334 n. 67) noted the need for a hermeneutic study of Alexander in early Christian literature. Previous scholarship had gone some of the way in answering this request and, with this study, I hope to have covered more ground and many gaps. Studying *exemplum* literature, for instance, has revealed a strong connection between early Christians and imperial education, which should not surprise us anymore. But Christian *exempla* also go much further than the Classicizing *topoi* in their use of "new" stories from Jewish texts. To understand these receptions, we need to move beyond and focus on other material that underpin the broader picture. The *Alexander Romance*, surely one of the most important and influential texts for Alexander's legacy, has normally taken priority for late antique Alexander receptions, but I hope to have shown that it is a worthwhile endeavor to cast wide nets elsewhere. The Christian Alexander was established in the late antique period and would influence the next millennium of Alexander literature in Europe and elsewhere. The nexus of themes was naturally expanded greatly and developed in later periods of Christian history— even continuing into the present day—but that is a story for another time.

References

Alonso Troncoso, V. (2010), "The Bearded King and the Beardless Hero," in E. Carney and D. Ogden (eds.), *Philip II and Alexander the Great: Father and Son, Lives and Afterlives*, 13–24, Oxford: OUP.

Amitay, O. (2010), *From Alexander to Jesus*, Berkeley, CA: UCP.

Amitay, O. (2017), "Alexander in Jerusalem: The Extra-Josephan Traditions," in P. Spilsbury and C. Seeman (eds.), *Judean Antiquities 11: Translation and Commentary*, 128–147, Leiden: Brill.

Anderson, A. R. (1932), *Alexander's Gate, Gog and Magog, and the Inclosed Nations*, Cambridge, MA: Mediaeval Academy of America.

Anderson, G. (1993), *The Second Sophistic: A Cultural Phenomenon in the Roman Empire*, London and New York: Routledge.

Andrade, N. J. (2018), *The Journey of Christianity to India in Late Antiquity*, Cambridge: CUP.

Angliviel, L. (2003), "Alexandre le Grand au IVe siècle apr. J.-C.," *Metis* n.s. 1: 271–288.

Asirvatham, S. (2012), "Alexander the Philosopher in the Greco-Roman, Persian, and Arabic Tradition," in R. Stoneman, K. Erickson and I. Netton (eds.), *The Alexander Romance in Persia and the East*, Ancient Narrative Supplementum 15, 311–326, Groningen: Barkhuis.

Asirvatham, S. (2018), "Plutarch's *Alexander*," in K. Moore (ed.), *Brill's Companion to the Reception of Alexander the Great*, 355–376, Leiden: Brill.

Atkinson, J. E. (1980), *A Commentary on Q. Curtius Rufus' Historiae Alexandri Magni, Books 3 and 4*, Amsterdam: J. C. Gieben.

Atkinson, J. E. (1994), *A Commentary on Q. Curtius Rufus' Historiae Alexandri Magni, Books 5 to 7*, Amsterdam: Hakkert.

Atkinson, J. E. (2009), *Curtius Rufus*, History of Alexander the Great, *Book 10*, with intro. and comm., trans. J. C. Yardley, Oxford: OUP.

Ausfeld, A. ([1907] 2009), *Der griechischen Alexanderroman*, ed. U. Bernays, Charleston, SC: BiblioBazaar.

Badian, E. (2012), *Collected Papers on Alexander the Great*, ed. R. Stoneman, London and New York: Routledge.

Barbantani, S. (2014), "'Mother of Snakes and Kings': Apollonius Rhodius' *Foundation of Alexandria*," *Histos* 8: 209–245.

Bar-Kochva, B. (2010), *The Image of the Jews in Greek Literature: The Hellenistic Period*, Berkeley, CA and London: UCP.

Barnes, T. D. (1985), "Constantine and the Christians of Persia," *JRS* 75: 126–136.

Baynham, E. (1994), "The Question of Macedonian Divine Honors for Philip," *Mediterranean Archaeology* 7: 35–43.

Bichler, R. (2010), "Wie lange wollen wir mit noch mit Alexander dem Grossen siegen?," in R. Rollinger and B. Truschnegg (eds.), *Reinhold Bichler: Gesammelte Schriften 3*, 207–240, Wiesbaden: Harassowitz Verlag.

Bichler, R. (2018), "Alexander's Image in German, Anglo-American and French Scholarship from the Aftermath of World War I to the Cold War," in K. Moore (ed.), *Brill's Companion to the Reception of Alexander the Great*, 640–674, Leiden: Brill.

Bickerman, E. J. (1967), *Four Strange Books of the Bible*, New York: Schoken Books.

Bickerman, E. J. (1988), *The Jews in the Greek Age*, Cambridge, MA: HUP.

Billows, R. (2000), "Polybius and Alexander Historiography," in A. B. Bosworth and E. Baynham (eds.), *Alexander the Great in Fact and Fiction*, 286–306, Oxford: OUP.

Bodenmann, R. (1986), *Naissance d'une Exégèse: Daniel dans l'Église ancienne des trois premiers siècles*, Tübingen: Mohr Siebeck.

Borg, B. (2013), *Crisis and Ambition: Tomb and Burial Customs in Third Century CE Rome*, Oxford: OUP.

Borg, B., ed. (2004), *Paideia: The World of the Second Sophistic*. Berlin: De Gruyter.

Bosman, P. R. (2007), "King Meets Dog: The Origin of the Meeting between Alexander the Great and Diogenes," *Acta Classica* 50: 51–63.

Bosman, P. R. (2010), "The Gymnosophist Riddle Contest (*Berol. P.* 13044): A Cynic Text?," *GBRS* 50: 175–192.

Bosworth, A. B. (1980–), *A Historical Commentary on Arrian's History of Alexander*, 3 vols., Oxford: OUP [Final volume edited by Pat Wheatley and Liz Baynham].

Bosworth, A. B. (1988), *Conquest and Empire: The Reign of Alexander the Great*, Cambridge: CUP.

Bosworth, A. B. (2011), "Anecdote, Apophthegm and the 'Real' Alexander," *Humanities Australia* 2: 44–52.

Briant, P. (2010), *Alexander the Great and His Empire: A Short Introduction*, trans. Amélie Kuhrt, Princeton, NJ: PUP.

Briant, P. (2012), *Alexandre des Lumières. Fragments d'histoire européenne*, Paris: Gallimard.

Briant, P. (2016), *Alexandre: exégèse des lieux communs*, Paris: Gallimard.

Briant, P. (2017), *The First European: A History of Alexander in the Age of Empire*, trans. Nicholas Elliott, Cambridge, MA: HUP.

Bridges, V. (2018), *Medieval Narratives of Alexander the Great: Transnational Texts in England and France*, Suffolk: Boydell and Brewer.

Broad, W. E. L. (2015), *Alexander or Jesus? The Origin of the Title "Son of God,"* Eugene, OR: Pickwick Publications (self-published).

Brown, P. ([2003] 2013), *The Rise of Western Christendom: Triumph and Diversity, A.D. 200–1000*, Hoboken, NJ: John Wiley & Sons.

Brown, P. (1992), *Power and Persuasion: Towards a Christian Empire*, Madison, WI: UWP.

Brown, P. (1995), *Authority and the Sacred: Aspects of the Christianisation of the Roman World*, Cambridge: CUP.

Brunell, C. (2017), "Alexander's Persian Pillow and Alexander's Cultured Commander," *CJ* 112.3: 257–278.

Budge, E. W. (1889), *The History of Alexander the Great: Being the Syriac Version of the Pseudo-Callisthenes*, Cambridge: CUP.

Buitenwerf, R. (2003), *Book III of the* Sibylline Oracles *and Its Social Setting*, Leiden: Brill.

Burgess, R. (2013), "The Date, Purpose, and Historical Context of the Original Greek and the Latin Translation of the So-Called *Excerpta Latina Barbari*," *Traditio* 68: 1–56.

Burgess, R. (2018), "Chronicles," in S. McGill and E. J. Watts (eds.), *A Companion to Late Antique Literature*, 177–192, Hoboken, NJ: Wiley Blackwell.

Burgess, R. W. and M. Kulikowski (2013), *Mosaics of Time: The Latin Chronicle Traditions from the First Century BC to the Sixth Century AD*, vol. 1, Turnhout: Brepols.

Cameron, Averil (1991), *Christianity and the Rhetoric of Empire: The Development of Christian Discourse*, Berkeley, CA: UCP.

Cameron, Averil (1997), "Eusebius' *Vita Constantini* and the Construction of Constantine', in M. J. Edwards and S. Swain (eds.), *Portraits: Biographical Representation in the Greek and Latin Literature of the Roman Empire*, 145–174, Oxford: OUP.

Cameron, Averil and Stuart G. Hall (1999), *Eusebius' Life of Constantine. Introduction, Translation and Commentary*, Oxford: OUP.

Carlsen, J., ed. (1993), *Alexander the Great: Reality and Myth*, Rome: L'Erma di Bretschneider.

Carney, E. (2015), *King and Court in Ancient Macedonia: Rivalry, Treason and Conspiracy*, Swansea: The Classical Press of Wales.

Carraroli, D. (1892), *La Legenda di Alessandro Magno*, Mondovi: Tip. G. Issoglio.

Cary, G. (1956), *The Medieval Alexander*, ed. D. J. A. Ross, Cambridge: CUP.

Cerrato, J. A. (2002), *Hippolytus between East and West: The Commentaries and the Provenance of the Corpus*, Oxford: OUP.

Chadwick, H. (2001), *The Church in Ancient Society: From Galilee to Gregory the Great*, Oxford: Clarendon Press.

Collins, J. (2016), *The Apocalyptic Imagination: An Introduction to Jewish Apocalypse Literature*, 3rd edition, Grand Rapids, MI: Wm. B. Eerdmans Publishing.

Coogan, M., M. Brettler, C. Newsom, and P. Perkins, eds. (2010), *The New Oxford Annotated Bible: New Revised Standard Version with the Apocrypha*, 4th edn., Oxford: OUP.

Corke-Webster, J. (2017a), "A Man for the Times: Jesus and the Abgar Correspondence in Eusebius of Caesarea's *Ecclesiastical History*," *Harvard Theological Review* 110 (4): 563–587.

Corke-Webster, J. (2017b), "The Early Reception of Pliny the Younger in Tertullian of Carthage and Eusebius of Caesarea," *CQ* 61.1: 247–262.

Corke-Webster, J. (2019), *Eusebius and Empire: Constructing Church and Empire in the Ecclesiastical History*, Cambridge: CUP [non vidi].

Cornell, T. J., ed. (2013), *Fragments of the Roman Historians*, 3 vols., Oxford: OUP.

Cracco-Ruggini, L. (1963), "Sulla Christianizzazione della cultura pagana: il mito greco e latino di Alessandro dall'età antonina al Medio Evo," *Athenaeum* 43: 3–80.

Cribiore, R. (2017), "Why Did Christians Compete with Pagans for Greek *paideia*?," in Karina Martin Hogan, Matthew Goff, and Emma Wasserman (eds.), *Pedagogy in Ancient Judaism and Early Christianity*, 359–374, Atlanta: SBL Press.

Croisille, J.-M., ed. (1990), *Neronia IV. Alejandro Magno, modelo de los emperadores romanos*, Bruxelles: Peeters Leuven.

Dahmen, Karsten (2007), *The Legend of Alexander the Great on Greek and Roman Coins* London and New York: Routledge.

De Focara, G. S. (2013), *D'Alexandre à Jésus: de la grandeur profane à la grandeur sacrée*, Paris: L'Harmattan.

Dellinger, G. (1980), "Alexander der Grosse als Bekenner des jüdischen Gottesglaubens," *Journal for the Study of Judaism* 12 (1): 1–51.

Demacopoulos, G. E. (2016), "The Eusebian Valorization of Violence and Constantine's Wars for God," in A. E. Siecienski (ed.), *Constantine: Religious Faith and Imperial Policy*, 115–128, London: Routledge.

Demandt, A. (2009), *Alexander der Grosse: Leben und Legende*, Munich: C.H. Beck.

Denuzzo, I. (2003), "Le storie dei Alessandro Magno nei papiri," *PapLup* 12: 69–98.

Di Berardino, A., ed. (2014), *Encyclopedia of Ancient Christianity*, 3 vols., Downers Grove, IL: IVP Academic.

Djurslev, C. T. (2018a), "Revisiting Alexander's Gates against 'Gog and Magog': Observations on the Testimonies before the *Alexander Romance* Tradition," in Richard Stoneman, Krzysztof Nawotka, and Agnieszka Wojciechowska (eds.), *The Alexander Romance: History and Literature*, Ancient Narrative Supplementum 25, 201–214, Groningen: Barkhuis.

Djurslev, C. T. (2018b), "Battling without Beards: Synesius of Cyrene's *calvitii encomium*, Arrian's *Anabasis Alexandri* and the Alexander Discourse of the Fourth Century AD," *Karanos* 1: 55–65.

Djurslev, C. T. (2018c), "Did Alexander Read Cratinus' *Eunidae* on His Deathbed?," *GRBS* 58.4: 542–560.

Döpp, S. (1999), "Alexander in Spätlateinischer Literatur," *Göttinger Forum für Altertumswissenschaft* 2: 193–216.

Doukifar-Aerts, F. (2010), *Alexander Magnus Arabicus: A Survey of the Alexander Tradition through Seven Centuries, from Pseudo-Callisthenes to Suri*, Leuven: Peeters.

Dräger, P. (2007), *Eusebios. Über das Leben des glückseligen Kaisers Konstantin*, Oberhaid: Museum Helviticum.

Dreyer, B. (2009), "Heroes, Cults, and Divinity," in W. Heckel and L. A. Tritle (eds.), *Alexander the Great: A New History*, 218–233, Oxford: Blackwell.
Edwards, M. J., M. Goodman, and S. Price, eds. (1999), *Apologetic in the Roman Empire*, Oxford: OUP.
Ehrhardt, A. T. T. (1945), "Jesus Christ and Alexander the Great," *Journal of Theological Studies* 46 (181–182): 45–51.
Eicke, L. (1909), "Veterum philosophorum qualia fuerint de Alexandro Magno iudicia," Rostock: typis academicis Adlerianus.
Engberg, J., A.-C. Jacobsen, and J. Ulrich, eds. (2014), *In Defence of Christianity: Early Christian Apologists*, Frankfurt am Main: Peter Lang.
Erskine, A. (2013), "Founding Alexandria in the Alexandrian Imagination," in S. L. Ager and R. Faber (eds.), *Belonging and Isolation in the Hellenistic World*, 169–183, Toronto: UTP.
Eshleman, K. (2012), *The Social World of Intellectuals in the Roman Empire: Sophists, Philosophers and Christians*, Cambridge: CUP.
Fears, J. R. (1974), "The Stoic View of the Career and Character of Alexander the Great," *Philologus* 112: 113–130.
Finn, J. (2014), "Alexander's Return of the Tyrannicide Statues to Athens," *Hist.* 63.4: 385–403.
Flower, R. (2013), *Bishops and Emperors in Late Roman Invective*, Cambridge: CUP.
Flusser, D. (1972), "The Four Empires in the Fourth Sibyl and in the Book of Daniel," *IOS* 2: 148–175.
Fraser, P. M. (1972), *Ptolemaic Alexandria*, 3 vols., Oxford: OUP.
Fraser, P. M. (1996), *Cities of Alexander the Great*, Oxford: OUP.
Frugoni, C. S. (1978), *La fortuna di Alessandro Magno dall'antichità al medioevo*, Florence: La nuova Italia.
Fulinska, A. (2012), "Oriental Imagery and Alexander's Legend in Art: Reconnaissance," in R. Stoneman, K. Erickson, and I. R. Netton (eds.), *The Alexander Romance in Persia and the East*, Ancient Narrative Supplementum 15, 383–404, Groningen: Barkhuis.
Gagé, J. (1975), "Alexandre le Grand en Macédoine dans la Ière moitié du IIIe siècle ap. J.-C.," *Hist* 24 (1): 1–16.
Garstad, B. (2011), "Barbarian Interest in the *Excerpta Latina Barbari*," *Early Medieval Europe* 19: 3–42.
Garstad, B. (2016a), "Euhemerus and the Chronicle of John Malalas," *International History Review* 38: 900–929.
Garstad, B. (2016b), "Nebuchadnezzar and Alexander in the *Excerpta Latina Barbari*," *Iraq* 78: 25–48.
Garstad, B. (2018), "Alexander's Circuit of the Mediterranean in the *Alexander Romance*," in R. Stoneman, K. Nawotka, and A. Wojciechowska (eds.), *The Alexander Romance: History and Literature*, Ancient Narrative Supplementum 25, 129–157, Groningen: Barkhuis.

Gassman, M. (2018), "Cyprian's Early Career in the Church of Carthage," *JEH* 1–17, available online at DOI: 10.1017/S0022046917002780.

Gaullier-Bougassas, C. (2011), *L'historiographie médiévale d'Alexandre le Grand*, Turnhout: Brepols.

Gaullier-Bougassas, C. (2014), *La fascination pour Alexandre le Grand dans les littératures européennes (Xe-XVIe siècle)*, 4 vols., Turnhout: Brepols.

Gero, S. (1993), "The Legend of Alexander the Great in the Christian Orient," *Bulletin of John Rylands Library* 75: 3–9.

Goez, W. (1958), *Translatio Imperii*, Tübingen: Mohr Siebeck.

Grafton, A. and M. Williams (2006), *Christianity and the Transformation of the Book*, Cambridge, MA and London: HUP.

Green, P. (1978), "Caesar and Alexander: *aemulatio, imitatio*, and *comparatio*," *American Journal of Ancient History* 3: 193–209.

Green, P. (2013), *Alexander of Macedon, 356–323 B.C.: A Historical Biography*, with a new preface and foreword, Berkeley, CA: UCP.

Gruen, E. (2013), "Polybius and Josephus on Rome," in B. Gibson and T. Harrison (eds.), *Polybius and His World: Essays in Memory of F. W. Walbank*, 255–266, Oxford: OUP.

Gunderson, L. L. (1977), "The Portrait of Alexander the Great in the *Sibylline Oracles*," in *Ancient Macedonia* II, 53–66, Thessaloniki: Institute for Balkan Studies.

Gunderson, L. L. (1980), *Alexander's Letter to Aristotle about India*, Meisenheim am Glan: Hain.

Hacikyan, A. J., ed. (2002), *The Heritage of Armenian Literature: From the Sixth to the Eighteenth Century*, vol. 2, Detroit, MI: WSUP.

Hamilton, J. R. (1969), *Plutarch's Alexander: A Commentary*, Oxford: OUP.

Hammond, N. G. L. (1983), *Three Historians of Alexander the Great: The So-Called Vulgate Authors, Diodorus, Justin and Curtius*, Cambridge: CUP.

Hammond, N. G. L. (1993), *Sources for Alexander the Great: An Analysis of Plutarch's* Life of Alexander *and Arrian's* Anabasis Alexandrou, Cambridge: CUP.

Hansen, M. H. (2002), *The Triumph of Time. Reflections of a Historian on Time in History*, Copenhagen: Museum Tusculanum Press.

Harf-Lancner, L., ed. (1999), *Alexandre le Grand dans les littératures occidentales et proche-orientales*, Paris: Actes du Colloque de Paris.

Hau, L. I. (2016), *Moral History from Herodotus to Diodorus Siculus*, Edinburgh: EUP.

Heckel, W. (2006), *Who's Who in the Age of Alexander the Great: Prosopography of Alexander's Empire*, Oxford: OUP.

Heckel, W. (2015), "Alexander, Achilles, and Heracles: Between Myth and History," in E. Baynham and P. Wheatley (eds.), *East and West in the World Empire of Alexander: Essays in Honour of Brian Bosworth*, 21–34, Oxford: OUP.

Hoffmann, W. (1907), *Das literarische Porträt Alexanders des Grossen im griechischen und römischen Altertum*, Leipzig: Quelle and Meyer.

Holt, F. (2003), *Alexander the Great and the Mystery of the Elephant Medallions*, Berkeley, CA: UCP.

Inglebert, H. (2001), *Interpretatio Christiana: les mutations des savoirs (cosmographie, géographie, ethnographie, histoire) dans l'antiquité chrétienne, 30–630 après J.-C.*, Paris: Institut d'Études Augustiniennes.

Janiszewski, P. (2006), *The Missing Link: Greek Pagan Historiography in the Second Half of the Third Century and in the Fourth Century AD*, trans. Dorota Dzierzbicka, Warsaw.

Janiszewski, P., K. Stebnicka, and E. Szabat, eds. (2015), *Prosopography of Greek Rhetors and Sophists in the Roman Empire*, Oxford: OUP.

Johnson, A. P. (2006), *Ethnicity and Argumentation in Eusebius' Praeparatio evangelica*. Oxford Early Christian Studies, Oxford: OUP.

Johnson, A. P. (2014), *Eusebius*, London: I. B. Tauris.

Jouanno, C. (2002), *Naissance et métamorphoses du Roman d'Alexandre: domaine grec*, Paris: CNRS Éditions.

Jouanno, C. (2016), "Alexandre à Jérusalem. Variations byzantines sur un thème hérité de Flavius Josèphe," *Anabases* 23: 75–95.

Kampers, F. (1901), *Alexander der Grosse und die Idee des Weltimperiums in Prophetie und Sage*, Freiburg: Herderische Verlagshandlung.

Karttunen, K. (1989), *India in the Hellenistic World*, Helsinki.

Kaster, R. A. (1988), *Guardians of Language: The Grammarian and Society in Late Antiquity*, Berkeley, CA: UCP.

Klęczar, A. (2012), "The Pagan King before the One God: The Alexander Narrative in Josephus, *Antiquitates Iudaicae* XI.8," *Classica Cracoviensia* 15: 137–150.

Klęczar, A. (2018), "Alexander in the Jewish Tradition," in K. Moore (ed.), *Brill's Companion to the Reception of Alexander the Great*, 379–402, Leiden: Brill.

Klein, R. ([1988] 2002), "Zur Beurteilung Alexanders des Grossen in der Patristischen Literatur," in R. von Heahling and K. Scherberich (eds.), *Richard Klein: Roma versa per aevum. Ausgewählte Schriften zur heidnischen und christlichen Spätantike*, 460–517, Zürich and New York: Georg Olms.

Koulakiotis, E. (2006), *Genese und Metamorphose des Alexandermythos: Im Spiegel der griechischen nicht-historiographischen Überlieferung bis zum 3. Jh. n. Chr.*, Konstanz: UVK.

Koulakiotis, E. (2017), "Plutarch's Alexander, Dionysus and the Metaphysics of Power," in T. Howe, S. Müller, and R. Stoneman (eds.), *Ancient Historiography on War and Empire*, 226–249, Oxford: Oxbow Books.

Kroll, W. ([1926] 2005), *Historia Alexandri Magni. Recensio vetusta*, Hildesheim: Weidmann.

Krueger, D. (1996), *Symeon the Holy Fool: Leontius' Life and the Late Antique City*, Berkeley, CA: UCP.

Kühnen, A. (2008), *Die in der römischen Politik (1. Jh. v. Chr.–3. Jh. n. Chr.)*, Münster: Rhema Verlag.

Lane Fox, R. (1973), *Alexander the Great*, London: Penguin.

Lane Fox, R. (1986), *Pagans and Christians: In the Mediterranean World from the Second Century AD to the Conversion of Constantine*, London: Viking.

Larsen, L. I. and S. Rubenson, eds. (2018), *Monastic Education in Late Antiquity: The Transformation of Classical* Paideia, Cambridge: CUP.
Lightfoot, J. (2007), *The* Sibylline Oracles: *With Introduction, Text, and Commentary on Books 1–2*, Oxford: OUP.
Lüschen, T.-E. R. (2013), "Alexander der Grosse, Gott und Gottessohn: Die religiöse Rezeption von der Antike bis ins frühe Mittelalter," diss., Fakultät für Geistes- und Erziehungswissenschaften der Technischen Universität Carolo-Wilhelmina zu Braunschweig.
Mann, K. ([1929] 1963), *Alexander, Roman der Utopie*, Munich: Nyphemburger Verlagshandlung.
Marrou, H. I. (1982), *A History of Education in Antiquity*, trans. G. Lamb, Madison, WI: UWP.
Mederer, E. (1936), *Die Alexanderlegenden bei den ältesten Alexanderhistorikern*, Stuttgart: Kohlhammer.
Merkelbach, R. (1977), *Die Quellen des griechischen Alexanderromans*, 2nd edn, Munich: C. H. Beck.
Molina Marín, I. A. (2018), *Alejandro Magno (1916–2015): Un siglo de estudios sobre Macedonia antigua*, Zaragosa: Libros Porticos.
Momigliano, A., ed. (1963), *The Conflict Between Paganism and Christianity in the Fourth Century* (Oxford-Warburg Studies), Oxford: Clarendon Press.
Momigliano, A. (1975), *Alien Wisdom: The Limits of Hellenization*, Cambridge: CUP.
Momigliano, A. (1977), *Essays in Ancient and Modern Historiography*, Oxford: Basil Blackwell.
Momigliano, A. (1979), "Flavius Josephus and Alexander's Visit to Jerusalem," *Athenaeum* 57: 442–448.
Monferrar-Sala, J. P. (2011), "Alexander the Great in the Syriac Literary Tradition," in D. Zuwiyya (ed.), *A Companion to Alexander Literature in the Middle Ages*, 20–40, Leiden: Brill.
Montaigne, J. (2014), "Persuasion, Emotion, and the Letters of the *Alexander Romance*," *Ancient Narrative* 11: 159–189.
Moore, K., ed. (2018), *Brill's Companion to the Reception of Alexander the Great*, Leiden: Brill.
Morgan, T. (2007), *Popular Morality in the Early Roman Empire*, Cambridge: CUP.
Mossman, J. (1988), "Tragedy and Epic in Plutarch's *Alexander*," *JHS* 108: 83–93.
Naiden, F. (2019), *Soldier, Priest, and God: A Life of Alexander the Great*, Oxford: OUP.
Nawotka, K. (2017), *The Alexander Romance by Ps.-Callisthenes: A Historical Commentary*, Leiden: Brill.
Niese, B. (1897), "Zum Würdigen Alexanders des Grossen," *Historische Zeitschrift* 79: 1–44.
Nock, A. D. (1933), *The Old and the New in Religion from Alexander the Great to Augustine of Hippo*, Oxford: Oxford Clarendon Press.

O'Loughlin, T. (2007), *Adomnán and the Holy Places: The Perceptions of an Insular Monk on the Locations of the Biblical Drama*, London and New York: Bloomsbury Press.

Ogden, D. (2011), *Alexander the Great: Myth, Genesis, and Sexuality*, Exeter: EUP.

Ogden, D. (2013), *Drakōn: Dragon Myth and Serpent Cult in the Greek and Roman Worlds*, Oxford: OUP.

Ogden, D. (2017), *The Legend of Seleucus: Kingship, Narrative, and Myth-Making in the Ancient World*, Cambridge: CUP.

Ogden, D. and C. T. Djurslev (2018), "Alexander, Agathoi Daimones, Argives and Armenians," *Karanos* 1: 11–21.

Ortmann, U. (1988), "Cicero und Alexander," in W. Will and J. Heinrichs (eds.), *Zu Alexander dem Grossen: Festschrift für Gerhart Wirth zum 60. Gerburtstag am 9.12.1986*, 2 vols., ii, 801–863, Amsterdam: Hakkert.

Parker, G. (2008), *The Making of Roman India: Greek Culture in the Roman World*, Cambridge and New York: CUP.

Pearson, L. (1960), *The Lost Histories of Alexander the Great*, New York: American Philological Association.

Pédech, P. (1984), *Historiens Compagnons d'Alexandre*, Paris: Les Belles Lettres.

Peltonen, J. (2018), "Church Fathers and the Reception of Alexander the Great," in K. Moore (ed.), *Brill's Companion to the Reception of Alexander the Great*, 477–502, Leiden: Brill.

Pernot, L. (2013), *Alexandre le Grand, les risques du pouvoir. Textes philosophiques et rhétoriques*, Paris: Les Belles Lettres.

Pernot, L. (2015), *Epideictic Rhetoric: Questioning the Stakes of Ancient Praise*, Austin, TX: UTP.

Pfister, F. (1976), *Kleine Schriften zum Alexanderroman*, Meisenheim am Glan: Hain.

Pfister, F. (1989), *Erinnerungen aus meinem Leben bis 1945: Mit einem Verzeichnis der volkskundlichen und religionswissenschaftlichen Schriften*, Würzburg: Bayer.

Pfrommer, M. (2001), *Alexander der Grosse: Auf den Spuren eines Mythos*, Mainz am Rhein: Philipp von Zabern.

Porter, P. A. (1983), *Metaphors and Monsters: A Literary-Critical Study of Daniel 7 and 8*, Old Testament Series 20, Uppsala: CWK Gleerup.

Potter, D. S. (1994), *Prophets and Emperors: Human and Divine Authority from Augustus to Theodosius*, Cambridge, MA: HUP.

Prandi, L. (2010), *Corpus dei papiri storici greci e latini. I papiri e le storie di Alessandro Magno*, Pisa and Rome: Fabrizio Serra Editore.

Prandi, L. (2013), *Diodoro Siculo. Biblioteca storica. Libro XVII. Commento storico*, Milan: Vita and Pensiero.

Quasten, J. (1950–1986), *Patrology*, ed. A. Di Bernadino, 4 vols., Westminster, MD.

Rapp, S. H. (2014), *The Sasanian World through Georgian Eyes: Caucasia and the Iranian Commonwealth in Late Antique Georgian Literature*, Farnham: Routledge.

Rebillard, (2012), *Christians and Their Many Identities in Late Antiquity, North Africa, 200–450 CE*, Ithaca and London: Cornell UP.

Reinink, G. J. (2005), *Syriac Christianity under Late Sasanian and Early Islamic Rule*, Aldershot: Ashgate.

Richter, D. S. and W. A. Johnson, eds. (2017), *The Oxford Handbook of the Second Sophistic*, Oxford and New York: OUP.

Rollinger, R. (2013), *Alexander und die großen Ströme*, Wiesbaden: Harrassowitz Verlag.

Ruina, D. T. (1993), *Philo of Alexandria in Early Christian Literature: A Survey*, Assen: Van Gorcum.

Sainte-Croix, M. ([1775] 1810), *Examen Critique des anciens historiens d'Alexandre-le-Grand*, 2nd edn., Paris: H. Grand, Bachelier.

Sauer, E., H. O. Rekavandi, and T. J. Wilkinson (2013), *Persia's Imperial Power in Late Antiquity: The Great Wall of Gorgan and the Frontier Landscapes of Sasanian Iran*, Oxford: Oxbow Books.

Saunders, N. J. (2006), *Alexander's Tomb: The Two-Thousand Year Obsession to Find the Lost Conqueror*, New York: Basic Books.

Schrekenberg, H. (1992), "Josephus in the Early Christian Literature and Medieval Christian Art," in H. Schrekenberg and K. Schubert (eds.), *Jewish Historiography and Iconography in Early and Medieval Christianity*, 1–138, Minneapolis, MN: Fortress Press.

Schubert, C. (2014), *Minucius Felix Octavius. Übersetzung und Kommentar*, Freiburg, Basel and Vienna: Herder.

Simmons, M. B. (1995), *Arnobius of Sicca: Religious Conflict and Competition in the Age of Diocletian*, Oxford: OUP.

Simonyan, H. (1989), *History of Alexander the Macedonian: Armenian Recensions* (in Armenian), Yerevan: Armenian Academy of Sciences.

Slotki, J. J. (1973), *Daniel. Ezra. Nehemiah*, London: Soncino.

Smith, R. (2011), "The Casting of Julian the Apostate in the Likeness of Alexander the Great: A *Topos* in Antique Historiography and Its Modern Echoes," *Histos* 5: 44–106.

Spencer, D. (2002), *The Roman Alexander: Reading a Cultural Myth*, Exeter: EUP.

Spilsbury, P. and C. Seeman (2017), *Flavius Josephus. Translation and Commentary*, vol. 6a: *Judean Antiquities* 11, Leiden: Brill.

Steinmann, M. (2012), *Alexander der Grosse und die "Nackten Weise" Indiens: Der fiktive Briefwechsel zwischen Alexander und dem Brahmanenkönig Dindimus*, Berlin: Frank and Timme.

Stewart, A. (1993), *Faces of Power: Alexander's Image and Hellenistic Politics*, Berkeley, CA: UCP.

Stoneman, R. (1994), "Jewish Traditions on Alexander the Great," *StudPhilon* 6: 37–56.

Stoneman, R. (2003), "The Legacy of Alexander in Ancient Philosophy," in J. Roisman (ed.), *Brill's Companion to Alexander the Great*, 325–345, Leiden: Brill.

Stoneman, R. (2007–), *Il Romanzo di Alessandro*, 3 vols., Milan: Mondadori.

Stoneman, R. (2008), *Alexander the Great: A Life in Legend*, New Haven, CT: YUP.

Stoneman, R. (2009), "The Author of the *Alexander Romance*," in M. Paschalis, S. Panayotakis, and G. L. Schmeling (eds.), *Readers and Writers in the Ancient Novel*, Ancient Narrative Supplementum 12, 142–154, Groningen: Barkhuis.

Stoneman, R. (2011), "Primary Sources from the Classical and Early Medieval Periods," in D. Zuwiyya (ed.), *A Companion to Alexander Literature in the Middle Ages*, 1–20, Leiden: Brill.

Stoneman, R. (2012), *Legends of Alexander the Great*, 2nd edn., London and New York: I. B. Tauris.

Stoneman, R. (2015), "Tales of Utopia: Alexander, Cynics, and Christian Ascetics," in M. P. Futre Pinheiro and S. Montiglio (eds.), *Philosophy and the Ancient Novel*, Ancient Narrative Supplementum 20, 51–64, Groningen: Barkhuis.

Straub, J. (1970), "Divus Alexander – Divus Christus," in P. Granfieldand and J. A. Jungmann (eds.), *Kyriakon: Festschrift Johannes Quasten*, 2 vols., 461–473, Münster, Westphalen: Aschendorff.

Szalc, A. (2011), "Alexander's Dialogue with Indian Philosophers: Riddle in Greek and Indian Tradition," *Eos* 98: 7–25.

Tarn, W. W. (1948), *Alexander the Great*, 2 vols., Cambridge: CUP.

Thomson, R. W. (1994), *Studies in Armenian Literature and Christianity*, Aldershot and Brookfield: Variorum.

Thorne, J. (2007), "Battles, Tactics, and the Emergence of the *limites* in the West," in P. Erdkamp (ed.), *A Companion to the Roman Army*, 218–234, Malden, MA: Blackwell.

Tolkien, J. R. R. ([1939] 2006), "On Fairy-Stories," in id., *Monsters and their Critics*, London: Harper Collins.

Torrey, C. C. (1925), "Alexander the Great in the Old Testament Prophecies," *BZAW* 41: 281–286.

Trapp, M. (1997), *Maximus of Tyre: The Philosophical Orations*, Oxford: OUP.

Usener, H. (1902), "Divus Alexander," *RhM* 57: 171–173.

Van Dam, R. (2007), *The Roman Revolution of Constantine*, Cambridge: CUP.

Van Nuffelen, P. (2012), *Orosius and the Rhetoric of History*, Oxford: OUP.

Wasserstein, A. and D. J. Wasserstein (2006), *The Legend of the Septuagint: From Classical Antiquity to Today*, Cambridge: CUP.

Watts, E. J. (2006), *City and School in Late Antique Athens and Alexandria*, Berkeley, CA: UCP.

Weber, F. (1909), *Alexander der Grosse im Urteil der Griechen und Romer bis in die konstantinische Zeit*, Leipzig: Borna.

Wienand, J. (2016), "The Cloak of Power: Dressing and Undressing the King," in J. Wienand (ed.), *Contested Monarchy: Integrating the Roman Empire in the Fourth Century AD*, 3–16, Oxford: OUP.

Welch, K. and H. Mitchell (2013), "Revisiting the Roman Alexander," *Antichthon* 47: 80–100.

Whealey, A. (2003), *Josephus on Jesus, The Testimonium Flavianum Controversy from Late Antiquity to Modern Times*, London: Peter Lang.

Wheatley, P. and R. Hannah, eds. (2009), *Alexander and His Successors: Essays from the Antipodes*, Claremont, CA: Regina Books.

Whitmarsh, T. (2001), *Greek Literature and the Roman Empire: The Politics of Imitation*, Oxford: OUP.

Whitmarsh, T. (2005), *The Second Sophistic*, Oxford: OUP.

Whitmarsh, T. (2013), *Beyond the Second Sophistic: Adventures in Greek Post-Classicism*, Berkeley, CA: UCP.

Will, W. and J. Heinrichs, eds. (1987–1988), *Zu Alexander dem Grossen: Festschrift für Gerhart Wirth zum 60. Gerburtstag am 9.12.1986*, 2 vols., Amsterdam: Verlag Hakkert.

Williams, Megan (2006), *The Monk and the Book: Jerome and the Making of Christian Scholarship*, Chicago, IL: Chicago UP.

Williams, Michael (2011), "Time and Authority in the *Chronicle* of Sulpicius Severus," in A. Lianeri (ed.), *The Western Time of Ancient History: Historiographical Encounters with the Greek and Roman Pasts*, 280–300, Cambridge: CUP.

Wirth, G. (1993), *Der Weg in die Vergessenheit: Zum Schicksal des antiken Alexanderbildes*, Vienna: Verlag der Österreichischen Akademie der Wissenschaften.

Wolohojian, A. M. (1969), *The Romance of Alexander the Great by Pseudo-Callisthenes*, New York: CUP.

Yardley, J. C. and W. Heckel (1997), *Justin: Epitome of the Philippic History of Pompeius Trogus*, vol. 1: *Books 11–12: Alexander the Great*, Oxford: Clarendon Press.

Yardley, J. C. and W. Heckel (2004), *Alexander the Great: Historical Sources in Translation*, Malden, MA: Blackwell.

Young, F. M. (1997), *Biblical Exegesis and the Formation of Christian Culture*, Cambridge: CUP.

Young, F. M., L. Ayres, and A. Louth, eds. (2004), *The Cambridge History of Early Christian Literature*, Cambridge: CUP.

Zecchini G. (1984), "Alessandro Magno nella cultura dell'età antonina," in M. Sordi (ed.), *Alessandro Magno tra storia e mito*, 195–212, Milan: Jaca Book.

Zuwiyya, D., ed. (2011), *A Companion to Alexander Literature in the Middle Ages*, Leiden: Brill.

Index Locorum

1. LITERARY TEXTS

a. Old Testament

Genesis
  1:14: 102
  1:27: 132
  1:31–2:4: 149
  3:24: 139
  10: 150
Exodus
  14:29: 137
  20:3–6, 15: 71
Deuteronomy
  5:7–10, 18: 71
Ezra
  7:12: 103
Psalm
  136:10–16: 137
Proverbs
  21:1: 126
Isaiah
  45:1: 130
Jeremiah
  5:6: 122
  13:23: 115
  50:8: 121
Ezekiel
  26:7: 103
Daniel
  2 (entire): 106–111
  2:37: 103
  2:46–8: 118
  4:33: 118
  4:36–7: 118
  7 (entire): 112
  7:6: 113
  7:7: 113
  7:8: 113
  7:9–12: 96
  7:11: 115
  7:12: 115
  7:13–14: 96
  8 (entire): 99–106, 107
  9:24–7: 135, 149
  10:1–12:4: 97
Nahum (Minor prophet)
  3:8–11: 92
Zechariah (Minor prophet)
  6:1–8: 124
  11:12–3: 102

b. Apocrypha

1 Maccabees
  1.1–10: 140–2
  6 (entire): 141

c. New Testament

Matthew
  24:42: 112
  27:54: 81
Mark
  3:17: 125
  13:35: 112
  13:37: 112
Luke
  2:1: 150, 191
  12:40: 112
John
  19:34–35: 81
Acts
  9:20: 182
  11:26: 152
  13:5: 182
  14:1: 182
  17: 182
  18:4: 182
  18:19: 182
  18:26–28: 182
  19:8: 182
  28:17–29: 182
2 Peter
  1:20–1: 94

Romans
    15: 182
    24: 182
    28: 182
Philippians
    2:10–11: 179
1 Thessalonians
    1.9: 190
1 Timothy
    6:15: 103
2 Timothy
    4:13: 40
Revelation
    (entire): 125–6
    1:1: 125
    17:14: 103
    19:16: 103

d. Non-scriptural authors and texts

Adamnán of Iona (628–704 AD)
    On Holy Places
    2.30.1: 93
    2.30.26: 93
Aelian
    Miscellaneous History (VA)
    3.23: 117, 151
    4.29: 190
    5.6: 53
    5.12: 76
    5.29: 77
    9.3: 200
    10.4: 116
    12.35: 161
    12.64: 73
    Nature of Animals (NA)
    5.54: 115
Aelian Tacticus
    Pref.6: 174
Aelius Aristides (Aristid.)
    Orations (Or.)
    26.26: 84
    32.39: 51
Aemilius Sura
    FRH 103: 110
Aeneas of Gaza
    Theophrastus
    p. 18: 60

p. 34: 76
Aeschines of Athens
    Against Ctesiphon
    §§ 107–112: 172
Alcuin of York (735–804 AD)
    On the Destruction of the Monastery at Lindisfarne
    9.35–6: 120
Alexander Romance α
    1.3.4: 67
    1.4–14: 168
    1.5–24: 199
    1.8.4: 72, 121
    1.12–24: 166
    1.13.4: 41
    1.17.1: 121
    1.18.6: 121
    1.26.4–6: 117
    1.31.1: 167
    1.30–34: 15, 86, 200
    1.35: 167
    1.46–7: 16, 166, 200
    2.15.2: 121
    3.4: 171
    3.5: 56–7
    3.17.37–8: 52, 63, 69, 175
    3.26.7: 52
    3.27–8: 63
    3.31: 200
    3.31.6–8: 186
    3.31–32.10: 77
    3.33.3: 182
    3.33.7: 121
    3.34: 15
    3.35.1: 143, 167, 171
Alexander Romance β
    1.1: 121
    1.14: 121
    1.31: 167
    1.34: 121
    1.38: 121
    2.7: 121
    2.20: 121
    2.23: 103
    3.5: 121
    3.25: 121
    3.35: 121
Alexander Romance ε
    24.2: 130

Ambrose of Milan
  Letter 7
    34–38: 54
Ammianus Marcellinus (Amm. Mar.)
    18.3.7: 45
    22.16.7: 84
    25.4.15: 200
Antipater of Sidon
  Epigrams
    7.246: 124
Aphrahat of Persia (270–345 AD)
  Demonstrations (*Dem.*)
    5.18–9: 114
Appian of Alexandria (App.)
  Civil War (*B. Civ.*)
    Prooemium.38.1: 13
    2.21.149: 138
Apsines of Gadara
  Art of Rhetoric
    1.19: 75
Aristobulus of Cassandreia (*FGrH/BNJ* 139)
    F6: 150
    F13: 167
    F33: 45
    F41: 52
    F47: 80
Aristotle
  History of Animals (*Hist. An.*)
    1.1.12: 116
    8.26.6–7: 115
Armenian *Alexander Romance* (*AR* Arm.)
    § 29: 41
    § 78: 167
    § 286: 121
Arnobius Afer
  Oration (*Or.*)
    1.5: 155
Arrian of Nicodemia (Arr.)
  Discourses of Epictetus (*Epict. Diss.*)
    1.6: 120
    2.13.24: 61
    3.22.92: 61
    3.23.38: 179
    3.24.69: 54
  History of Alexander (*Anab.*)
    1.1–6: 200
    1.1–9: 166, 200
    1.13–16: 167
    1.17: 166

    1.26.1–2: 137
    2.16.1–24.5: 167
    3.2.1: 86
    3.3.2: 64
    3.3.3: 167
    3.16.7–8: 85
    4.7.4: 40
    4.9.2: 48
    4.14.3: 45
    4.14.4: 44
    5.1.2: 200
    5.16.5: 171
    6.11.5: 150
    7.1.3: 180
    7.1.4: 185, 200
    7.1.6: 201
    7.2.1: 60
    7.3.1: 53
    7.9.2: 103
    7.10.6: 171
    7.15.5: 180
    7.24–30: 201
    7.27: 76
    7.28.1: 167, 171
    7.28.2–3: 200
    7.30.1–3: 120
  Periplus of the Black Sea (*Peripl. M. Eux.*)
    §§ 21–23: 79
Athenaeus of Naucratis
  Sophists at Supper
    6.57: 80
    10.44: 186
    10.49: 53
    12.55: 74
Athenaeus the Mechanic
  Tactica
    § 5: 54
Athenagoras of Athens
  Embassy (*Leg. Pro. Christ.*)
    § 28: 65
Augustine of Hippo (August.)
  City of God (*De Civ. D.*)
    4.4: 159
    8.5: 64
    12.11: 64
Aulus Gellius (Gell.)
  Miscellany (*NA*)
    9.2.1–11: 40

9.3.3–6: 51
Basil of Caesarea
   Letters
      9.3: 61
   Philocalia
      23.5: 101
Bede, the Venerable (672–735 AD)
   Commentary on Proverbs
      2.22: 42
Bemarchius (*FGrH/BNJ* 220)
   202
Bottius of Antioch (*FRH* 98)
   F1: 153
Callisthenes of Olynthus (*FGrH/BNJ* 124)
   F12a-d: 66
   F14a: 150, 162
   F31: 137
   T1: 46
   T6: 46
   T13: 81
   T16a-18f: 46
   T18a: 44
Cassius Dio
   77.8.5: 188
Chares of Mytilene (*FGrH/BNJ* 125)
   F19a: 53
Cicero (Cic.)
   On Duties (*Off.*)
      2.16: 41
   On the Orator (*De or.*)
      2.341: 41
   On the Republic (*Rep.*)
      3.24: 159
   Tusculan Disputations (*Tusc.*)
      4.79: 48
Clement of Alexandria (Clem. Al.)
   Exhortation (*Protr.*)
      2.11.3: 103
      4.54.2: 71
      4.54.5: 75
      6.77.4: 161
      10.96.4: 74
   Miscellany (*Strom.*)
      1.21.106.3: 69
      1.21.128.3: 147
      1.24.158.3–159.6: 179
      3.4.30.2: 69, 175
      6.4.38: 58
      7.10.59.3: 179
   Pedagogue (*Paed.*)
      1.7.55: 42
Cornelius Nepos
   On Kings (*Reg.*)
      § 3: 101
Curtius Rufus, Quintus (Curt.)
   3.6.17–20: 157
   3.12.6: 166
   4.2–4: 167
   4.7.10–1: 167
   4.7.25: 64
   4.8.6: 86
   5.1.3: 150
   6.6.1–10: 40
   8.1.20–2.3: 46
   8.6.16: 200
   8.8.22–3: 44
   10.2.4: 200
   10.5.12–14: 187
   10.5.26: 156
   10.5.34–36: 185
   10.5–10: 201
Cyril of Alexandria
   Commentary on Nahum (*Comm. Nah.*)
      2.56–7: 94
   Commentary on Zechariah (*Comm. Zech.*)
      2.359–60: 110, 124
Demades of Athens (*FGrH/BNJ* 227)
   T82: 76
   T93: 75
Didache
   16.1: 112
Dio Chrysostum
   Orations (*Or.*)
      4.70–2: 103
      49.4–5: 51
Diodorus Siculus
   1.3.3: 146
   1.13.3: 67
   16.92.5: 75
   17.Preface: 44
   17.1.3: 199
   17.8.2–14.4: 166, 200
   17.19–21: 167
   17.21.7: 166
   17.40–46: 167
   17.52.5–6
   17.75–6: 167

17.77.5: 40
17.85: 171
17.93.4: 69
17.96: 171
17.107: 62
17.109.1: 200
17.117.5: 167
17.117–118: 77, 201
Diogenes Läertius (Diog. Laert.)
  5.5: 45–6
  5.2–27 (Aristotle): 51
  6.32: 60
  8.73: 39
  9.60: 81
Diognetus, Letter to (Diogn.)
  5: 4
Ephippus of Olynthus (FGrH/BNJ 126)
  F3: 186
Ephorus of Cyme (FGrH/BNJ 217)
  F70: 72
Epiphanius of Salamis
  Ancoratus
    § 60.4: 76
Eratosthenes of Alexandria (FGrH/BNJ 241)
  F1 a: 147
  F30: 40
Eusebius of Caesarea
  Chronicle (Chron.)
    Discussed: 165–72
  Church History (Hist. eccl.)
    1.1.7: 164
    1.13: 5
    2.2.1–2: 76
    2.15–16: 87
    2.24.1: 87
    3.24.18: 125
    3.49: 98
    4.26: 145
    4.29: 10
    4.30.3: 7
    Book 6 (Origeniana): 7, 9
    6.7.1: 97
    8.1–2: 6
    9.9.5–7: 138
  Demonstration of the Gospel (Dem. evang.)
    8.2.67: 134, 135
    15.1.20: 118

15 F 1: 109
Life of Constantine (Vit. Const.)
  1.7: 183–4
  1.8: 185
  1.11: 185
  1.38: 138
  4.73: 201
Onomasticon (Onom.)
  p. 40: 186
Preparation for the Gospel (Praep. evang.)
  1.4.2–4: 145
  3.2.6–7: 67
  6.11.25: 101, 109
  7.21: 120
  8.14: 120
  9.4.6–9: 137
  9.5.5: 53
  9.6.7: 89
  9.15.1: 186
  10.11.27: 186
  10.12.23: 70
  10.14.17: 35
  13.12.1: 89
  13.13.15: 186
  13.13.42: 186
Eusthatius of Thessalonica (1115–1195 AD)
  Commentary on the Iliad (Il.)
    13.29: 137
Excerpta Latini Barbari
  1.6.6: 153–4
Fragmentum Sabbaiticum (FGrH/BNJ 151)
  F 1.2: 138
Frontinus (Frontin.)
  Stratagems (Str.)
    2.3.19: 151
George the Sinner (fl. mid-ninth cent.)
  Chronicle (Chron.)
    p. 32: 137
Greek Chronicle of 334
  149
Hecataeus of Abdera (FGrH/BNJ 264)
  F 21: 137
  F22: 84
Herennius, Rhetoric to
  4.31: 16, 73

Herodotus
  2.3: 65
  2.10: 66
Hilarianus, Quintus Julius
  On the Course of Time
  p. 169: 141
Hippolytus of Rome
  Against Heresies
  1.24.7: 55
  4.5.5: 35
  Commentary on Daniel (Comm. Dan.)
  2.12.1–7: 108
  4.3.5–4.1: 114
  4.7.3: 112
  4.26.2–7: 99–100
  On the Antichrist
  § 24: 100, 126
  § 28: 111, 126
  § 32: 119
  § 49: 141
Homer
  Iliad (Il.)
  5.340: 80
  18.129: 110
Ignatius of Antioch (Ign.)
  Letter to the Magnesians (Magn.)
  10.1–4: 152
  Letter to the Romans
  3.3: 152
  5.1: 115
  Letter to the Philadelphians (Phld.)
  6.1: 152
Irenaeus of Lyons (Iren.)
  Refutation of Heresies (Haer.)
  1.4.4: 78
  1.23.5: 78
  3.21.2: 91
  5.30.1: 125
Isho'dad of Merv (fl. c. 850 AD)
  Commentary on Daniel (Comm. Dan.)
  11:3: 129
Isidore of Seville (560–636 AD)
  Etymologies (Etym.)
  15.1.34: 92
Itinerary of Alexander (It. Alex.)
  § 6: 156
  § 20: 86

§ 50: 64
§§ 107–108: 171
Jerome of Stridon (Jer.)
  Against Jovian (Jov.)
  2.14: 62
  Commentary on Daniel (Comm. Dan.)
  1.2.34: 109
  1.2.47: 135
  2.7.6: 100, 115–116
  2.7.7b: 107
  2.8.8: 100
  2.8.9a: 101, 104
  3.9.24: 135, 143
  3.10.20b: 104
  3.11.2: 105
  3.11.3–4: 172
  Commentary on Hosea (Comm. Os.)
  2.9.5–6: 93
  Commentary on Isaiah (Comm. Is.)
  5.20.1: 100
  Commentary on Jeremiah (Comm. Jer.)
  1.6.8: 124
  1.95: 123
  Commentary on Nahum (Comm. Nah.)
  3.8–9: 92
  Letters
  33: 181
  71.5: 136
  98.9: 181
  107.4: 42
  Life of Hilarion (Vit. Hil.)
  Preface: 100
  On Illustrious Men
  § 8: 87
  § 11.3: 87
  Tractate on the Psalm (Tract. Ps.)
  14: 181
John Chrysostum
  2 Homily on 2 Corinthians 26
  73, 182
  Homily on 1 Thessalonians
  1.8–10: 189
  Against the Jews (Adv. Jud.)
  5.7.1: 100
  5.7.4: 101
John Malalas (Malalas)
  Chronograph (Chron.)

8.1: 153
8.6–8: 91–2
John Moschus (fl. seventh cent.)
  Spiritual Meadow
  § 77: 85
Josephus, Flavius (Joseph.)
  Jewish Antiquities (*AJ*)
  2.348: 137
  10.195–210: 108
  10.209: 109
  10.269–76: 102
  11.304–46: 129
  11.305: 134
  11.313: 134
  11.320: 134
  11.323: 168
  11.333–35: 200
  11.340–45: 168
  11.345: 134
  12.70: 134
  12.11–118: 89
  14.114: 84
  20.415: 134
  Jewish War (*BJ*)
  2.487–8: 84
  7.244–5: 136
  Against Apion (*Ap.*)
  1.179: 53
  1.200–5: 137
  2.35–44: 84
  2.45–7: 89
  2.70–72: 84
Julian
  Against Heraclides
  § 8: 61
  Caesars
  321a: 185
  To Uneducated Dogs
  6.20: 61
Julius Africanus (Jul. Afr.)
  Chronograph (*Chron.*)
  F65: 149
  F73: 149
  F82: 148, 165
  F84: 149
  F86: 92
  Miscellany
  F12.1: 173
  F12.2: 172

  D(ubia)17: 172
Julius Valerius
  1.31: 167
Justin (Just.)
  Epitome of the Philippic Histories
  (*Epit.*)
  1.2.9: 171
  7.6.10: 71
  9.7.1–6: 200
  10.3.7: 167
  11.2.4: 116
  11.3.6–4.8: 166, 200
  11.6.8–13: 167
  11.6–7: 44, 46
  11.9.11–16: 158
  11.10.10–14: 167
  11.11.1–8: 64, 68
  11.11.11–12: 40
  12.2.3: 69
  12.4: 77
  12.6.7–11: 48
  12.15–6: 201
  13.5.3–4: 200
  15.3.3–7: 46
Justin Martyr
  1 Apology (*Apol.*)
  1.32: 91
  Dialog with Trypho (Dial.)
  § 1: 40
  § 9: 40
  § 68: 91
  § 69: 72
  § 80: 126
Juvenal (Juv.)
  10.168–73: 73
  14.308–12: 61
  15: 72
Khachatur Kecharetsi (1260–1331 AD)
  History of Alexander
  Preface: 176
Lactantius (Lactant.)
  Divine Institutes (*Div. Inst.*)
  1.6.8: 162
  2.7.18–19: 36
  7.15.12–3: 110
  7.15.19: 110
Leon of Pella (*FGrH/BNJ* 659)
  Collected fragments: 64

Libanius of Antioch
　Orations (Or.)
　　11.16: 152
Liber de Morte (LM)
　§ 97: 77
Livy
　9.18.9: 156
　45.9: 12, 182
Lucan
　10.21: 113, 159
　10.25–28: 73, 187
　10.34: 186
　10.41: 187
　10.48–52: 185
Lucian of Samosata
　Dialogs of the Dead (DMort.)
　　12.6: 76
　　No. 13: 49
　　13.1–2: 73
　　13.2–3: 76
　Herodotus (Herod.)
　　§§ 4–7: 81
　Parliament of the Gods (Deor.
　　Conc.)
　　§§ 8–10: 72
　Peregrinus (Peregr.)
　　§§ 11–14: 48
　The Ship (Nav.)
　　§§ 28–40: 56
　True Story (Ver. Hist.)
　　2.9: 188
Lucius Ampelius
　Liber Memoralis
　　16.2: 12
Manetho (FGrH/BNJ 609)
　F18: 67
Manilius
　On Astronomy
　　3.22–3: 12
Marcus Aurelius (M. Aur.)
　Meditations (Med.)
　　2.3: 120
　　4.9: 120
　　4.33: 177
　　5.8: 120
　　6.18: 177
　　6.24: 177
　　8.3: 61, 177
　　10.27: 177

Maximus of Tyre (Max. Tyr.)
　Orations (Or.)
　　2.6: 197
　　8.4: 197
　　14.8: 197
　　23.7: 197
　　28.1: 197
　　29.2: 66, 197
　　32.9: 197
　　36.6: 197
　　41.1: 66, 197
Megathenes (FGrH/BNJ 715)
　F34a: 53
Menander Rhetor (Men. Rhet.)
　p. 327: 185
　p. 387: 185
　p. 426: 178
Methodius of Olympus
　On the Resurrection (Res.)
　　§ 28: 147
Metz Epitome
　§ 34: 171
　§§ 78–84: 57
Minucius Felix
　Octavius (Oct.)
　　21.3: 66
　　25.9–12: 110
Nearchus of Crete (FGrH/BNJ 133)
　F4: 53
　F23: 52
Nicanor (FGrH/BNJ 146)
　F1a: 161
　F1b: 162
Nonnus of Panopolis
　Dionysiaca
　　7.117–28: 71
Onesicritus of Asypalea (FGrH/BNJ
　　134)
　F17a: 38
Origen
　Commentary on Genesis
　　1.8: 101, 109
　Contra Celsum
　　2.4: 95
　　2.8: 95
　　2.12: 95
　　2.15: 95
　　2.28–9: 95
　　2.30: 145

2.36: 80
2.37: 95
2.79: 95
3.17: 95
3.22.1: 72
3.36: 77
4.39: 90
5.50: 131, 200
6.19: 90
7.4: 95
Orosius, Paul
  3.7.5: 157, 167
  3.16–20: 156–8
  3.18.5: 167
  3.23.6: 156
  3.23.14: 158
  4.1.13: 157
  6.21.19–20: 157
Ovid
  Ibis (*Ib.*)
  297–8: 77
Oxyrhynchus historian, the (*FGrH/BNJ* 255)
  F6: 166
  F7: 167
  F 9: 148
Palladius of Helenopolis
  Life of the Brahmans
  Discussed: 58–59
  2.1: 191
  2.30: 120
  2.34: 121
Parian Marbles (*FGrH/BNJ* 239)
  B-C2: 166
  B5: 170
Pausanias (the geographer)
  1.11.1: 71
  10.12.9: 161–62
  10.37.5–6: 172
Phaedrus (the fabulist)
  3.2: 115
Philo of Alexandria
  Every Good Man is Free (*Prob.*)
  § 96: 54
  Life of Moses (*Vit. Mos.*)
  2.3: 179
  2.29: 89
  2.191: 94
  2.278: 119

On the Cherubim (*Cher.*)
  § 63: 139
Philostratus (Philostr.)
  Life of Apollonius of Tyana (*VA*)
  1.18: 55
  2.9: 55
  2.10: 55
  2.12: 55
  2.23–41: 58
  2.24: 55
  2.33: 56
  2.43: 56, 58
  3.16: 55–6
  Lives of the Sophists (*VS*)
  § 7: 48
  § 481: 8
  § 507: 8
Philostorgius
  Church History (*Hist. Eccl.*)
  F 1.1: 141
Photius of Constantinople
  Library (*Bibl.*)
  Cod. 40: 141
  Cod. 44.9b: 55
Phylarchus (*FGrH/BNJ* 81)
  F41: 74
Pliny
  Natural History (*HN*)
  4.13: 79
  12.62: 42
  30.149: 77
  35.92–3: 186
Plutarch
  Life of Alexander (Plut. *Alex.*)
  2.1: 166, 168
  4.5–7: 188
  7.6–7: 43
  8: 43, 201
  11.4–6: 166
  11.6–13.15: 166, 200
  14.5: 60
  14.6–7: 69
  16: 167
  17.1: 166
  22.9–10: 41
  24–5: 42, 167
  26.8–10: 86
  28.3: 81
  31.6: 150

45.2: 40
48–55: 44
50–55.2: 46
55.8–9: 51
64: 57
77.1–3: 52, 77
Life of Eumenes
13.3–4: 200
Life of Theseus
5.4: 173
Moral Essays (Plut. *Mor.*)
65d: 44
96c: 44
179e-f: 42
180b: 103
181c-d: 171
329b-c: 43
329f-330a: 40
330d: 113
331f-332a: 60
397a: 161
446d-e: 190
449e: 48
458b: 44
605d-e: 60
782b-c: 60
Pollux
Onomasticon (*Onom.*)
4.85: 110
4.88: 110
Polyaenus of Macedon
Stratagems (*Strat.*)
4.3.1: 38
4.3.2: 173
4.2.3–4: 167
4.3.6: 151
4.3.24: 200
4.3.29: 171
Polybius of Megalopolis (Polyb.)
8.17.3: 120
10.11.9: 120
Porphyry of Tyre (*FGrH*/*BNJ* 260)
Against the Christians
F37: 107
F82: 6
Life of Plotinus
§ 3: 9
Praxagoras of Athens (*FGrH*/*BNJ* 219)
T1: 176

Ps.-Clement of Rome
Homilies
6.23.1: 78
Recognitions
10.21.5: 72
10.25.2: 78
Ps.-Cyprian of Carthage
Idols are not gods (*Idol.*)
§ 3: 64, 68
Ps.-Ephrem
Commentary on Daniel (*Comm. Dan.*)
7:7: 113
Ps.-Hegesippus
On the Fall of Jerusalem (*De Ex. Urb. Hier.*)
2.9: 185
3.5: 137
5.19: 120
5.50: 136
Ps.-Hippolytus of Rome
Collection of Chronologies (*Chron.*)
§ 9: 150
§ 17: 150
§ 18: 150
§ 715: 150
§ 717: 151
§§ 742–56: 151
Ps.-John Chrysostom
Homily on Luke 2.2: 101
Ps.-Justin Martyr
Exhortation
§ 5: 52
§ 12: 35, 89–90
Ps.-Scyllax
Periplus
§ 37: 172
Ptolemy I, son of Lagus (*FGrH*/*BNJ* 138)
F10: 150
F11: 173
F17: 45
Quintilian (Quint.)
Institutions of Oratory (*Inst.*)
1.1.9: 42
5.10.42: 146
12.10.27–37: 110
Rufinus of Aquileia
Origen's on First Principles (*Orig. Princ.*)
Pref.2: 181

Seneca the Elder (Sen.)
　1.pr.1: 12, 73
　1.5: 81
Seneca the Younger (Sen.)
　On Anger (*De Ira*)
　　3.17: 44
　On Benefits (*Ben.*)
　　1.13: 39, 113, 159
　　5.4.4: 61
　Letters (*Ep.*)
　　53.10: 39, 159
　　59.12: 81
　　83.23: 77, 186
　　94.62: 156
　　119.7: 73
　Natural Questions (*QNat.*)
　　6.23.2–3: 4
Sextus Empiricus (Sext. Emp.)
　Against the Academics (*Math.*)
　　1.263: 77
　　5.89: 35
Sibylline Oracles
　3.381–400: 163, 186–87
　4.88–94: 164
　5.6–7: 74, 164
　11.102–108: 164
　11.118: 186
　11.195–219: 164, 168, 170, 186–87
　11.232–35: 170
Socrates of Constantinople
　Church History (*Hist. eccl.*)
　　3.23.54–6: 177
　　7.13: 85
Soterichus of Oasis (*FGrH*/*BNJ* 153)
　F14a: 175
Strabo (Str.)
　1.4.9: 43
　14.3.9: 138
　15.1.35: 117
　15.1.61: 52
　15.1.64: 38
　15.1.66: 52
　15.1.68: 53
　16.1.3: 150
　17.1.6: 86
　17.1.14: 167
　17.1.43: 150, 162
Suda (Byzantine Greek Lexicon)
　Σ 361: 162, 177

Suetonius (Suet.)
　Life of Augustus (*Aug.*)
　　8.1: 84
Synesius of Cyrene
　Encomium of Baldness (*Enc. Cal.*)
　　§§ 15–16: 173
Tacitus (Tac.)
　Annals (*Ann.*)
　　2.73: 156
Tatian (Tat.)
　Exhortation to the Greeks (*Ad. Gr.*)
　　§ 2.1–2: 43–50
　　§ 35: 50
　　§ 36: 147
　　§ 45: 50
Tertullian of Carthage (Tert.)
　Against the Jews (*Adv. Jud.*)
　　§ 7.7: 180
　　§ 8: 143
　Against Marcion (*Marc.*)
　　1.7.2: 180
　Against the Valentinians (*Adv. Valent.*)
　　15.3: 77
　Apology (*Apol.*)
　　§ 11.15: 41
　　§ 18: 4, 91
　　§ 46.15: 50, 72
　On the Philosopher's Mantle (*Pall.*)
　　4.6: 39
　On the Soul
　　§ 50.3: 77
Theodore of Mopsuesta
　Commentary on Nahum (*Comm. Nah.*)
　　3.8: 93
Theodoret of Cyrrhus
　Commentary on Daniel (*Comm. Dan.*)
　　8.5: 106
　　8.8: 101, 106
　Commentary on Jeremiah (*Comm. Jer.*)
　　50:8–10: 121
　Commentary on Nahum (*Comm. Nah.*)
　　3.8: 93
　Cure of Greek Maladies (*Graecarum affectionum curatio*)
　　8.60–61: 74
　Questions in Numbers (*Qu. Num.*)
　　44.1: 141

Theophilus of Antioch
   Letter to Autolycus
      (*Autol.*)
    1.14: 119
    3.17–27: 152
Valerius Maximus (Val. Max.)
    1.1.ext1: 36
    1.1.ext5: 36
    1.4.ext1: 86
    4.3.ext4: 61
    6.4.ext3: 191
    7.2.ext13: 76
    8.14.ext2: 190
    9.3.ext1: 44
Velleius Paterculus
    1.6.6: 110

Vitruvius
   On Architecture (*De arch.*)
    2.preface.4: 86
    8.3.16: 77
Zosimus (Zos.)
    1.1.2: 120

2. PAPYRI

P.Berol. 13044: 57
P.Genev.inv.271: 57
P.Hamb. 129: 15

3. INSCRIPTIONS

SEG 33.802: 15

General Index

Abgar V 5, 7
Abraham 32, 153, 164–5, 169
Achamoth 78
Achilles 42, 71, 79, 110
Adam 152–3, 165
Adamnan 92–3
Aelian 76, 115–16, 172
Aelius Aristides 8, 51, 84
Agesilaus 41
Agnes, saint 54–5
Alans 136, 172
Alexander I of Macedon 123
Alexander III of Macedon, 'the Great' *passim*
Alexander IV 163
Alexander Romance 11, 14–15, 41, 52, 56, 58, 62–3, 67, 69, 113, 121–2, 130, 134, 137, 143, 147–8, 154, 172, 175, 177, 186, 194–6, 201–2
Alexander Severus 8, 25–6, 75, 114, 148–9, 151
Alexandria 6, 9, 12, 15, 18–19, 22–3, 25, 27–8, 66, 72, 83–8, 92–5, 122, 130, 134–5, 142–3, 148–9, 151–4, 157, 167–70, 172, 175, 181, 183–4, 191, 193, 196, 200–1
Ambrose of Milan 54–5, 139, 160
Ammon 12, 14–15, 63–4, 71–2, 74, 77, 121, 157, 162, 167–8, 186, *see also* Zeus
Amos, prophet 122, 196
Amyntas 158
Anaximenes 171
Andromachus 167, 169
Antigonus, successor 86, 100–1, 116
Antioch 21, 28, 84, 115, 151–4, 189–90
Antiochus IV Epiphanes 95, 97, 99–102, 107, 113, 127, 140–3, 149
Antipater 77, 173
Aornus Rock 55, 167, 171
Apelles, painter 186
Aphrahat of Persia 114, 195
Aphrodite 81

Apollo 68–9
Apollonius of Tyana 55–6, 58, 175
Aquila of Sinope 91
Arbela 12, 150, 174
Aristeas, letter of 88–9
Aristippus 43, 50
Aristobulus 13–14, 45, 52–3
Aristotle 18, 22–3, 30, 35, 38, 41, 43–4, 47, 49–54, 63, 77, 90, 115, 184
Armenia 5, 116, 177, 194–5
Arnobius 'Afer' of Sicca 27, 29–32, 154–6, 160, 187
Arrian 13–15, 44–7, 53, 57, 59, 60, 77–9, 120, 137, 146, 150, 170–2, 180–1, 185, 197
Asclepius 72, 78
Asia Minor 1, 3, 40, 100, 104, 134, 137, 156
Assyria *or* Assyrians 64, 109–10, 153, 155, 164, 179, *see also* Syria
Athenagoras of Athens 22–3, 27, 65–8, 88
Athene 59, 121
Athens 7–8, 23, 35, 55, 85
Augustine of Hippo 2, 65, 68–70, 160
Augustus 6, 13, 84, 143, 145, 150–1, 183, 199
Aulus Gellius 51, 172

Babylon *or* Babylonians 12–13, 47, 55–6, 74, 77, 85, 96, 100, 104, 106–9, 112, 121–2, 124, 141, 147, 149, 153, 163–4, 167–8, 170–1, 191
Bactria 12, 47, 155
Bardesanes of Edessa 7, 25
Basil of Caesarea 61, 102
Bede, Venerable 42, 194
Berossus of Babylon 22, 147
Bethlehem 33, 85
Bottius 153–4
Brahmans 55–6, 59–60, 62, 192
Britain 142, 185, 200
Byzantium 98, 136, 194

Caesarea (Palestine) 7, 28, 31, 88, 133
Cain 139
Calanus 53–5, 57, 59, 62, 139
Callisthenes 13–14, 43–9, 51, 57, 66, 81, 150, 158, 162, 184
Caracalla 188
Caranus 148, 151, *see also* Calanus
Carthage 26, 40, 66, 117, 124, 134, 154, 157
Cassander 77, 163
Cato the Elder 41
Celsus 72, 77, 80–1, 90, 95, 131
Ceres 36, 63
Chaldeans 121, 124, 153, 164
Christians *passim*
Cicero 27, 41, 44, 159, 164
Clement of Alexandria 9, 23–4, 42, 58, 60, 69, 71–2, 74–9, 88, 90, 103, 147, 172, 175, 179, *see also* Pseudo-Clement
Cleopatra VII 143, 170
Clitarchus of Alexandria 13–14
Clitus 43, 44, 46–9, 51, 158, 184
Commodus 8, 22, 66
Constantine I 2–3, 5–6, 19, 30–1, 61, 74, 114, 138–9, 176, 183–5, 188–9, 191, 195, 199–202
Constantinople 61, 98, 165
Constantius I 199–200
Corinth 60–1, 174
Craterus 117, 173
Croesus 41–2
Curtius Rufus 13, 40, 46, 62, 159, 166, 185–7
Cyril of Alexandria 85, 94–5, 110, 124–5
Cyrus the Great 41, 96, 102, 124–5, 127, 129–30, 150, 152, 183, 185, 188–9

Dandamis 53, 59–60
Daniel, Book of 25, 28, 32, 95–119, 121–3, 126–30, 135, 139, 141–4, 149, 154, 160–1, 165–6, 170–1, 183, 188, 190, 193–6
Danube River 116, 200
Darius I 146, 180
Darius III 12, 15, 47, 99–102, 104–5, 114–15, 124–5, 129–31, 140, 149–50, 153–4, 157–8, 165–7, 169–72, 200
Delphi 69, 162

Demeter *see* Ceres
Demetrius (Poliorketes) 100–1, 114
Demetrius of Phaleron 88
Demetrius, bishop 28, 88
Demosthenes 41, 90, 164
Dindimus *see* Dandamis
Dio Chrysostom 51, 61, 174
Diocletian 153, 175
Diocletianic persecutions 6, 29–31, 155
Diodorus Siculus 13, 16, 46, 62, 67, 83–4, 113, 140, 146
Diogenes Laërtius 51–2, 60
Diogenes the Cynic 37, 43, 49–50, 60–2, 76–7, 192
Dionysius, tyrant of Syracuse 43, 50
Dionysus 39, 40, 72, 77–8, 171, 201
Domninus 153

Egypt *or* Egyptians 9–10, 14, 23, 49, 63–7, 71, 85–6, 89, 91–3, 100–2, 105, 110, 122, 130, 134, 143, 146, 149, 152–4, 156, 163–70, 185
Empedocles 39–40
Ephorus of Cyme 72, 146
Epicureans 103
Epicurus 171
Ethiopia *or* Ethiopians 5, 66, 165, 185
Euhemerus of Messene 66
Eunapius of Sardis 8–9
Euphrates River 186
Eusebius of Caesarea 3, 5–10, 19, 23–5, 27–8, 31–3, 69, 87, 90, 97–8, 102, 109, 118, 127, 133–40, 148, 164–71, 183–9, 199–202
Ezekiel, prophet 122, 126, 196

Gabriel, archangel 99, 102–3, 112
Galerius 31, 114
Ganges River 58, 116–17
Gaugamela 105, 150, 168, 170, 200
Gaza 95, 129, 132, 134
George Syncellus 25, 166–8
Gordian Knot 16, 132
Granicus River 12, 46, 104, 167–8
Greece *or* Greeks 22–3, 41, 43, 51, 53–4, 56, 59, 67, 69, 71, 86–7, 93, 96, 99, 103–4, 107–8, 110, 112–15, 124, 140, 149, 152, 154–6, 164, 166, 171, 174, 177, 179, 183–4, 195–6, 200

Gregory Nazianzen 102
Gregory the Illuminator 195
Gymnosophists 52–60, 88, 105, 117, 192, 201

Hannibal 49
Harmodius 85
Harpalus 167, 171
Hector 79
Hegesippus 32, *see also* Pseudo-Hegesippus
Heliopolis 11, 63, 65
Hephaestus 67
Hephaistion 46–7, 173, 187–8
Hera 67
Heracles *see* Hercules
Heraclitus 57, 177
Hercules 41, 72, 78, 171, 179, 201
Hermes Trismegistus 23, 65–6
Hermes 63
Herodes Atticus 8, 40
Herodotus 23, 27, 65–6, 72, 146, 189
Hilarianus 141
Hippias of Elis 50
Hippodamia 71
Hippolytus of Rome 24, 32–3, 35–7, 55, 60, 97, 99, 100–1, 103, 105, 108, 111–12, 114–17, 119, 125–7, 141, 143, 149, *see also* Pseudo-Hippolytus
Holophernes 180
Homer 28, 71, 79
Hosea, prophet 122, 196
Hydaspes River 168
Hyphasis River 55, 117
Hyrcanians 136, 167, 170

Icarus 56
Illyria *or* Illyrians 116, 166, 171, 182
India *or* Indians 4, 12, 22, 38, 47, 51–6, 58–60, 63, 88, 105, 116, 121–3, 165, 168, 171–2, 175, 182, 185, 199
Indian Ocean 116, 182
Indus 1, 52, 167, 171, 182, 186
Iollas 77
Irenaeus of Lyons 7
Iron Maiden 1
Isaiah 100, 122, 126, 130, 189, 196
Isidore of Seville 92–3
Issus 12, 104, 124–5, 157, 168, 200

Jaddus, High Priest 129–35, 138, 167
Jeremiah 85–7, 121–3, 196
Jerome of Stridon 18, 26–33, 42, 62, 68, 87, 91–3, 95, 97–100, 103–5, 109–10, 115–17, 120, 122–7, 135–6, 141–3, 160–1, 164–8, 171–2, 181–3, 194
Jerusalem 19, 25, 28–9, 83, 85, 88, 95, 122–3, 126, 129–36, 138–9, 141, 152, 165, 168–70, 184, 191, 193, 200
Jesus Christ 5–8, 11, 23, 27–31, 42, 72–4, 76, 79–81, 85, 91, 94–5, 97, 102–3, 108, 125–6, 128, 131–3, 143, 145, 149, 151–2, 155, 162, 176–7, 179–82, 189, 191, 197, 200–1
Jews 5, 18–19, 37, 53–4, 83–8, 94–7, 107, 121, 126, 128–34, 138–9, 149, 152, 165, 169, 180, 196, 198
Jewish diaspora 83, 85–6, 107, 193
John Chrysostom 62, 73, 75–6, 182–3, 189–90
John Malalas 91, 153
John the Baptist 11
John, apostle 125
Josephus, Flavius 18, 83–5, 87, 89, 91, 102–3, 108–11, 126, 128–40, 146, 149, 167, 169, 193
Judah *see* Judea
Judas Maccabeus 97
Judea 76, 83, 87, 95, 102, 122–4, 133, 167, 169, 181
Julian 61
Julius Africanus 25–6, 32, 34, 91–2, 148–51, 153, 164–5, 168, 172–5
Julius Caesar 84, 157
Jupiter *see* Zeus
Justin Martyr 4, 21, 40, 52
Justin, epitomizer 13, 46, 62, 158–9, 171
Juvenal 73, 79

Lactantius 3, 30–2, 36–7, 68, 110, 138, 161–3
Lawrence, saint 55
Leon of Pella 62–9, 192
Leonidas of Epirus 41–4, 50
Levantine Coast 129, 134
Livy 12, 120, 182
Lucan 159, 184–7
Lucian of Samosata 8, 48–51, 56, 61, 72, 76, 79, 188, 192

Lucius Ampelius 12–13, 104, 150
Lucius Verus 152, 174
Lyncestis River 78
Lysimachus 45–6, 101

Macedon *or* Macedonians 12–13, 28, 41,
　45, 52–5, 62, 64, 67, 78, 92, 100,
　103–5, 109–10, 114–15, 119,
　129–30, 132, 134, 137, 143, 147–51,
　155, 157, 162, 164–7, 169, 171–4,
　182–3, 185, 189–91, 201
Mandamis *see* Dandamis
Manetho 67, 152
Manlius Torquatus 171
Marcion of Sinope 7, 91, 180
Marcus Aurelius 2, 22, 61, 66, 152, 174,
　177, 191, 197
Mardia *or* Mardians 167, 170
Mark, evangelist 87
Maxentius 138, 200
Maximus of Ephesus 61
Maximus of Tyre 8–9, 66, 197
Media *or* Medes 96, 99, 104, 107, 109–10,
　123–4, 140, 143, 153, 170
Melito of Sardis 125
Memphis 63, 65, 67, 134, 201
Menander of Samaria 78
Menander Rhetor 16, 178
Methodius of Olympus 28–9, 146
Michael, archangel 96
Midas 56
Miletus 36
Milvian Bridge 138
Minucius Felix 26–7, 65–9, 110–11
Momus 72
Moses 89–90, 137–8, 146, 152–3, 179
Mosollamus 137

Nahum 92–3, 122, 196
Nebuchadnezzar II 96, 106, 118, 127, 135,
　180
Nectanebus 14–15, 168
Neoptolemus 71
Nero 8, 125
Nicanor 162–3
Nicomedia (Bithynia) 30
Nile River 66, 93, 117
Noah 150, 152–3, 161, 163
No-Amon 92–4

Nonacris River 77–8
North Africa 27, 40, 66, 71, 134, 154

Octavian *see* Augustus
Octavius of Cirta 27, 66–7
Olympias 12, 41, 52, 63–5, 71–2, 117, 166,
　168
Olympus 28, 72
Onesicritus of Astypalea 38, 52, 59
Origen 7–9, 23–5, 27–8, 31–4, 77, 79–81,
　88, 91, 95, 97–8, 101–3, 109, 125,
　127, 131–6, 164, 167, 181, 183
Orosius, Paulus 30, 154–61, 168, 187–8
Osroëne 4
Oxydracae 56

Palladius 58–60, 93, 191
Pamphilius 31, 133
Pamphylian Sea 137
Pantaenus 23, 88
Parmenio 47, 158, 173
Patroclus 79
Paul, apostle 19, 28, 40, 152, 181–3, 190
Pelagia, saint 54–5
Pella 12, 62, 73
Pericles 41
Persaeus of Citium 62, 67
Persepolis 51, 141, 157
Perseus of Macedon 12, 148, 182
Persia *or* Persians 1, 12, 14, 41–2, 47, 57,
　64, 73, 90, 96, 99–100, 103–10, 112,
　114–15, 119, 123–4, 130–1, 134,
　138–41, 143, 147, 149, 151, 153,
　155–6, 165, 167–70, 174, 181, 183,
　191, 201
Peter, apostle 94, 152
Philip I, 'the Arab' 28
Philip II of Macedon 12, 14, 16, 41–2, 45,
　49, 51, 65, 67, 72, 74–6, 90, 100, 104,
　140, 146, 157, 165–6, 168, 171, 173,
　199–200
Philip III Arrhidaeus 52, 114, 116, 148
Philip V 12
Philo of Alexandria 54, 87, 89–90, 119–20,
　139
Philostorgius 141, 177
Philostratus 8, 55–6, 58,
Philotas 47, 158
Phoenicia 28, 134

Phroates 56
Phryne 50
Pinarus River 125
Plato 27, 29, 35, 38, 43, 48, 50, 52, 89–90, 105, 155
Plotinus of Lycopolis 9, 97
Plutarch 13–15, 38, 40–1, 43, 48, 51–2, 56, 58, 60–1, 69, 71, 81, 103, 119–20, 150, 168, 173, 177, 188
Polyaenus 151, 173–4
Polycrates 41
Pompeius Trogus 13, 146, 158
Pompey the Great 41, 177
Pontius Pilate 76
Porphyry of Tyre 6, 9, 29, 97, 107–8, 135
Porus 56, 105, 167–8, 171
Praxagoras of Athens 176, 202
Prodicus of Ceos 67
Proserpina 36
Proteas 186
Pseudo-Clement 71–2, 78
Pseudo-Cyprian 66–70
Pseudo-Ephrem of Syria 98, 113, 195
Pseudo-Hegesippus 136–7
Pseudo-Hippolytus 149–51, 170
Ptah 67
Ptolemy Chennus 172
Ptolemy I Soter 13–14, 45, 84, 86, 88, 100–2, 114, 116, 134, 149–50, 170, 173–4
Ptolemy II Philadelphus 88–9
Ptolemy of Macedon 186
Ptolemy VI Philometor 149
Ptolemy VII Euergetes II 149
Ptolemy XII Auletes 151
Pyrrhus 36
Pythagoras 89

Quintilian 42, 50, 146–7

Roman Empire *see* Rome
Rome *or* Romans 3–8, 11–13, 21, 24–6, 29–30, 36, 39–42, 48, 50, 56, 58, 63, 66, 68, 76, 78, 80–1, 84, 87, 91, 107–11, 114–17, 120, 123–4, 132–4, 136, 140, 143, 145–7, 150–6, 158, 164–5, 170–1, 174, 177–8, 180–2, 185, 189–91, 194, 200–1
Roxane 47

Samaria 124, 169
Sardanapalus 41, 179
Sardis 12, 166, 172
Satan 126
Scipio Africanus 41, 49
Scythia *or* Scythians 71, 172–3, 185
Seleucus I 84, 100–1, 114, 116, 152, 173
Seneca the Elder 12, 73
Seneca the Younger 39, 44–6, 159, 184, 186, 195
Septimius Severus 23, 25
Serapis 15, 121, 200
Sextus Empiricus 35–7, 77
Sibylline Oracles 74–5, 83, 107, 138, 161–4, 168, 170, 177, 184, 186–7
Sicca 29, 154
Sicily 23, 134,
Simon Magus 78, 169
Siwah Oasis 63–4, 66, 68, 93, 134–5, 159, 162, 167, 171
Socrates 27, 41, 43, 48, 50, 90, 177
Solomon 85–7, 152, 180
Sophia, goddess 59, 120–1
Sphines *see* Calanus
Strabo 14, 38, 43, 84, 87, 117, 137–8, 150, 162
Successors of Alexander 19, 45, 84, 86, 89, 95, 99–102, 105, 107, 112, 115–16, 127, 140–2, 146, 149, 151, 156, 158, 163, 165, 170, 182
Sulla 41
Susa 12, 40, 54
Susanna 25, 96, 102
Symmachus the Ebionite 91
Synesius of Cyrene 173–4, 176
Syria *or* Syrians 6–7, 21, 23, 53–4, 106, 133–4, 137, 182, *see also* Assyria

Taprobane 58
Tatian of Assyria 10, 18, 21–2, 26, 33, 43–52, 147, 184
Taxila 52
Taxiles 167, 171
Tertullian of Carthage 4, 26–7, 33, 39–42, 50–1, 66–7, 72, 77–8, 143, 180–1
Tetrarchy 30
Thaddeus, disciple 5
Thebes (Egypt) 65, 92–3
Thebes (Greece) 16, 51, 54, 103–4, 134, 154, 156, 166, 171, 175, 200

Thecla, saint 54–5
Themistocles 41–2
Theocritus of Chios 74–5
Theodoret of Cyrrhus 73–4, 93, 106, 121, 141
Theodotion of Ephesus 91
Theophilus of Antioch 152, 154
Theophrastus 54
Thrace *or* Thracians 166, 171, 182
Tiberius 76
Tiridates III (Trdat) 195
Trajan 85, 174, 199
Trier (Germany) 30
Tyre 28, 31, 95, 129, 134, 167

Valentinus of Alexandria 7, 78
Valerius Maximus 14, 36–7
Varro 63, 161–3
Vespasian 13, 134
Victorinus of Pettau 125
Virgil 27, 29
Vulgate, Alexander historiography 13, 15
Vulgate, Bible 91, 93

Xerxes 155

Zechariah 122–3, 196
Zeus 67–8, 70–2, 77, 154, 162, 168, 186, *see also* Ammon

www.ingramcontent.com/pod-product-compliance
Lightning Source LLC
Chambersburg PA
CBHW052035300426
44117CB00012B/1826